# *Period Piece*

all the life of Cambridge
( a society small & exclusive!

lovely things now improved
away!

when all experience, even for all its
apparent formality, was individuated
no man, no media

imagine
letters
Expansive

loving language

# PERIOD PIECE

by

## GWEN RAVERAT

*Ann Arbor Paperbacks*
THE UNIVERSITY OF MICHIGAN PRESS

First edition as an Ann Arbor Paperback 1991
Copyright © by Gwen Raverat 1952
All rights reserved
Published in the United States of America by
The University of Michigan Press
Manufactured in the United States of America

1994   1993   1992          4   3   2


**Library of Congress Cataloging-in-Publication Data**

Raverat, Gwen, 1885–1957.
    Period Piece / by Gwen Raverat.
        p.   cm. — (Ann Arbor paperbacks)
    Originally published: New York : Norton, 1976.
    ISBN 0-472-09475-0 (cloth : alk. paper). — ISBN 0-472-06475-4
(paper : alk. paper)
    1. Raverat, Gwen, 1885–1957.   2. Wood-engravers—England—
Biography.   3. Cambridge (England)—Social life and customs.
NE1147.6.R28A2   1991
769.92—dc20
[B]                                                    91-29510
                                                          CIP

To
FRANCES

# Contents

# *Preface*

This is a circular book. It does not begin at the beginning and go on to the end; it is all going on at the same time, sticking out like the spokes of a wheel from the hub, which is me. So it does not matter which chapter is read first or last. On the next page is a list of the people in the book.

# *My Mother's Family*

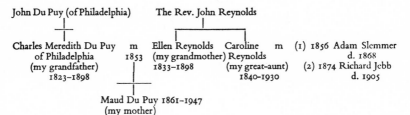

John Du Puy (of Philadelphia)          The Rev. John Reynolds

Charles Meredith Du Puy      m      Ellen Reynolds    Caroline      m      (1) 1856 Adam Slemmer
 of Philadelphia   1853 (my grandmother) Reynolds    d. 1868
 (my grandfather)     1833–1898 (my great-aunt) (2) 1874 Richard Jebb
  1823–1898         1840–1930    d. 1905

Maud Du Puy 1861–1947
(my mother)

# My Father's Family

```
                          ─William            m       Sara Sedgwick
                           1839–1914         1877      1839–1902
                          (Uncle William)            (Aunt Sara)

                          ─Henrietta          m       R. B. Litchfield
                           1843–1929         1871      1832–1903
                          (Aunt Etty)                (Uncle Richard)
                                                                    ┌─Gwen m Jacques Raverat
                                                                    │  b. 1885
                                                                    ├─Charles m Katharine Pember
                          ─George             m       Maud Du Puy ─┤  b. 1887
                           1845–1912         1884      1861–1947   ├─Margaret m Geoffrey Keynes
Charles Darwin            (my father)                (my mother)   │  b. 1890
1809–1882                                                          └─William m Monica Slingsby
(my grandfather)          ─Elizabeth                                  (Billy) b. 1894
 m 1839 ──┐                1847–1925
Emma Wedgwood             (Aunt Bessy)
1808–1896                              ┌1874  Amy Ruck ─┐┌─Bernard m Elinor Monsell
(Grandmamma)                           │      1850–1876  ││  b. 1876
                          ─Francis    m┤1883  Ellen Crofts ┼─Frances m Francis Cornford
                           1848–1925   │      1856–1903   │  b. 1886
                          (Uncle Frank)│     (Aunt Ellen)
                                       └1913  Florence Maitland
                                              d 1920
                                       ┌1882  Elizabeth Fraser
                          ─Leonard    m┤      1846–1898
                           1850–1943   │     (Aunt Bee)
                          (Uncle Lenny)└1900  Mildred Massingberd
                                              1868–1940
                                              (Mildred)       ┌─Erasmus
                                                              │  1881–1915
                          ─Horace             m       Ida Farrer ──┼─Ruth m W. Rees Thomas
                           1851–1928         1880      1854–1946   │  b. 1883
                          (Uncle Horace)              (Aunt Ida)   └─Nora m Alan Barlow
                                                                      b. 1885
```

*Period Piece*

# CHAPTER I

## *Prelude*

In the spring of 1883 my mother, Maud Du Puy, came from America to spend the summer in Cambridge with her aunt, Mrs. Jebb. She was nearly twenty-two, and had never been abroad before; pretty, affectionate, self-willed, and sociable; but not at all a flirt. Indeed her sisters considered her rather stiff with young men. She was very fresh and innocent, something of a Puritan, and with her strong character, was clearly destined for matriarchy.

The Jebbs, my great-uncle Dick, and my great-aunt Cara,  lived at Springfield, at the southern end of the Backs, and their house looked across Queens' Green to the elms behind Queens' College. Uncle Dick was later to be Sir Richard Jebb, O.M., M.P., Professor of Greek at Cambridge, and all the rest of it; but, at that time, he held the chair of Greek at Glasgow, and so had been obliged to resign his Trinity fellowship and the post of Public Orator at Cambridge. However the Jebbs spent only the winters in Glasgow, and kept on their Cambridge house for the summers, while they waited hopefully for old Dr. Kennedy to retire, so that Uncle Dick might succeed him in the Cambridge Professorship. This was the Dr. Kennedy who wrote the Latin Grammar, which we all knew very well in our youth, and he had not the slightest intention of retiring; neither was it by any means so certain as the Jebbs chose to consider it, that the succession would fall to Uncle Dick. However, after keeping them waiting for thirteen years, Dr. Kennedy died in 1889, and Uncle Dick came into his kingdom at last.

The earliest Cambridge that I can remember must have been seen by me in reflection from my mother's mind, for it is the same picture as that which she draws in a series of artless letters, written to her family in Philadelphia in this summer of 1883, two years before I was born. In this, the first Cambridge in the mirror of my mind, the sun is always shining, and there are always ladies and gentlemen sitting in the garden under the trees, very much occupied with each other. It was quite a different Cambridge which I saw later on, when I looked at it with my own eyes.

My mother had fallen into a world which was very strange to her. She wrote home: '*I am at last at the Utopia of all my fondest dreams.*' It was a Utopia of tea-parties, dinner-parties, boat-races, lawn-tennis, antique shops, picnics, new bonnets, charming young men, delicious food and perfect servants; and it almost seems too good to be true. I suppose there must have been some difficulties, even in those days; and indeed all the right sleeves of my mother's dresses would keep on getting too tight, from the constant tennis; and the helpings of ice-cream were far too small for an American; but, otherwise, you would really think, from the letters, that Un-requited Love—other people's Unrequited Love—was the only serious trouble. And even the broken hearts of which we are told seem to have been very quickly mended.

The Du Puys were of a good family of Huguenot descent; but they were not well off. There were many children, and Maud could not possibly have accepted her aunt's invitation, if her fare to Eng-land had not been paid by her elder brother. He was now getting on well, and was generous to his sisters. The girls had been sent to fairly good schools; but in the case of my mother at any rate, Education, like an unsuccessful vaccination, had not *taken* very well. It was not a question of schooling, but of temperament. But my mother arrived in England with a great respect for culture, and eager to learn all she could. We find her struggling to read Browning and Tennyson and Shelley; battering her way with pride and tenacity through *La Petite Fadette*, and preaching the virtues of learning French to her younger sisters. But with all her respect for education

My mother was tall and had golden-brown hair and dark blue eyes and such a lovely complexion that people often thought that she was made up; which would of course have been improper.

—and no one could respect it more—learning was never her strong point. However, she got on perfectly well without it.

In these early letters my mother told her family everything, higgledy-piggledy, helter-skelter, with the most perfect simplicity. And much of the information must have been quite mysterious to them, as she never explained at all about the unknown people of whom she wrote: neither who they were, nor what they did, nor where they lived. But then, even in later life, my mother assumed that you knew all about the people who came into her letters or

'Sketching is such a nice occupation for a young lady', as they used to say in those days.

conversation. If you didn't, you ought to; and anyhow it didn't matter much. In these first letters, both the spelling and the grammar are rather shaky, but, after a lecture from Aunt Cara, stern endeavour improved them very much.

# Prelude

In writing to her sisters, Maud was always careful to tell them anything which might be useful to them, if they should come to England in their turn. She sends a list of words not to use: *somewheres, anywheres, fix* (as fix my dress), take it *off of* the table; '*Dick* [Jebb] *says* location *is not a good word.*' She did a good deal of painting in oils, mostly of round ornamental plaques of her own designs of flowers; these are rather smudgy, but have some feeling for pattern and colour. Maud tells her young sister Carrie how she sketched King's Chapel, and suffered very much in the process from cows, little boys and rain. She goes on, in a kind, but patronizing way: '*I was ever so glad to hear about your reading. Aunt Cara said that every one who is not musical ought to be fond of poetry. So you ought to cultivate your taste in that direction. I am reading Browning, but think he is awfully hard to understand.*' [*Too hard for you* is implied.] '*You could not help liking Shelley and Tennyson.*'

The records of this first summer deal very largely with the fluctuations of two or three love-affairs among her new acquaintance; for to the very end of her life, affairs of the heart were of the greatest interest to my mother. At the end of the summer the letters culminated in the exciting proposal of a certain Mr. T. to herself; and with his rejection she left Cambridge. During this time, after a slow start, she grew to like my father more and more; and, though she never considered him romantic, he gradually became an intimate friend, so that he was consulted at once about Mr. T.'s proposal. But all that summer Romance, for my mother, fluttered lightly round the figure of a much younger man, Mr. G., who was so charming and so intelligent, and who looked so well in his flannels; even though her aunt unkindly noticed that he had bow legs and turned one foot in. However, nothing came of this affair. Mr. T., Mr. G., and my father, George Darwin, were all three Fellows of Trinity.

My father was at that time thirty-eight; the second son of

## Prelude

Charles Darwin, who had recently died. His health had been bad as a young man; in fact he had never expected to live. His complaint sounds like some sort of nervous dyspepsia (perhaps a gastric ulcer?) but it is impossible now to make out what was wrong, or how

My father at this time. He is wearing an unnaturally fierce photographic expression. In very early days I was much confused because his beard and the tobacco he smoked seemed to be of exactly the same colour and texture. Did he perhaps smoke his own moustache? His hair was made of a rather darker kind of tobacco.

much was physical, how much hypochondria. He had been Second Wrangler in the Tripos, and had held a Trinity fellowship. He was then called to the Bar, but was not strong enough to practise. He became interested in various scientific questions, involving mathematics; and specially in the movements of the moon and the tides. In this year, 1883, he had just been elected Plumian Professor of Astronomy; and was also re-elected to a Trinity Fellowship. Maud writes: '*G.D. had a dinner-party after he was made a fellow—and it passed off most pleasantly. In consequence he was ill all the next day—too much for his nerves and his stomach.*'

But he was really now better in health, and being of a warm, open, affectionate nature, wished very much to get married.

Here is my mother's description of her first sight of my father; it is written on 18th of May 1883, the day after her arrival in Cambridge: '*Jane came to tell me that Aunt C. wished me to come downstairs to meet Mr. Darwin. I ran down and opened the door quickly before I could lose courage, and G.D. quickly stepped forward blushing rosy-red*

*and shook hands. The first thing that struck me was his size. He is little.*
[My father was over five foot ten inches in height, but thin and slight.] *He is intensely nervous, cannot sit still a minute. He is full of fun, and talks differently from an American man. They are so different in everything.'* In her next letter she says: *'After any exertion he seems utterly exhausted. He comes in to see Aunt C. every day, and sometimes twice a day and is very convenient to do little errands and to take us out.'* Aunt Cara was evidently educating my father for ladies' society, which was probably very good for him. Aunt Cara writes: *'He is wonderfully improvable; already he has thrown off entirely the little thoughtless ways that used to strike one. I laughed at him about talking instead of waiting on the tea-table; now he says the mere sight of a tea-pot brings him to his feet in an instant; he hands cups and cake without inter-mission.'*

Maud did not think much of English girls. Of a certain brilliant and much admired girl she writes: *'I don't call her beautiful at all; in America I think with one accord we should call her homely.'* And again: *'The English girls are so awfully susceptible; if a man speaks to them almost, they instantly think he is desperately in love with them.'* Of herself she truly says: *'I am not at all susceptible; and that is one differ-ence between* [English girls] *and me.'*

But from the beginning she liked English men—or gentlemen, as she generally called them, in accordance with the custom of her time. Though she thought them very cold: *'Englishmen are strange creatures. I doubt if they ever really fall in love; they marry of course; but generally from a prudent motive.'* In spite of this defect, she admired them exceedingly: *'The gentlemen all seem so simple and no boasting in their manners, and one thing I notice in particular, they are all so careful not to hurt each others' feelings. Aunt C. says that no boasting in their talk and manners is because they have their position in life generally, and are not obliged to talk and act to keep it. When I think of these men and compare them with the class of gentlemen that are in society in West*

# Prelude

*Philadelphia, I "weaken". If we could only transport a dozen girls what belles they would be. I do not think the English girls can begin to be compared to the American girls, but the gentlemen seem to be better. Not in a society sense, for many of them are quite embarrassed; but in themselves. They read more and think more and know more. The ones that we should call ordinary, they call handsome and those we think handsome they call ordinary. Except of course Gerald Balfour whom all call handsome.'*

Gerald Balfour was a younger brother of Arthur Balfour, and was later on Home Secretary for a time. He was often at Cambridge and Aunt Cara was much dazzled by him; but he was perhaps now beginning to be rather tired of her; for Maud wrote shrewdly, that *'Aunt C. does not like it very much'*, because, when she charged him with preferring his sister-in-law, Lady Frances Balfour, to herself, he did not deny it! At first Maud, too, was much impressed by him. She writes: *'He is just what you would imagine an English Lord to look and be like. . . . He is so beautiful.'* But presently the Spirit of American Independence breaks out: *'He is really the most conservative man that I have yet met. Believes the higher set of people, the Lords etc., set a good example to the lower class of people—and ever so much more stuff that I had read of but never met anyone that believed it.'*

There seem to be some indications that Aunt Cara had originally intended another of the Darwin brothers, Frank the botanist, for Maud; hoping perhaps to keep George under her own sway; for Maud writes: *'Aunt C. had picked out Frank Darwin for me* [at a party]. *She tried to be entertaining, but evidently Frank was not entrapped, for he appeared at the* [boat] *races with his sister and a Miss Cross* [Crofts]. *Aunt C. thought he was very attentive to her. Aunt C. did not like it, she wishes to have him as attentive to herself as G.D. So yesterday she asked him to tennis on Monday, when I anticipate watching a great deal of fun. It is wonderful to me to watch the way she makes people admire her, she is a fascinating woman.'* But alas, before Monday, Frank's engagement to Miss Crofts was announced; so there

22

was an end to Aunt Cara's little plot. Of this marriage was born my cousin Frances Darwin, later to be Frances Cornford.

There is a long letter about a visit to London to see an amateur performance of a Greek play in 'Lady Freak's house' [? Freke].

'The Fatigue and Brainwork of Shopping.' Aunt Cara and my mother buying a bonnet.

*'At 12 we were all packed, I with my gray dress and red velvet hat on, and lavender dress in a valise—Aunt C. in her best black silk dress, with her Spanish lace dress in her box. We were seated in the cab* [American for railway carriage] *when suddenly I was aroused by Aunt C. saying in stentorian tones, "I have forgotten the tickets for the Greek play".'* After

some agitation they '*decided to run the risk of being turned away*' and went off shopping to '*Picadolly* [sic] *and Regent Streets*'. Here Aunt C. purchased for herself '*a little black and gold-braided bonnet, with four yellow roses and a little narrow black velvet ribbon,*' for which she paid two pounds. There is something so succulent about this bonnet that I have not the heart to omit it, as I have all the numberless other things they bought. In the evening they '*had no difficulty in getting in. . . . Gladstone, Sir Isaac Newton* [sic], *Sir Frederic Leighton and some other great codger sat immediately in front of us.*' [Query: Who can Sir Isaac Newton have been?] '*Gladstone looks exactly like the caricatures of him, only his collar is a little larger and his eyes are so keen and bright and twinkle so when he laughs. Sir F. Leighton had charge of the scenic effects and succeeded very well, only all the rouge and powder and Greek dresses could not make perfect beauties of the English girls. The play was called* The Tale of Troy, *and this night was spoken entirely in Greek.*' [Of which, of course, she knew not a word.] '*Mr Stephen* [J. K. Stephen] *was Hector and acted remarkably well. Lionel Tennyson as Ulysses would have been better had he known his part. I enjoyed the play very much and equally so the people. Such dresses! ! ! Words fail me for description.*'

This account has been extracted in fragments from an enormous entanglement of to-ing and fro-ing in cabs, while they looked for rooms for the night. They got them at last at '*the St Pancreas Hotel*'. I was delighted to find this spelling so early, as, to the end of her days, my mother always considered the Saint and the Internal Organ as identical. Next day they continued their delightful shopping expeditions, and ended up at the Royal Academy, to see the Millais and the Leightons: '*and I think it quite rested Aunt C. after the fatigue and brainwork of shopping.*'

They were obliged to hurry back to Cambridge as they were dining out. '*There was a Mr Foster* [afterwards Sir Michael Foster, the physiologist] *who sat near me and "chaffed" (English word) me*

*till I almost lost my patience. I did not understand that he was teasing me,
but thought he had taken a little too much wine, which amused Aunt C.
immensely. But he insisted and insisted in such a grave way that I really
thought he did not know what he was talking about and that he was either
a fool or a little out of his mind. If I meet him again won't I turn the tables
and see if he "chaffs" me again!!* Mr Verrall [Dr. Verrall, Greek scholar]
*took me out to dinner and proved very pleasant (married men or little
men are generally the ones that I like, he was the former). I wore my
lavender which Aunt C. thinks very becoming but an inartistic colour.
I never saw Aunt Cara look better in my life. She really did not look over
30.'* [She was then forty-three.]

The grain of this letter has been extracted out of many pages of
details; on the other hand my mother could at times be admirably
terse. She sums up her account of a visit to Ely Cathedral, by saying: '*The architecture was very good.*' I don't see what more anybody
could say after that.

Maud was a good deal puzzled by Cambridge habits when she
first came to England. She had never learnt to dance, and was
afraid that some of her family would be shocked, when they heard
that she had been to a ball. She seems only to have been to one ball
at King's that summer; and even later there is very little mention
of dances. This is probably because she never learnt to dance well;
certainly not because she disapproved of dancing. She writes that
she has not 'yet' played games on Sunday; though she was able
to enjoy very bad riddles on that day. 'Why are women like tele-
grams? Because they are in advance of the mails in intelligence.'
'Why are men like telescopes? Because women draw them out,
look through them and shut them up.' This is characteristic, for all
her life she loved puzzles and riddles. One Sunday she went to the
Round Church, which was '*almost as old as the hills*'; but '*the English
service is so long; they repeat always two creeds and the Lord's Prayer
three and often four times, and they never combine the Royal Family in*

*one prayer, but always there is one for Victoria and then another for the Prince of Wales. And the sermon was rediculous* [sic]. *I think I shall go to the chapel hereafter. They have a short service, no sermon and good music. The college people never go to any of the churches. Aunt C. made G.D. go to chapel for the first time for a dozen years on Sunday. She says he is what they call an a r g o n a i s t* [sic]. I think *that is the word.* [Agnostic?] *But it means an infidel who does not try to make other people infidels. So many of the people here are that kind. They, or at least a few, go to chapel, but only for the music.'* This does not seem to shock her at all.

The gaieties, dinners and tennis continue all the summer, till in mid-September Maud went with Aunt Cara to pay some visits in Scotland. But first she bought a new coat. *'After looking at lots of dowdy things, at last we were shown an exceedingly pretty brown brocaded velvet, a kind of coat and yet a mantle, trimmed with lovely fur —I think it was black fox which was brown. But the price was very extravagant—seven guineas. The fur cost a guinea a yard, the clerk said. There were about ten yards of fur on it.'* This kind of arithmetical puzzle—ten yards of guinea-a-yard fur on a seven-guinea coat— would never have troubled my mother at all. Aunt Cara evidently pressed her to buy it, but my mother remained firm. It was *'too good'*. So she bought a three-guinea coat, of *'mixed red and blue cloth in stripes'* with *'a feather trimming'* and *'capey sleeves'*, *'as stylish as can be'*.

This was the period of the 'aesthetic' dresses—(*Patience* had appeared first in 1881)—but both Aunt Cara and Maud considered them affected and ridiculous. Maud writes: *'There were quite a number of aesthetic or ascetic* [sic] *costumes, at a Newnham Garden Party.* Those she describes sound rather charming, though floppy. She says: *'Aunt C. has a simply perfect tea-gown; not aesthetic, but so graceful and lovely.'* Her own favourite gown was *'my white albatross'*, whatever that may be.

# Prelude

At this time Uncle Dick's mother was very ill: *'In a selfish mood both Aunt C. and I hope that she will not die at once, for we should have to give up our tour to Scotland.'* This danger was averted, and they went off to meet George at Edinburgh, where they had two days' sightseeing with him: *'The Scotch look sturdy, but their features are not at all good. Their noses so lumpy and their mouths big. George D. was very nice. In good spirits. I can see how nice he is as a brother and a friend, and he would make a good husband, but somehow the romantic view of a lover is left out of his disposition.'*

My father was always at his best when travelling; he enjoyed it so much and was so full of enterprise and enthusiasm, that it was no wonder that Maud now began to find him more interesting. If not romantic as a lover (though I believe that she presently changed her mind even about that), he was extremely romantic as a sight-seer and I can't think of anyone—except Sir Walter Scott himself—with whom I would rather have seen Edinburgh.

After their return to Cambridge at the end of September, the crisis of Mr. T.'s proposal occurs rather unexpectedly. There is a tremendously involved account of everything that happened for several days before the event, most of it quite irrelevant. It is contained in a letter to Dear Mamma, marked *Private*, with a list of only eight near relations to whom it may be shewn; *'and that is all, all.'* *'Well, in the morning I was in my tub when Jennie came to my door and said, "Miss Maud, here is a note which I will put under the door." I easily got it and to my* amazement *it was a* proposal!' She encloses the actual letter, which I expected to find marked with the bath-water; and also a photograph of Mr. T. He is rather handsome and looks intelligent and virtuous, but dull; his beard, however, was vast and flowing, a great attraction in those days. But alas, alas! he was forty-one and his legs were very short indeed.

Aunt Cara writes: *'Why is there something always queer about the legs of those attractive creatures, which catches straight the eyes of the in-*

*different and makes them think our heroes common?'* [Mr. G., you remember, had crooked legs, too.] '*T. is very manly, a good shot, Alpine climber, tennis player, has an income of, I fancy, about £2000 a year'*—and Aunt C. here goes into details of what a very good match it would be. But Maud was quite clear that it would not do,

Mr. T., from the photograph which my mother sent to Philadelphia. His hair and beard were considered very attractive, and his legs fortunately don't show here.

even though Mr. T. had rashly bought a large house, hoping to live there with her. George was consulted at once; it must have been difficult for him. Maud writes: '*Dick [Jebb] asked G. D. to find out something about Arcturus* [the star] *which Dick wished to write in his book. So G.D. came after dinner. . . . They retired to Dick's study. To my great amusement, instead of talking about Arcturus, they talked about me and Mr T.; G. D. thought Dick had been told. Dick said, "Why it is a splendid match. He is rich, and is a very able man." Age did not make any difference to him evidently.'* But George need not have been worried by all this, for Maud writes again: '*Speaking truthfully I am nearly a half-head taller than he is. He is rather stout. His hair is a beautiful wavy dark brown, and he has a nice soft brown beard; I like him as a friend, but nothing more. He is too little; imagine me marrying a man shorter than myself. A short man though will be my fate, as it is only that kind that like me.'*

So Aunt Cara wrote a beautiful letter of refusal for Maud to copy; only it must have been rather too beautiful, for Mr. T. did not take it seriously. Aunt Cara writes: '*He admires her frankness and candour (I wrote the letter myself) and he thinks her answer encouraging!*

# Prelude

*Heaven save the mark! Can't any man understand a "NO" unless it is shouted at him? The answer to this* [second] *letter can't be misunderstood. Still I don't believe he will give it up, unless Maud becomes engaged to someone else. Englishmen are given to take these things more seriously than Americans. . . . His legs are perfectly* straight, *which is so much to the good, and his head and shoulders are fine.*' Aunt Cara obviously still thought it a pity to throw away such a good bargain; she thinks Maud *'might get to like him'*, but Maud (as usual) was firm, not to say obstinate. She writes: *'Now don't think I am going to marry Mr T. for I have no idea of so doing. In the first place I do not want to marry over here, in the second I do not like him enough, in the third he is too little, and lastly I should fulfil my predestination and be an old maid, which I ..end to do. . . . That is all, and I have probably refused the only offer I shall ever have.'*

So Maud copied out a second refusal; but still Aunt Cara did not give up hope for Mr. T. She writes: *'He is by no means a brilliant match, but I do think he is superior to anyone you are likely to meet in America. As a husband, I believe he would make a woman happier than would G.D. for instance, whose health would always be a very serious drawback. Still, the match is not brilliant; but then think how rarely brilliant matches come in one's way.* "Sure, the world is askew", *where matrimony is concerned.'* She followed this later with a reminder: *'I do pity N. in West Philadelphia, and you too, if you have to go there. It must be* awful *to see year after year slip by and to live in a place where nothing can happen. Mr T. would be better than* that.' Aunt Cara clearly thought that a bird in the hand was worth two in the bush, for she was not yet sure how serious George might be, though she was very fond of George, and in discussing him had written: *'George has by nature the straightest of lines, a very well-proportioned figure, and a really beautiful forehead. Nobody could call him ugly.'* And again: *'Gerald* [Balfour] *says he has the sweetest, most unspoilt nature.'* But she was also rather afraid of appearing to press his claims, in case—as she wrote to George himself, just after his engagement had actually taken place—'*the Darwin family might think this was a match of my making. And it wasn't* one bit, *mind that.* . . . . *If there is a suspicion I utterly and entirely repudiate, it is that of being a match maker.*'

But Maud's views of marriage were less business-like than Aunt Cara's; she had begun to care for George, and Mr. T.'s chance was gone. So poor Mr. T. never married at all, and lived for the rest of his life alone in the large house he had bought.

It is always a fascinating problem to consider who we would have been, if our mother (or our father) had married another person; it is, however, too large a subject to enter into properly here; and I must merely remark that if our father had been Mr. T. we should certainly have had magnificent beards. But then beards are very little use nowadays, especially to females; and we should have lost over the roundabouts—I mean the legs—which are now very important indeed. So no doubt things were all for the best.

After this stirring event the summer ended, and Maud went away and travelled on the Continent, with a different and highly irritating aunt—(whose portrait can be seen on page 114). And my father pursued her; and though he was barely three years younger than Mr. T. and of only medium height, they got engaged at Florence in March 1884. And I must hasten to add that my father's legs were *perfectly straight* and that he was two or three inches taller than she was. Though, by that time, I believe she would have married him, even if his legs had been crooked.

# CHAPTER II

# *Newnham Grange*

---

So they were married in the summer of 1884, at Erie, Pennsylvania; where the local paper described my mother as 'a Philadelphia belle of the first water'. And on the whole they were very happy. My mother's calmness, good spirits and unshakable courage were very soothing to my father's overstrung nerves; and in all the more important things she submitted her strong will to his better judgment. She was always kind and sympathetic to him when he was ill, and took his ailments perfectly seriously; but, unlike a Darwin, she did not positively enjoy his ill-health; she would really have preferred him to be well; and as a consequence he did get very much better. Perhaps, in some ways, she might have been happier with a younger, stronger, gayer man; and he with someone nearer his own intellectual level; but on both sides there were compensations, which made up for what was lacking.

That first winter of 1884–5 they rented the Jebbs' house, Springfield, while the Jebbs spent the winter in Glasgow; and they then began to look for a house of their own. They first made an offer, through a friend, for the house so recently acquired by Mr. T. This strikes me as rather tactless; at any rate Mr. T. seemed determined not to lose his house as well as his lady, for he answered that he was going to live there himself. Aunt Cara writes, in unconscious rhyme: '*He will think a wife is easier to find, than another house so exactly to his mind.*'

Then my father bought the family house and business place of the Beales, just across the road from Springfield. They were

Newnham Grange as I first remember it. There was then a railing down the road; later on the windows on each side of the door were built out; otherwise it is little changed. It makes my blood run cold to remember how we used to run, chasing each other, along the top of the nine-foot garden wall, and jump down from that height.

Cambridge corn and coal merchants—there is still a coal-merchant of that name in the town—and their granaries, warehouses, cow-houses, stables and yards ran along the west bank of the Cam, up-stream from Silver Street Bridge. The house had no name, nor had the road; all that part of Cambridge was simply called Newn-ham; so my father named it *Newnham Grange*. It was certainly a good investment, but I am sure that he really bought the place because he fell in love with it and all its romantic associations.

It is a late eighteenth-century house, probably built over an older one; it faces north up the Backs; and on the south side stands on a branch of the Cam, about half-way between the King's Mill and

The river side of Newnham Grange.

the Newnham Mill. There was a water-door under one of the granaries, to which the barges used once to bring their loads. However, though corn still sometimes came by barge to Foster's Mill (the King's Mill) it no longer came any farther, and the Beales' business had all moved down to the station. The place was now too big for the two old Misses Beales, who still lived there, so my father bought the whole estate. And my mother took to it with enthusiasm; which was characteristically brave of her; for most mothers would have thought the situation damp, and the river both dangerous and smelly.

And so it was; I can remember the smell very well, for all the sewage went into the river, till the town was at last properly drained, when I was about ten years old. There is a tale of Queen

The King's Mill (Foster's Mill) from the end of our garden near Silver Street Bridge. From here we used to watch the corn sacks being hoisted up into the Mill, from barges or wagons. The Mill was pulled down in 1928.

Victoria being shown over Trinity by the Master, Dr. Whewell, and saying, as she looked down over the bridge: 'What are all those pieces of paper floating down the river?' To which, with great presence of mind, he replied: 'Those, ma'am, are notices that bathing is forbidden.' However, we lived at the upper end of the town, so it was not so very bad. That was why the bathing places were on the upper river, on Sheeps' Green and Coe Fen.

In those days both the mills were in use. I still now feel that there is an unnatural gap in the landscape, where Foster's Mill used to stand before it was pulled down; and I find it hard to believe that the boys, who now sit fishing on the parapet, have no idea that there once was a great mill behind them. We used to spend many hours watching the fat corn-sacks being hauled up by a pulley into

The view up the river from our windows. Newnham Mill is in the distance. The cows used to ford the river here four times a day, coming and going to and from their pasture on Sheep's Green.

the overhanging gable, sometimes from a barge, but more often from the great yellow four-horse wagons, which stood beneath the trapdoor. The sacks butted the trapdoors open with their own noses, and the doors fell to, with a loud clap, behind them. At night there was a watchman in the mill who used to divert himself by

trying to play the flute. It was a doleful sound to hear at three in
the morning, especially as he had not advanced very far in his
studies. My father, always a bad sleeper, was much worried by his
aimless tootlings, but felt it would be cruel to protest; however, in
the end, they came to an agreement which suited them both.

My father repaired the house and altered the kitchens, making
them still more vast and stony than they were before. He pulled
down some of the granaries and stables; and made a tennis-court
where there had been a cobbled yard. And he built two wooden
bridges across branches of the river, to reach the two islands. For
the river here becomes exceedingly complicated, with mill-races
and weirs and millpools and various old channels and ditches, all
wandering about in the Fen. He 'threw out' a bay-window to the
drawing-room; this was a pity, as it spoilt the Georgian symmetry
of the house. But architects did not think much of eighteenth-
century architecture in those days.

From that window you could look up the river, under the arch-
ing trees, and see far off the cows crossing the ford below the Newnham Millpool, as they went to and from their stables to be milked,
four times a day; a very pretty sight. My mother loved watching
them; she loved the whole place, and in her romantic fervour she
hopefully asked one of the old Misses Beales if there were not a
ghost in the house? The old lady replied: 'Oh, we never speak about
it! I can't tell you anything about that.' And would say no more.
So my mother assumed that there was a ghost of some kind. Years
later, this first old lady having meanwhile died, my mother met
the surviving sister, and said: 'I wish you would tell me the story
of the ghost. Your sister would not tell me anything about it.'
Miss Beales seemed displeased and surprised; and hummed and
hawed for some time; but at last she said: 'Did my sister really
imply that there was a ghost there? That was just like her. She had
a very curious sense of humour.' Which was the Victorian way of

saying, that she had been pulling my mother's leg. But whether this was really her little joke, or whether both sisters knew of some story they wished to conceal, we were never able to find out. No one ever saw a ghost; but we children all knew very well where the ghost would have lived, if there had been one; by the dark cupboard, on the top landing. The house had a ghostly feeling anyhow.

The architect turned one of the river granaries into a long narrow gallery, overlooking the tennis-court. This court has not proved large enough for the fury of the modern game, but it was quite big enough for the pat-ball tennis of those primitive times, when young and old hopped about together in a gentle and unprofessional manner. He had intended tennis parties to sit in this gallery to watch the game; but as it faces north, it has always been far too cold for that. Also, as he was a really good architect, he naturally built an elegant, carved, stone bow window in the latest Victorian-Gothic style, on to the outer wall of this plain old Georgian granary. This gives an agreeable exotic flavour to the building; in fact, it is so absurd as to be rather charming. But what very odd minds architects do have!

In summer tea was in the garden, under the great copper-beech by the river. It was here that Miss Cecilia Beaux, a well-known American artist, painted my mother's portrait in pastel. She was a fine portrait-painter in the Impressionist tradition, more or less after Manet; and this portrait of my mother is very charming. Miss Beaux was a great friend of my mother's, and was one of the ladies I sometimes used to chaperon (*see* Chapter VI). She was certainly one of the very few visitors whom I really liked; I believe I was even then interested in her painting.

At the end of the tennis-court stood the one big empty granary, which had not been pulled down. My mother being nothing if not ingenious, used this granary in a number of experimental ways. Sometimes she planned to grow mushrooms on the upper floors;

sometimes the first floor was a drying-room for the washing, and the washing was done on the ground floor, with water which the maids had to pump up from the river. (They did not like this at all.) Sometimes the first floor was a hen-house. The granary was built

Cecilia Beaux making a pastel portrait of my mother under the copper beech tree.

over a kind of cellar, which was always liable to flooding; so the hens lived on the first floor, and a small door-hole was knocked through the wall for them, from which a sort of ladder ran down to the ground. The poor hens were supposed to go down this ladder across the stable-yard, out through another hole in the great carriage-door, and across the road to pasture on Queens' Green.

## Newnham Grange

I don't know whether this journey was too complicated for their well-known lack of intelligence, or whether they found the ladder too difficult to climb, or whether they were run over by the fiery hansom-cabs and butchers' carts of those days, but anyhow, the plan did not succeed; and the hens were soon moved to a salubrious period residence on the Big Island, where my mother designed for them a little bridge of their own, across the ditch to the Lammas-land meadow. It was rather like the Bridge of Sighs, made in wire-netting; and with a little instruction they learnt to negotiate it.

But the hens' hole in the granary wall remained, and one of our favourite pastimes was to swarm up a drainpipe and wriggle through the hole into the loft; and my worst nightmares still have to do with the time when I got stuck in the hens' door-hole, because I was too fat, and had the greatest difficulty in getting out alive.

When I was about nine the granary became so dilapidated that something had to be done about it; so my mother had the idea of turning it into a flat, or upstairs house, and letting it. Then for a long time, we had glorious fun with scaffolding rising up out of the river, and ladders, and mortar, and workmen, and mess. Underneath the house, the ground floor was made into a coach-house and stable for the horse my mother always intended to keep some day, and never did. I still often feel as if the present garage is haunted by the wistful ghost of a horse, who never was there at all. The house is most ingeniously full of my mother's beloved gadgets: tricks for opening the front door without going downstairs, and for drawing up the bread in a basket; though, of course, the architect insisted on following the well-known Victorian principles of making the dining-room as far as possible from the kitchen, and the bathroom as far as possible from the hot-water boiler. This particular architect was quite explicit about it: he wrote a book on house design, in which he said: '*The coal store should be placed as far as possible from the kitchen, in order to induce economy in the use of fuel.*' This house was named the Granary.

Beyond the Granary, there was another strip of garden running along the river bank, and from the very end of it I can remember seeing, in the twilight of a June evening, the procession of boats, which used to end the May races. The eights were dressed up with flowers and flags, and came up into the Millpool to turn there, before going down again. It must have been in 1892, the last time the procession took place.

The Grange was, of course, modernized inside, for my mother was always on the side of progress. She had an enormous coal-bin built beside the nursery door, to which the coalmen carried their sacks up the narrow back stairs and along the wriggling round-about passages, making a terrible mess as they went. This was to save the maids' labour, but they did not like the plan at all, more because it was unusual than because of the coal dust. There was now a bathroom, too, with the bath, all decently encased in mahogany, so that you could not see its legs. She had installed a system of speaking tubes from the nursery to the hall; but these were never used at all, because shouting up the short back stairs was so much simpler, if less refined.

Anyhow our house never was the sort of place where you rang the bell for the maid to put coal on the fire. My mother always sent a child to ask for what was wanted, if the child could not itself do what was necessary. I don't say she never rang the bell herself when the supply of children ran short; but it was far more likely that she would call out to someone passing by the door to come and do what she wanted. For like a true American, she always left the doors ajar; no doubt she felt it dull if they were shut. One of the four big rooms downstairs was called the smoking-room, for smoking was not yet quite respectable, though of course my father really smoked everywhere. It was later on the schoolroom.

## Newnham Grange

There was gaslight in the nurseries and passages and bedrooms; hissing, unshaded gas-burners as a rule; where the brown middle of the flower-like flame always fascinated me. There was a Colza oil lamp in the drawing-room, and tall candles in the dining-room. But as soon as it was possible we had the new electric light put in, though it was considered very expensive and much too extravagant

The weir, with Foster's Mill, Silver Street Bridge, and Queens' College seen in the distance.

for the kitchens and the attics; and such passage lights as there were must never be left on. We had the telephone, too, so early that we were Number 10 on the list. In the kitchen, near the vast iron range happily roaring the coal away, stood the clockwork roasting-jack, behind its shiny screen; though the screen was now chiefly used to shelter the troughs of dough, when the bread was put down before the fire to rise; for our bread was all made at home of stone-milled flour from Grantchester Mill.

41

## Newnham Grange

Here at the Grange I was born in the summer of 1885, and here I and my brothers and sister spent all our youth.

From the big night nursery window we could look right down on to the slow green river beneath us; and if a boat went by it was reflected upside down, as a patch of light moving across the ceiling; and the ripples always purled in a dancing rhythm there, when the sun shone. Across the Little Island we could see up to the weir and the footpath along the Upper River, where I always thought the Lord walked when he led his flock to lie down in green pastures. Here we were never out of hearing of the faint sound of the water running over the weir; and on windy winter nights, when we were in bed, we could hear, a long way off, the trucks being shunted at the station and the whistling of the engines on the line. That was when you couldn't sleep because you had a 'feverish attack' and, wonderfully, there was a fire in the night nursery, throwing up the flickering criss-cross of the high fender on the ceiling; and you were glad to be safe in bed, because of the lonely dreadfulness of the night outside. And in the dark early morning we could sometimes hear from the Big Island the crowing of the cocks, which disturbed my father so much.

From the day nursery window we looked across the road to the grass bank and the lime trees opposite; and over Queens' Green to the great elms of the Backs. The level of the Green was then lower than the road, and the horses grazed on the smooth ancient turf, which can only be made by hundreds of years of pasturing animals. It seemed to me the original place about which had been written the poem, which I then thought so lovely:

> *Buttercups and daisies—*
> *O the pretty flowers!*
> *Coming ere the spring-time,*
> *To tell of sunny hours.*

42

# Newnham Grange

Then the Town Council decided that the level of the Green must be raised; and for a long time—two or three years—it was in a most repulsive mess, while cart after cart dumped refuse there. The horses used to flounder about and often fell on the slippery mud; and then they would lie there as helpless in their harness as fallen knights in armour. I used to watch them with horrified and exaggerated pity. I should not have minded nearly so much if they had been men; but I identified myself with the horses. At last the grass grew on the Green again; but the old, old turf was gone and most of the daisies, too; and it has never been so beautiful since the level was raised.

Once I was taken out of bed and carried down to the front door in my nightgown to see the water covering the road and the Green, when a flood had risen suddenly one night. My parents had gone out to dinner on foot, but the frightened maids sent a four-wheeler to fetch them back in a hurry. The water came up to the hubs of the wheels, but was not very deep on the pavement. The cellars were awash, and my father had to wade out into the garden to rescue a cat which was marooned on top of a wall. We had several very delightful floods in my youth, but unfortunately the water never quite came into the house; nor did it in the Great Flood of 1947.

Gunning records, in his *Reminiscences of Cambridge*, that there was a very high flood in February 1795. '*There was a ball given by the Freemasons on that evening, and a carriage was waiting to take Mrs Beales and her party to it. The coachman (in order to save his own life and that of his horses) was obliged to drive away, leaving the company behind. Monsieur Corneille, a celebrated hair-dresser, whose presence was anxiously awaited by several parties in the town, could not leave Mr Beales's house, but was obliged to take up his residence there for the night.*' It is clear that this refers to the Grange; and also it is pretty plain, from the context, that, apart from the cellars, the house itself was not flooded even then; though from the height the water reached in the

43

Queens' Cloister Court, it must have been higher than any flood we ever saw.

If you looked to the left out of the day-nursery window you could see Springfield, and the beginning of Sidgwick Avenue; it was still being made then, and we called it *The New Road*. Here, at the crossroads of the Backs, the lame crossing-sweeper plied his trade, limping, all crooked, across the road with his broom.

And if you looked to the right there was a small builder's yard and two little houses, before you got to the tall trees and Silver Street Bridge, and Queens' Essex Building. But you could not see the little Tudor cottage which stood among the trees. Another early memory is of a fire at night in the builders' yard opposite, and of my father in agitation about the sparks, which were flying across the road to the Granary.

There were railings along the road leading to the bridge, lovely Georgian railings, now improved away; and often people were glad to dodge behind them to escape from the terrified and terrifying herds of cattle, which were driven with bangs and shouts, through the streets to the Monday cattle-market. There had always been some sort of bridge, where the bridge is now, and Desiderius Erasmus himself must often have walked down our road when he went out from Queens' to take the air.

In the summer the thick white dust came powdering in at all the windows; rising in clouds from the horses' hooves, and whitening the grass and the trees across the road. And in the winter the oozy, jammy mud sloshed about, and the street-cleaners scraped it up in delicious soupy spoonfuls, and threw it into their carts. And everywhere and all the time there was the smell of horses; it came in at the windows with the dust; not very nice, but not nearly so nasty as the petrol and exhaust smells are now. And often we heard the clattering of the feet of the hansom-cab horses and the jingling of their bells, as they cantered by; for they were mostly retired New-

44

market race-horses, and so they always had to pretend to gallop, to satisfy the undergraduates, however slowly they might really be going. My cousin Nora said she knew the faces of every one of those horses.

Then there was the rush and rattle of the butchers' traps and their furious little ponies, whom we believed to be fed on meat to make them fierce; and the yellow milk-carts, like Roman chariots, with their big brass-bound churns of milk and their little dippers hooked on at the side; and the hairy-footed shire horses, who drew the great corn-wagons in from the country. And on Saturdays, market days, the farmers came trotting by in their traps; and the carriers' carts plodded in with their slow horses from villages as much as fifteen miles away. Sometimes they were hooded carts, sometimes they were just open carts, with planks for seats, on which sat twelve cloaked and bonneted women, six a side, squeezed together, for the interminable journey. As late as 1914 I knew the carrier of Croydon-cum-Clopton, twelve miles from Cambridge; his cart started at 6.30 in the morning and got back about ten at night. Though he was not old, he could neither read nor write; but he took commissions all along the road—a packet of needles for Mrs. This, and a new teapot for Mrs. That—and delivered them all correctly on the way back.

All day long the slow four-wheelers used to go clip-clopping along to the station. And sometimes, even slower, even heavier, yet more dismal, there was the Plop, Plop, Plop, of the feet of the oldest horses in the world, as they plugged along, pulling the funereal Girton cabs out to Girton with four melancholy students in each; while the drab Newnham girls skurried to and fro to their lectures on foot. And all the time there were dons going 'to lecture, with the wind in their gowns'; and undergraduates in their Norfolk jackets, setting out in pairs to do the 'Grantchester Grind' for exercise.

# Newnham Grange

Nearly every day we could watch the Master of St. Catharine's riding by on his small black pony. He was a little old man, and made an antique and lonely figure in his clerical clothes. Even we children knew that he had been cut by all the university, ever since the rumours about his election to the Mastership in 1861, thirty years before; and it was said that he had been passed over when his turn came to be Vice-Chancellor. It was believed that, at the college election, he and another Fellow had each promised to vote for the other. The voting was equal between these two, but when it came to the point, Dr. Robinson voted for himself, thus becoming Master by two votes; the affair, however, has never been very clear. My parents used to greet him, if they met outside, for the sake of poor Mrs. Robinson, but he was never invited to parties. Often his daughter Mary rode out with him, on a taller horse, yet even this only seemed to enhance his solitude.

There were still occasional old workmen riding by, with their plaited straw bags of tools, on their high penny-farthing bicycles. Sometimes there were lovely organ-grinders; or a stray Italian boy, with a little shivering monkey, or even a dancing-bear. Every night the lamp-lighter came with his long pole to turn on the gas-lights. Sometimes, of a summer night, there were the beautiful scarlet Volunteers, marching by in all their glory; beautiful, but vaguely frightening, casting a kind of shadow image of what war might be, into my childish mind. And the sound of their brass band, and of their marching feet going over the bridge, made my heart turn right over in my stomach.

There was plenty to see; nearly all the life of Cambridge flowed backwards and forwards over our bridge, and before our house.

CHAPTER III

# *Theories*

From 1878 onwards, the Revised Statutes, which allowed Fellows of colleges to marry without losing their fellowships, came into force in one college after another. Till then, with a few exceptions, only Heads of Houses and Professors could marry, so that the children of the university remained few in number. But after 1878 families began to appear; thus, though not among the eldest, I belong to the first hatching of Fellows' children, and was born into a society which was still small and exclusive. The town, of course, did not count at all.

I was also born into the trying position of being the eldest of the family, so that the full force of my mother's theories about education were brought to bear upon me; and it fell to me to blaze a path to freedom for my juniors, through the forest of her good intentions.

I don't believe that my mother was more subject to attacks of theories than many other parents of her time; indeed many children of my acquaintance had parents who were more addicted to them than she was; and, worse still, many of those parents were much more efficient in enforcing their theory-based laws. There were some children who might not ride bicycles, and others who were forbidden to go in boats; some who were forced to play the violin, and others who always had to wear mufflers; some who might not eat currant buns, and others who were obliged to have cold baths:

all kinds of fads and foolishnesses. There were even some children who were forced to go barefoot, and others who were forbidden to do so. Now, my mother's theories often passed off quite quickly; and in any case there were always (thank Heaven) a good many holes and by-passes through the walls built by her pronouncements. Also she was often out, or away from home; and Nana, though loyal, was eminently humane and reasonable in practice. So that, on the whole, we were rather more free than many of our contemporaries.

Her sturdy American belief in Independence made my mother encourage us to do things for ourselves, unlike the well-brought-up English children of our class, some of whom simply did not know that you *could* make a bed yourself. No doubt it was chiefly because it happened to be convenient, that I was occasionally given a holiday to turn out and clean the locked store-cupboard; but the theory that we could make our own beds, or clean our own bicycles was a great advance. We even sometimes were made to polish our own boots, which we rather enjoyed. We were supposed to learn to cook, too; but that is impossible, where there is an affectionate cook in the kitchen with you, to tell you exactly what to do, and to manage the fire for you. Once, when Margaret had had a course of cooking lessons, she undertook, in the cook's absence, to roast a goose for dinner; and the goose gradually froze to death as the fire went out. There were no gas-cookers then! But the company remarked on the delicious tomato sandwiches she made for tea that afternoon; though it was afterwards discovered that they had been well sprinkled with Keating's Insect Powder, in mistake for pepper. It was partly in consequence of these views of my mother's that when, in 1940, we all came down with a thump to the bare facts of life, we were not quite so helpless as some of our contemporaries; though still idiotic enough, Heaven knows.

Even when I first married it would never have occurred to me that I could possibly be the cook myself, or that I could care for my baby alone, though we were not at all well off at that time. It was not that I was too proud to work—I would not have minded in the least what I did—it was simply that I had not the faintest idea how to begin to run a house by myself, and would not have thought it possible that I could do it, in spite of all my mother's efforts to train us in housework. Of course I disapproved of having servants on principle, even when they were treated with affection and respect, as ours were at home. But this was just an abstract theory; for I had never considered in the least how we should get on without them; in fact it seemed to me quite inevitable that they should be there, a necessary and very tolerable arrangement, both for them and for us. What a distance we have travelled in the last forty years!

Another excellent thing was that we were sometimes left to shift for ourselves, more than was usual for children in our class and time; though this was only partly in consequence of my mother's views on independence. It was also largely a result of the casual happy-go-luckiness—not unaccompanied by laziness—which was one of her most attractive qualities. She was of course inexhaustibly energetic about anything that interested her. She would go to great trouble and make long expeditions to find a cook for someone else; but if a cook for herself was needed, she was bored, and would go to almost equal trouble to get someone else to do the tiresome job for her. 'Very important' committee meetings used sometimes to prevent her from accompanying us on the great family move, when we went to a hired house in Yorkshire, for part of the summer holidays. It was my father who organized and conducted the awful journey, with changes at Ely and York, and piles of luggage and the maids and the dogs and the pram and the parrot and the cot and the bath and us children; particularly Billy, who was always sick in the train. And when we at last got to the house, it was Nana and I who arranged everything; and my mother would arrive comfortably a day or two later, and find us all nicely settled in. We enjoyed doing it, and we did it perfectly well, so all was for the best. But most mothers would have thought it their duty to do more of the fussing themselves.

It was always so. In a sense the maids ran the house; and so long as they showed a certain tact towards her private economies and foibles, she was glad they should do so. But it was very definitely *her* house all the same; only that was the way she ran it. And on the whole it was a success; it was comfortable, the food was always excellent, and the maids stayed for years: the great Mrs. Phillips for nearly thirty years. (Mrs. was a courtesy title, of course.) It was the most hospitable of houses; the sort of place where you could bring five extra people in to lunch unexpectedly, without upsetting anyone. Of course, during her reign, Mrs. Phillips really ran the house completely, but appearances were always preserved. You should have seen the skill with which Mrs. Phillips and my mother avoided each other if they happened to be annoyed. But even Mrs. Phillips herself had to go through the farce of asking for every pot of jam or box of matches to be given out of the store cupboard, for she herself was never allowed to hold the key for a single instant.

The Inviolability of the Locked Store Cupboard was the rock bottom of all my mother's sacred theories of housekeeping. The Opening of the Cupboard was an unpredictable ceremony. First my mother had to be caught at a propitious moment; then the Key had to be found; and then due application had to be made by each maid in turn for the necessaries of their crafts. If my mother was away, or ill, I was trusted with the Key and performed the rites; when I always gave out twice as much as was asked for, as I thought that being given one piece of soap at a time made things rather difficult for the housemaid. However, with that adaptability which is the chief asset of the human race, the maids soon learnt the ropes: they asked for more than they needed and made little hoards against the future; or they ostentatiously left no soap in my mother's own bedroom; or saw to it that it was the dining-room sugar-basin that was empty. No one really suffered; and her Bad Angel, whose name was Economy, was appeased by the show of worship; while her Good Angel, whose name was Serenity, reigned in all essentials.

This Good Angel also made her allow us to go about alone more than most other children did. By the time I was eleven or twelve, I was even allowed to bicycle alone down the Backs after dark, when I came home from having tea with my cousins. It was very quiet and lonely there at night; it may not have been too safe, but she was always singularly fearless.

*I* was afraid; but, of course, I never spoke of my fear; for it was above all things necessary to me to see my cousins, and I was more afraid of having my freedom curtailed than of all the terrors of darkness and solitude.

The Backs were a frightening place, even by daylight, because it was there, more than anywhere else, that Mad Dogs were liable to occur; or so my cousin Frances said, and *she knew*. For she had seen there a very mysterious figure, who was connected with mad dogs: a girl with *red-flannel soles* to her shoes. (I cannot imagine who she was, unless she was the Goddess of Hydrophobia?) The possibility, the probability, of Mad Dogs was very much in our minds; slinking about, with their red tongues hanging out, slobbering and whining; like Caldecott's picture of *the dog it was that died*. Of course there were real mad dogs in those days; and sometimes our dogs had to be muzzled for a time; so we had some excuse for our fears.

Even when we were older, and the Backs were less terrifying by day, it was perfectly appalling at night, to have to ride through the great gulfs of blackness between the faint gas-lamps; while shadowy lovers were hiding in pairs behind the great elm trunks. Or perhaps worse than lovers? Murderers? Or footpads? We only had candle or oil bicycle lamps then, and to make matters worse they were blown out by every breath of air; but I clenched my teeth and rode like the wind, and hoped to get through alive. Freedom was worth any heroism. None of my cousins were allowed to do this, so I had the recompense of feeling rather grand about it.

But when all is said and done, our liberty was only relative; we were only just a little more free than some of our contemporaries, and I have no hesitation in saying that all our generation was much too carefully brought up. As we grew towards adolescence the restrictions became steadily more painful, for they prevented us from growing in the natural way, just as the binding of the feet of a Chinese girl prevents growth. Our cousins, Ruth and Nora, were very much more carefully brought up than we were; and they suffered, both then and later, more than we did. Frances was the sheltered and adored only child, and though she was less unhappy at the time, she too suffered in the end from the over-protection.

My own private theory is, that it is better to let children's teeth or morals suffer from *laisser-aller*, than to be too vigilant about them. But no doubt people who have been really hurt by neglect in their youth will disagree with me. For this is a matter in which it is impossible ever to be in the right.

Dear Reader, you may take it from me, that however hard you try—or don't try; whatever you do—or don't do; for better, for worse; for richer, for poorer; every way and every day:

THE PARENT IS ALWAYS WRONG

So it is no good bothering about it. When the little pests grow up they will certainly tell you exactly what you did wrong in their case. But, never mind; they will be just as wrong themselves in their turn. So take things easily; and above all, *eschew good intentions*.

By all accounts I was a charming baby. As I have never been considered particularly charming since then, I think it only just to myself to set this on record. It fairly makes me blush to read the pages of admiration in the old letters—not only those of my mother, but others as well. How I have gone off since then! My mother writes of some visitor at Down: *'For the first time I have met a typical English husband, according to our American ideas. Cross, bad-tempered and very prejudiced. . . . But even he was charmed by Gwen!'*

But there are dangers attached to charm. In another letter she tells how my cousin Bernard Darwin liked playing with me, when I was one year old and he ten. *'When Gwen is older, it will be difficult to keep her away from Dubba (B.D.). There is such a strong liking on both sides of George's family to marry first cousins, that I shall dread Gwen's living so near Dubba (at Cambridge). . . . There is plenty of time, but when Gwen is seventeen I am going to send her away.'* This precaution did not prove necessary; by the time I was seventeen my charm was no longer so dangerous to the male sex.

My mother was always throwing out new ideas; some of them were rather wild; others were so simple and sensible that they very nearly amounted to genius; but the application of them was sometimes rather autocratic. For instance, she rightly held that children should lead a simple life, without over-indulgence. Of course we never had fires in our bedrooms, unless we were really ill; but then neither did the grown-ups, so that was all right and fair. In spite of the huge coal fires in the sitting-rooms and the hall, the whole house was much colder and draughtier than would now be considered tolerable.

But surely our feeding was unnecessarily austere? We had porridge for breakfast, with salt, not sugar; and milk to drink. Porridge always reminds me of having breakfast alone with my father, when I was so small that I put the porridge into the spoon with my fingers, while he told me stories in French. My mother came down later, perhaps with the sensible idea of avoiding me and the porridge and the French. There was toast and butter, but I never had anything stronger for breakfast, till I tasted bacon for the first time in my life when I went to stay with Frances, at the age of nearly ten.

It is true that twice a week we had, at the end of breakfast, one piece of toast, spread with a thin layer of that dangerous luxury, Jam. But, of course, not butter, too. Butter and Jam on the same bit of bread would have been an unheard-of indulgence—a disgraceful orgy. The queer thing is that we none of us like it to this very day. But these two glamorous Jam-days have permanently coloured my conception of Sundays and Wednesdays, which are both lovely dark red days. Though Wednesday, being also Drawing Class Day, is much the redder of the two. Sunday's delicious jam colour has been considerably paled down by Church.

Just occasionally our father used to give us, as a breakfast treat, a taste of a special food, called by us *Speissums*; but, schismatically, by our cousins: *Purr Meat*. There was a continual controversy over the correct name. Fortnum and Mason called it *Hung Beef*. Some of it was freshly grated every morning into a fluffy pile on a plate; and you put a bit of toast, butter side down, on it, and some of it stuck on. It was delicious. But that was later on, when the decay of morals had set in. Margaret got it when she was quite young. I didn't.

There was only bread-and-butter and milk for tea, as Jam might have weakened our moral fibre; and sponge-cakes when visitors came. One of my major crimes was a propensity for nibbling the edges off the sponge-cakes before the visitors arrived. Our cousins did not consider that our tea-parties were very good; they were rather sorry for us. We were generally given one piece of Maple Sugar after tea; my mother imported it from the States. It was delicious, but not nearly enough; and we might not ever buy sweets, which were considered very unwholesome; except, oddly enough, butterscotch out of the penny-in-the-slot machines at the railway stations. There was a blessed theory that the slot machines were pure, that the Railways guaranteed their Virtue. But we did not travel often, so I was obliged to steal sugar whenever I could. Certainly I was greedy, but one really had to do the best one could for oneself, in those days, when sugar was thought to be unwholesome; and fruit, though a pleasant treat, rather dangerous.

As we grew older, our moral fibre was weakened by having either Jam or very heavy dough-cake for tea. But not both; never both. However, this relaxation was the beginning of the end; under our continual pressure the food laws wore thinner and thinner, till by the time they got down to Billy—who is nine years younger than I am—there were no regulations left at all, and he could eat whatever was going for breakfast and tea, just like the grown-ups themselves. And I cannot see that his character is any the worse for it; in fact, he is probably less greedy than I am. Ah, innocent child, he little knew how much he owed to my self-sacrificing campaign for liberty, equality and fraternity over the victuals.

My mother's attacks of theories were often short, but some of them were permanent. For instance, we were never allowed to drink tea at all; for, as a good American she considered it most dangerously stimulating, though coffee was perfectly harmless. But we always drank great quantities of milk, till suddenly one day, a mischief-making doctor promulgated the revolting theory that all milk must be BOILED! Because of *Germs*; of which we now heard for the first time, and in which we vehemently declined to believe. So, when cold, boiled milk, *with the skin on it*, was put before us, there was a regular riot of disgust, and we refused to touch it; and went on refusing—with Nana's covert sympathy—till the vile enactment was allowed to lapse, and the Theory faded back into that limbo where Theories wander, while they are waiting for their next incarnation. And in two or three months' time we were happily drinking our nice, fresh, tuberculous milk again.

That was a short bout, though a sharp one. The Theory that

# Theories

Beef was Bad and Mutton was Good died harder; though even my mother's 'muttonic habits' passed off in time; and the Theory that Gingerbread Pudding gave you cancer caused us very little trouble, as we did not much like Gingerbread Pudding anyhow. But there was a permanent ban on brown sugar, because it was made by negroes, who were dirty. We used to tease her by saying that she thought the negroes' skins were not fast colour, so that the brown came off them. I don't believe she really thought that; but, anyhow, I have been left with an unsatisfied brown-sugar complex to this very day.

My mother would have been a keen teetotaller, if my father had not happened to like wine in moderation. She used to explain to us that he only took it for the good of his digestion; but we knew very well that that was Nonsense. All the same we were not allowed to have brandy-butter with our plum-puddings; and she used to tell us a really shocking story, of how her own mother, when she had to dose her children with castor oil, used to give it in Whiskey, in order to make them take a dislike for drink. I believe that my mother felt rather guilty because she did not do the same by us; but mercifully she did not. Castor oil *and* whiskey together would really have been too much, so dreadful as they both were! Modern children have no idea of the horrors they have escaped, in not being brought up on castor oil. We were always having doses of it. 'So safe', they used to say; and yet now the doctors consider it dangerous. Sugar is good now and castor oil bad! How happy those ideas would have made us in our day. But I expect it is only a matter of time, till the wheel comes round again, and the doctors reverse the verdict.

My own especial horrors were *powders*, which modern children don't have either. It was a most unpleasant shock to be woken up, when the elders went to bed, and to have a teaspoonful of pink powder—just like plate-powder—with a dab of jelly on top, suddenly presented under your sleepy nose. The powderiness of it sometimes made me really sick.

Another health theory was that, as sea-bathing was wholesome, salt in our bath-water would do just as well as a visit to the sea-side. So some handfuls of Dr. Tidman's Sea Salt—little round pebbles—were put into the tub we had in front of the day-nursery fire, twice a week. As the salt was only put in when we got in ourselves it did not have time to melt; and we disliked it exceedingly, because the pebbles were so painful to stand or sit on. I suppose this was pure magic? I must put on record here a cure for chilblains, which a friend tells me was practised by her father's nurse. A red-hot poker was put into 'that which is beneath the bed', and, as the nurse said, 'it was most mysteerus', but a certain cure. And even in the year 1947 *a fried mouse* was most earnestly recommended to me as a cure for whooping cough. I dare say it is as good as any other cure; the only difficulty is to believe in it.

Our mother was always faithful to Our Doctor, who was the only good doctor in the world. His lightest word was enshrined like a fly in amber, and remained a gospel truth for ever and ever; and as for Our Dentist, in London, he was practically a god. Our Pram, too, was sacred. It was a 'baby-carriage', brought for me from America in 1885, along with several rocking-chairs. The pram was made of basket-work, very high and light and rattly, with clattering wooden wheels. Many a battle did she have with her grandchildren's nurses in the nineteen-twenties, when they refused to be seen by the other nurses 'pushing such a peculiar-looking object'. I believe that even Nana herself, in her day, had something to bear on that head.

Of course, we children had a few theories of our own. One was that the gum of cherry or plum trees was delicious, and must be eaten as a great treat. This is a mistake, as it is quite incredibly nasty; and so is snow with jam, which we also believed to be nice. Another theory was, that if you swallowed the smallest speck of cork, it would swell and swell inside, till it filled you right up and you died. There was also the now disproved idea that bulls were infuriated by red rags; for this reason I used to bite in my supposedly red lips if ever I met the oldest and mildest cow; and I remember carefully concealing the red halfpenny stamps on any letters I might be taking to the post, for the same reason. And of course we believed, as I think all nurses and children do, that if you cut, or even scratched, the fold of skin which joins your thumb and first finger, you got lockjaw at once, and died in agonies.

Another theory of my mother's was that the punishment should fit the crime. And so once, when I had bitten the nursery-maid, I had my mouth washed out with soap and water; and another time when I had slapped her, I had socks tied down over my hands and had to come down to lunch and be fed in public with a spoon, when I was quite old. A dreadful punishment for a shy child. And when I cut off my own hair, I was made to go about with it as it was, for several days, before I was allowed to have it cut properly. 'It looks as if a dog had bitten it off', my mother said, as I sat on her knee. She had a very queer look on her face, and I suddenly realized that she was trying not to laugh at me, which mortified me very much.

I was only once spanked that I can remember. I had been put to rest after lunch on my mother's bed, under the muslin curtains, which fell down from the hanging canopy. Now resting is a foolish theory, from which many parents suffer. It is far too exhausting for children, it is really only suitable for the old. I used to get absolutely worn out inventing games to play during the ages when I was condemned to 'rest'; so that by the time the rest was over, I really did need a rest. However, this time I enjoyed myself. I found on the dressing-table a stick of red lip-salve. The white wall-paper was neatly framed by the bed-curtains; so I began a fine, bold wall-painting, in enormous swoops and circles. It was like frescoing the walls of Heaven. But I was interrupted, and my father was told to spank me with a slipper. It didn't hurt and I did not mind a bit. But I never forgot the joy of wall-painting.

## CHAPTER IV

# *Education*

---

My mother's theories of education were so revolutionary and sensible, that modern thought has hardly caught up with them even now. I find her writing, before I was six months old: *'I believe in every girl being brought up to have some occupation when they are grown-up, just as a boy is; it makes them much happier. Gwen is to be a mathematician.'* But, later on she, for once, was defeated; and, strange to say, retired baffled before my obvious mathematical idiocy. This was most exceptional, for as a rule she was quite convinced that anyone could do anything they wished to do. For instance, till the very last year of her life, she was always pressing me to make a lot of money by drawing comic pictures of undergraduates, to be published as post cards. 'What nonsense. Of course you could do it. It is quite easy for anyone who can draw. Very silly of you not to try.' But I disappointed her in that way, as in so many others. It makes me sorry now to think of it. I really ought once to have tried to draw an undergraduate climbing a lamp-post. But I never did.

She also held strongly that the education of the hands developed the mind. But we conservative children did not agree at all; though perhaps that was because the minds of our governesses had not been properly developed. At any rate their efforts to teach us handicrafts were not a success. As usual the theory was right, but the practice went wrong. We objected very strongly to being reft away from proper lessons, such as sums or Latin grammar, to make weak and waggly baskets, which nobody wanted; or to fold up pieces of paper while our governess tried to make out from the Book, what we were supposed to do next with them. It bored us passionately, and offended our dignity. It was simply not Right to have to do things like that in lesson time. And sewing was downright wicked slavery.

The worst of it was that there was a strong theory that day-schools for girls were Bad; so, though Charles went fairly young to 'Goody's [St. Faith's], we girls were condemned to the dull confinement of the schoolroom at home, under a series of daily governesses. This was partly because the Perse School for Girls was not well spoken of, at that time; but, still more, because my aunts would not have dreamt of sending my cousins there. The upper classes did not approve of day schools, though boarding schools for older girls might sometimes be allowed. The Aristocracy, however, did not even hold with boarding schools, for a peeress of our acquaintance once roused my mother to fury, by snubbing her with the words: '*We* do not send our daughters away to school.' However, I believe that the real reason why we were kept at home all those years was that my mother herself had been unhappy at school; for if she had felt strongly that we ought to go, she would have sent us, in spite of a hundred aunts or a million peeresses.

But really I longed to go to school, though of course I never said so. Anything would have been better than the schoolroom at home. I can't imagine why we four cousins of the same age could not have had a class together? Margaret was a good deal younger, but there were Ruth and Nora and Frances and I, all of a suitable age. Surely it would have been exclusive enough, even for our refined family? And it would have been such fun for us. But it was never even thought of, as far as I know; and there were we four girls, shut up in three separate schoolrooms, with three separate governesses. It was fantastic.

## Education

Unlike our cousins, we had daily governesses; they did not live in, chiefly because my mother thought it would be a bore to have them in the house; and she also had a theory that they would value their independence. But, though they were mostly Scotch, they had not really reached the independence level, in spite of all their wha-haeing. *Whahaeing* is one of the chief pursuits of the Scotch, as Burns states in his difficult poem beginning *Scots wha hae*. These ladies lived lonely and uncomfortable lives in lodgings; and were generally in love, though they thought we did not know it; and some of them had Family Circumstances; and some of them had Religion as well, which made it much worse, both for them and for us. And they whahaed about Bruce and Wallace, and rubbed in spiders and tartans and porridge and the insufferable and universal superiority of the Scotch (No, I will NOT say Scots) to such an extent, that we could only get into corners and thank our stars that we had not one drop of Scotch blood in our veins. And it was many, many years before any of us was able to look with unprejudiced eyes at anything Scotch again. Always excepting Scott's novels, which we loved. I write this on purpose, so that any surviving Scotch governesses may take warning, and learn to draw it milder. Our Nana was Scotch—her name was Helen Jean Campbell—but she had never lived in Scotland, or learnt the Scotch doxology.

They were all kind, good, dull women; but even interesting lessons can be made incredibly stupid, when they are taught by people who are bored to death with them, and who do not care for the art of teaching either. But, of course, if these ladies had had any ambition they would not have been teaching us, but would have made a career of it, by teaching at a school. However, thank heaven, I also went to one or two special lessons with real teachers, who were interested in what they were teaching.

Our daily walks with the governess were quite paralysing with dulness; for in the winter our only form of exercise was walking, now that we were growing too old for playing pirates and climbing trees. Ruth and Nora had a governess, who insisted on their walking with very short steps, because you got more exercise that way.

But, anyhow, there was always Miss Mary Greene's Wednesday Drawing Class, which was the centre of my youthful existence. I lived in those days from Wednesday to Wednesday; for it was not only that the drawing was an ecstasy, but that Miss Greene's warm, generous, appreciative nature was a great release and encouragement to me. Besides it was such fun; the three cousins came, too, and we did exciting things, such as exploring the vast cellars of the Cast Museum with a box of matches, when we were supposed to be drawing *The Dying Gladiator*; or getting locked into the Round Church with a lunatic, when we were learning about Norman architecture.

We did all kinds of things with Miss Greene; it was not just sitting and drawing in the studio—though that in itself was passionately interesting, especially when we had a real model. She took us out to draw buildings and streets and trees and animals, and we learnt about architecture and perspective and anatomy; and she gave us lectures about the great painters, and showed us reproductions of their work. I can still remember nearly all the lecture on Hogarth; how he ran away with his master's daughter, and the meaning of all the queer figures in *Calais Gate*, and all about *Gin Lane* and how he hated cruelty. Every week we had homework to do: a drawing from life, and a composition on a set subject. Charles's best composition was on the subject *A Surprise*: three vermilion devils in a row, cocking snooks at a poor little man on a horse, which was rearing up in most natural alarm. A very striking work; though we did not usually consider Charles one of our best artists. I admired Frances's pictures most of all. They seemed to me exactly like real life, which was then my simple criterion of art; though I do just remember thinking that she did not draw human legs quite right, the backs of the thighs seemed to bulge in a curious way; otherwise her pictures were perfectly beautiful.

From the time I was nine, when the Drawing Class began, I always kept a sketchbook going, and drew everything I saw. They were bad drawings; still I suppose I learnt something from the habit—observation, if nothing else. Nobody had ever told me that drawing is not copying, and I should probably not have understood if they had; but it took me a long time to find it out for myself. All the people round me thought that pictures ought to be photographically like reality; so of course I thought so, too. Yet every now and then I would suddenly see a picture in my head—usually a vision of a landscape, not a remembered scene—and when I drew it, I did realize that it turned out better than the landscapes I copied so laboriously from nature. But I did not realize why this was. I am sure that no one would have picked me out of the class as a promising artist; my colour was even worse than my drawing; there was nothing to notice about me, except my keenness.

I was just thirteen when I was first taken abroad; we passed through Amsterdam, where a big Rembrandt exhibition was being held. I went absolutely mad, and set out to copy as many of the paintings as I could, in pencil, in a grubby little sketchbook. After that, someone gave me a little book of reproductions of Rembrandt's drawings and etchings, and I carried it about in my pocket and slept with it by my bed for several years. If I had been asked then what I wanted to do in later life, I should have answered: 'to make pictures of people doing things' (i.e. working). Some time after this, as a result of a lecture on Turner by Miss Greene, I went all by myself to the FitzWilliam Museum, and asked to see the Turner water-colours which are kept there. This required considerable courage. They brought out some of those painted on blue-tinted paper, and picked out with body-colour. I did not understand them then, and was much disappointed. Rembrandt remained my God. But by the time I went to the Slade, I had begun to perceive that Turner's finest works were abstract paintings, and that he was one of the great painters of the world. Of course, I could not have used the word *abstract* then, but it was what I meant, when I was bowled over by such compositions as 'Interior at Petworth', or 'The Sea Monster'.

I always liked pictures, as long as I can remember anything; and I always liked poetry, and knew that it did not matter whether I understood it or not. But music left me quite cold; or, worse than that, I thought it a terrible bore. We used occasionally to be taken to children's concerts, where I struggled with agonies of sleepiness, or played games with my fingers and watched the clock. It had never occurred to me to listen, till one evening, when all the concert-party were ragging about in the Backs on the way home, I heard a boy say: 'Oh, do shut up, I want to think about the music.' I was quite astonished. I knew that you could think about painting or poetry, but I did not know that you *could* think about music. But even after that I only listened with my mind, not with my ears. Music moved me sensually a good deal, but in a way which I disliked; especially brass bands, and church organs, and Mrs. N. playing Beethoven on the piano, in her most powerful manner. (Not that I knew that it was Beethoven then, I only assume it now.)

I was a remarkably poor performer on the piano myself; I was, however, apparently able to impress Margaret, when she was but young; for once we raided her diary and discovered the following entry: '*Gwen played the piano very beautifully, and Olwen and I lay on the floor and had pure sad thoughts.*' We tormented Margaret about her pure sad thoughts for many a long year.

I was so ignorant and uninterested in music that when I went away to school, at the age of sixteen, and was asked in a General Knowledge Paper, which were my three favourite composers, I had the greatest difficulty in naming as many as three altogether!

65

# Education

And I had no idea what any of them had written. It was my own fault that my development was so lopsided; one does not assimilate what one does not find interesting.

Music, in our nursery, was represented by a barrel-organ, on which you put round yellow cards with little holes in them, through which iron teeth came bobbing up when you turned a handle to grind out 'The Minstrel Boy' or 'She Wore a Wreath of Roses'. Only Charles always insisted on making it more interesting by putting on the cards upside down, so that the tunes were played backwards. He was a great adept at doing things backwards; I still remember the beginning (or rather the end) of the Greek alphabet backwards, as he taught it to me on the platform of Rugby station: Agemo, isp, ik, if, nolispu, uat, etc. At about this time he also invented a new language, which had *none but irregular verbs*.

But I have wandered a long way from our governesses. My mother was a good deal of a feminist, and she would have liked to have inspired them with the ambition to take up some of the new professions, which were beginning to be open to women; but she had no success. There was however *one* governess, of whom my mother might in time have made something; she at any rate had enterprise.

She came to us as a holiday governess, for only a short time, and did not have to teach us seriously, which was probably why she took the job. Miss Z. was tall and athletic, with rolling black eyes and an incredibly high starched collar; and she had an enormous bag of golf-clubs. Her manners were rather slapdash, and we did not much like her, but there was a kind of 'I could an if I would' flavour about her conversation, which was intriguing. I remember her threatening, in joke, 'to let down our drawers and smack our bottoms'. We thought this vulgar, but it was interesting, as being so different from anything the other governesses could possibly have said. She also taught Margaret (who was six) to sing a parody

66

of 'After the Ball is Over', which ran 'See her take off her false hair', and so on. My mother did not like her, but let her stay till the end of the time for which she had been engaged.

Some time afterwards a case was noticed in the paper, in which this same Miss Z. sued a man for libel. He had been a guest in the house where she was acting as governess, and he told her employer that he recognized her as having been a parlourmaid in another house which he had visited. She denied this, but it proved to be true, and she lost her case. Apparently she had been in the habit of taking temporary jobs, sometimes as governess, sometimes as parlourmaid. The gulf between a servant and a governess was then unbridgeable; it was as if a shrimp had tried to turn into a tiger. We used to wonder afterwards whether she had stolen all those golf-clubs, though I don't believe there was much reason to think that she had done anything worse than misrepresent her status as that of a lady; Heaven knows that was bad enough! My mother laughed about it all: 'Well, thank goodness, she was with us so short a time, that she can't have done the children any harm.' The other governesses had done much more harm, though with the best possible intentions.

The Classics at their most classic—studies not of literature but of words and grammar—were then considered by public school-masters as the only proper learning for boys; anything outside Latin and Greek were frivolous hors-d'œuvres. When Charles won a prize for history at Marlborough, the headmaster wrote in his term's report: '*This shews that he is not a mere mathematician.*' Charles was very much hurt, and my father sympathized with him. He believed in a wider education.

So he took care that we should learn to speak French well. He was justly proud of his own French; and one of my earliest memories is of the stories he used to tell us in French, about some children who walked along a *falaise* (a cliff) and saw a *taupe* (a mole)—words I never forgot. We always had French nursery-maids under Nana (poor Nana!). They were always homesick, poor things, and used to cry and sniff in the housemaids' cupboard. By a provision of Providence they were always called Eugenie, so that when a new one came she could be called Newgenie. My father had a great friend, an aristocratic French senator, whose children used to come to stay with us, and scandalize Nana by having a grown-up dinner when we were going to bed. But I scandalized them by learning Latin with Charles, which they thought most un-feminine, and really indecent.

Later, just before Charles went to Marlborough, we were sent together to Hanover to learn German. There I attended a drawing class, where the 'nude' model was decently clothed from head to foot in pink tights; and the street boys used to pursue us and stone us, under the very noses of the stout and haughty policemen, with cries of '*Engeländer, Engeländer, die Booren kommen*'—for this was during the Boer War. Here, too, we heard of the death of Queen Victoria, which surprised me; for though I knew it was impossible that she should live for ever, yet at the same time I had thought that perhaps she might! She had been Queen since a long time before my father was born, and he always seemed to me immensely old. She might well have turned out to be immortal, I thought.

Here, too, I was revolted by the slave treatment of the servant at the flat where we stayed in Hanover. The girl slept in a windowless attic, up a ladder out of the kitchen. While we were there, everyone had influenza rather badly; when the girl fell ill she just went up into her dog-kennel, and stayed there, alone in the dark, for several days. Nobody went near her or did anything but curse at her, for the presumption of supposing that she was not able to do her usual work. Of course she could have done it; she was only a peasant, and consideration was quite wasted on peasants; they were animals, alto-gether beneath humanity. Indeed I must admit that those Hanoverian peasants did look less intelligent than a well-bred cow, as they staggered about with huge loads of firewood on their backs and heads. But I was horrified by the German callousness, and once shocked a peasant woman exceedingly by helping her to pick up some wood she had dropped. She suspected me of the most sinister motives for my action.

My father came to visit us while we were there, and I remember overhearing him say, that he had been struck by the number of stories of bullying and cruelty which he had heard since he had been in Germany, particularly of the ill-treatment by parents of one among their children. It was a new idea to me that this was possible. He was also astonished to find that the well-known professors, whom he had come to see, were all Jingo and Imperialist, and that they were passionate admirers of the Kaiser.

As long as Charles remained at Goody's, there was a breath of fresh air blowing into my life from the world outside. But when he was sent away to school I missed him dreadfully, and the stuffiness became almost intolerable. At last, when I was nearly sixteen, I went to my parents and asked if I could not go away to school, too. I could not think of any other plan of escape; and though I was not very happy at school, still I felt I was seeing the world from a new angle, and that I had not stopped growing, as I had at home.

School upset me very much at first, and I did not think that I could survive it, when the poison gas of homesickness settled down over my head, with its indescribable nausea. Though it was not really *home*-sickness, for I did not want to go home, only to escape into an air which I could breathe. I remember the first morning, kneeling at prayers (an alarming rite to me), and staring out of the window, when my eyes ought to have been tight shut, and thinking: 'If only I could get out into that garden, perhaps I might feel better; anyhow there are some quite ordinary trees there, and some real grass'—for everything inside the house seemed to be tainted with a nightmare horror.

For the first six months the fog hardly lifted at all; and for much of that time I was physically unwell from misery; then my cousin Nora joined me at school; and that one little corner of understanding made an immense difference to me. Nora adapted herself to school far more easily than I did.

But the smell of the poison-gas never really went away, and I still now sometimes get a whiff of it when I have had to visit a school or stay with incongruous people. I must confess that once, when I was quite old and had gone to call on some strangers, the alien feeling of the furniture became so appalling to me, after the maid had left me alone in the drawing-room, that I scrambled disgracefully out of the window and ran away down the drive and never returned. I can't imagine what the lady and the maid thought when they came in and found the room empty. Perhaps I have become their family ghost.

I was sent to a small private school; an excellent one in its way no doubt; but it was not my way. The emphasis was all on Young-lady-hood, slightly tinged with Christianity (C. of E. variety), and I should never have felt comfortable there if I had stayed there for a million years. When, a little later, I went to the Slade School, I felt perfectly happy there at once; and I was at ease with the students, though many of them came from backgrounds which were quite unfamiliar to me. But that seemed like my own country. At boarding-school I was always a foreigner.

Not that I wanted to leave school; I wanted to stay on, if only I could manage to bear it; for I was very curious about the extraordinary habits of the girls. For instance, that first day, they were all singing: 'I am the Honeysuckle, You are the Bee.' Why? What on earth was it? (I had never heard a popular song in my life.) And they were all busy making hat-pin knobs out of coloured sealing-wax. Now why in the world did they like doing that? Nearly everything they did mystified me.

It took me some time to realize that it was considered queer to be interested in anything whatever except horses, or things like hat-pin-knobbing; or, of course, games or gossip. However, presently I began to enjoy hockey myself, and I even got into the team, and

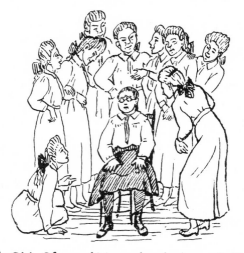

The Génie. Of course this is not what school was really like, but it is what it felt like to me.

felt very grand with my red cap (like a boy's cap) pinned on to my hair. We played in white blouses and blue skirts, which had to clear the ground by six inches; and our waist-belts were very neat and trim over our tight stays. And when we came in from a game —and our play was most ferocious—all covered with mud and streaming hot, we had to go straight into school, without having time to change, or wash, or comb our hair, at all.

As soon as I dared I began to take part in the gossip, too, with all the bewildered avidity of an anthropologist trying to understand the minds of the natives. But I never really succeeded. Once, after I had married Jacques, I dreamt that I had got to go back to school, and take him with me, and *explain him to the Girls*. Only Nora, who knew both Jacques and The Girls, can fully realize the nightmare impossibility of this task.

I always felt that the girls' comments on my appearance and character were perfectly fair, though they did not err on the side of mildness, for I knew that I was raw and uncouth. School criticism certainly improved my manners a good deal; but my social self-confidence, never very strong, was badly and permanently shaken by it. And my school nickname hurt me deeply. They called me, in the Anglo-French which we had to talk all day long, *The Génie*; a hybrid term, neither The Genius, nor yet *Le Génie*. This name was ostensibly given me because I was put into rather high classes on my first arrival; actually because they thought me queer. How that name did sting! I suppose that was why it stuck all through my career. Yet I passionately wanted to be an Ordinary Person; and I tried very hard, and quite ineffectually, to conceal all my real interests from their contempt and mockery.

For the chief thing I learnt at school was how to tell lies. Or rather, how to try to tell them; for, of course, I did it very badly. Still, I did my best to pretend that I did like what I didn't and that I didn't like what I did. But it was no good; they knew perfectly well that there was something wrong about me, so that I always felt inferior and out of it, just as I did at a party. The truth was, that while I was desperately anxious to appear exactly like everyone else, yet at the same time, I intended at all costs to keep alive the precious little grain of *me*, which was inside. And no one can succeed in running with the hare and hunting with the hounds for very long.

Besides the hare got out sometimes. Once we had a debate: 'that unhappiness is better for the character than happiness.' I could not bear what I considered the sanctimonious falsity of this conception of life; and Nora and I both made impassioned speeches against the motion; but the whole school out-voted us, and, in spite of our scorn, revelled in the purifying effects of sorrow.

There was another outburst in a French lesson. Mademoiselle M. used to set us to write compositions on such subjects as 'Le berceau et le tombeau' or 'L'honneur'. When she set: 'Le Mariage est une loterie' we were very indignant, and Nora said, with her English accent: 'Ce n'aye par vraye, Mademoiselle,' and we both argued fiercely that marriage was a perfectly reasonable proceeding, not subject to the laws of chance. Nora was a great comfort to me at school.

Mademoiselle was the most vivid person there. We were all rather afraid of her tired, yellow face, above her perpetual plaid blouse and grubby lace necktie; for when a French woman decides to be shabby, she does it better than anyone else. She had a burning passion for teaching; a vocation, a mission to make us learn French thoroughly. In class she would point her finger at you suddenly, and command: 'Les cinq temps primitifs de *moudre*' (or some other of those anarchic verbs); and if you did not instantly reply: 'Moudre moulant, moulu, je meuds, je moulus'—her fury could make any of us cry, even the captain of the hockey team. The headmistress herself, a most fiery and imperial lady, thought twice before going through Mademoiselle's classroom if she were giving a lesson there.

Every morning, after Prayers, we were asked: 'Will anyone who spoke English yesterday hold up her hand.' Generally about three people held up their hands and got their bad marks; for our consciences were not too particular about a word here or there; though there was one girl, who had scruples, and who held up her hand every day. I believe that she did this chiefly to annoy the authorities; in which, of course, she succeeded; though they always ignored her gesture with dignified blindness. But Mademoiselle's unsleeping ardour could be trusted to make her come pouncing out of the study, if ever anyone in the farthest corner of the house (or so it seemed) spoke English, or said shocking things like: 'Je vais faire mon cheveu'; or 'Etes-vous froid?' And she really did teach us to speak French without false shame, which is half the battle.

For the rest, school is rather a dim memory to me; all hurry and scurry; beginning in the morning with the sound of the house-maids' feet racing along the passages, as they carried great cans of water for the saucer-baths, which they pulled out from under our beds; and then, all day long, running myself like a hare, from place to place, at the sound of the bell, in the hopeless endeavour not to be late. And then, the continual strain, the effort, of trying to understand, to imitate, to conciliate the indigenous population of that foreign land, where I never could get higher than the tolerance of 'It's only old Génie' from the kinder inhabitants. And when at last the anxious, crowded day was over, there came the distasteful duty of *kissing* five or six mistresses good night. They stood in a row after Prayers, to endure this unhygienic operation from the whole school. (How could they bear it?)

In all that time there is only one vision that I keep: a flash, seen through the garden hedge, of some sheep in the next field, with the frosty, winter light running along their backs. It seemed like something from another world: the real world, to which I should escape again some day. It kept me alive.

I must not be ungrateful: I did learn a great deal at school, and grow and widen, too. I am glad I went there. But it is no use denying it: I don't like boarding schools; although they are better than governesses. Day schools might be better still, but I never went to a day school.

# CHAPTER V

## *Ladies*

When my granddaughter Anne was about five, she said to me one day: 'Grandmamma, when I am grown up, I think I shall be a witch. There are too many ladies, don't you think?' Well, I suppose there are still too many ladies; but there were many more too many ladies when I was young. My whole life was surrounded by them; but from the very beginning I was determined, like Anne, never, never to be one. I remember thinking how pretty my mother's hands were—white, slender and charming, with her big diamond ring on her pink-tipped finger; and I thought: 'When I'm old, I don't want to have hands like that; I want to have hands like Nana's, all brown and wrinkled.'

Ladies were ladies in those days; they did not do things themselves, they told other people what to do and how to do it. My mother would have told anybody how to do anything: the cook how to skin a rabbit, or the groom how to harness a horse; though of course she had never done, or even observed, these operations herself. She would cheerfully have told an engine-driver how to drive his engine, and he would have taken it quite naturally, and have answered: 'Yes, ma'am,' 'Very good, ma'am,' 'Quite right, ma'am,' and then would have gone on driving his engine exactly as before, with hardly even an inward grin at the vagaries of the upper classes; while my mother would certainly have thought his driving much improved. But then they would both have been experts at their own jobs, and tolerant of each others' little whims.

For instance, my mother had a theory, founded on intuition, that lard was dirty; and it was strictly forbidden in our kitchen. But the cook always had plenty of lard—I suppose called by some other name in the account book—and it was quite safe, for my mother would not have recognized the stuff if she had seen it on the kitchen table. The cook knew well enough that part of her job was to listen to her mistress talking about lard, or any other fad; after which she did exactly what she had always intended to do, and got on with her work in her own way.

I remember once sitting by, much embarrassed, during the call of an acquaintance, who held a high official position connected with the Admiralty. My mother told him, in detail, exactly what had been done wrong in the Archer-Shee case—that now historic scandal—about which she knew nothing whatever, except from the newspapers; while he must have known all about it at first hand. And as she told him what ought now to be done to set things right, he listened, smiling and assenting, and privately enjoying the joke, for I am sure he liked her and was amused, not irritated, by his scolding.

I can never remember being bathed by my mother, or even having my hair brushed by her, and I should not at all have liked it if she had done anything of the kind. We did not feel it was her place to do such things; though my father used to cut our finger-nails with his sharp white-handled knife, and that we felt quite pleasant and proper. Anyhow, there was no need for my mother to do such things, for Nana hardly ever went out, and if she did the housemaid or the nurserymaid was left in charge of us. About once in two or three years there was an appalling calamity, and Nana left us poor little orphans, while she went away for a week's holiday; but it was all arranged beforehand, and my mother did nothing extra herself, except perhaps a little more *telling* than usual.

The only manual work I can ever remember her doing was un-picking old dresses for the dressmaker to re-fashion; and, once or twice of a summer evening, holding the nozzle of the garden-hose before handing it over to one of us. But I must state, most em-phatically, that she did not avoid work because she felt it beneath her; it was because it bored her. So she always got someone else to do it for her. As far as appearances went, she would have walked about with a coal-scuttle on her head without turning a hair. She used to laugh at Uncle Dick for refusing to carry a parcel in the street. But she was lazy in some ways; it was the other side of her comfortable calmness.

There is however one letter from my mother to my father, writ-ten from Philadelphia shortly before her marriage: it contains an account of an episode which was unique in her career. '*Just now I am resting from painting—not artistic painting, but practical painting. I thought it would be a pleasant little surprise for Mamma to come home and find the dining-room entirely repainted. So I bought the paint and have been brushing it on all the morning. . . . Now I have given it to one of the maids to finish. It is tiresome work.*' And I feel quite certain that she never did any practical painting again.

There was also the memorable occasion when she made Corn Beef Hash. It was in her first summer in England, when she was staying with the Jebbs, and Gerald Balfour was coming to dinner. She writes that '*Dick was "nervous". He asked about the dinner. Only G.B. was expected. Aunt C. intended having soup, fish, roast beef, pud-ding, fruit and cheese. Dick objected at not having an entrée. It was too late to send to college and we racked our brains to think of something easily made. Aunt C. said how good hashes used to taste in Philadelphia. And then in fun I suggested corn-beef hash, as we had had corn-beef in the luncheon. So, in fear and trembling I went into the kitchen, and made it the*

*way I thought it ought to be. Dick and Gerald ate it as if they enjoyed it.*
*Aunt C. asked Dick afterwards for his opinion, and he said he thought it*
*was good, but looked "improvised".'*

The regular round of formal dinner-parties was very important
in Cambridge. In our house the parties were generally of twelve
or fourteen people, and everybody of dinner-party status was invited strictly in turn. The guests were seated according to the Proto-
col, the Heads of Houses ranking by the dates of the foundations of
their colleges, except that the Vice-Chancellor would come first
of all. After the Masters came the Regius Professors in the order of
their subjects, Divinity first; and then the other Professors according
to the dates of the foundations of their chairs, and so on down all the
steps of the hierarchy. It was better not to invite too many important people at the same time, or the complications became insoluble
to hosts of only ordinary culture. How could they tell if Hebrew
or Greek took precedence, of two professorships founded in the
same year? And some of the grandees were very touchy about their
rights, and their wives were even more easily offended.

The latest bride had to wear her wedding-dress, and was taken
in by the host. It was terrifying for her, poor young thing, to walk
out before all those hawk-eyed matrons; and to remember to be
ready for the hostess to 'catch her eye' at the end of dinner. This
was the signal for the ladies to gather up their belongings and to
sweep demurely out of the room, leaving the gentlemen to their
wine. And it was worst of all for her in the drawing-room, where
the ladies all fell into intimate, low-voiced conversations about their
illnesses, their children and their servants; for she had as yet no illnesses, nor children, and knew very little about servants. At the
end—about 10.15—no one could leave until the bride rose; and
cases have been known of the bride being so petrified by fear that,
after a long wait, the kindest of the elder ladies had to rise and pro-
pel her into doing her duty.

# Ladies

We children used to huddle on the stairs in our nightgowns to watch the formal procession going from the drawing-room to the dining-room, led by my father with the principal lady on his arm, while my mother brought up the rear, on the arm of the most important gentleman. After they had all swept grandly by, we could dash down and warm ourselves by the drawing-room fire, before taking up our stations by the serving-hatch to help finish up the good things as they came out. The strident roar of conversation pointed by the clatter of knives and forks came through the hatch in bursts, cut off suddenly when it was closed.

Dinner was at 7.45, and there were eight, nine, or even ten courses: I have some of the menus. Such dinners needed good organization, especially as they were all prepared and served by our own ordinary three servants, with very little extra help, beyond a waitress. Some people had special dishes sent in from the college kitchens, but my mother considered that extravagant. Here is a dinner given by my parents on 31st October 1885, when Sir William and Lady Thomson (the Kelvins) came to stay. This is clearly rather a grand dinner.

> Clear Soup
> Brill and Lobster Sauce
> Chicken Cutlets and Rice Balls
> Oyster Patties
> Mutton, Potatoes, Artichokes, Beets
> Partridges and Salad
> Caramel Pudding ⎫
> Pears and Whipped Cream ⎬
> Cheese Ramequins ⎫
> Cheese Straws ⎬
> Ice
> Grapes, Walnuts, Chocolates and Pears.

## Ladies

But on 1st April 1885, there were only four people at dinner: my mother, my father, Edmund Gosse and Dew Smith, and yet they had:

> Tomato Soup
> Fried Smelts and Drawn Butter Sauce
> Mushrooms on Toast
> Roast Beef, Cauliflower and Potatoes
> Apple Charlotte
> Toasted Cheese
> Dessert: Candied Peel, Oranges, Peanuts,
> Raisins and Ginger

I know this because after dinner my mother left the three men alone and came into the drawing-room and wrote it all down in a letter to her sister. This was five months before I was born; she was twenty-three, and she clearly felt very grand and grown-up, with three servants of her own.

There was a cook who would not use the cream-whipper or the egg-beater—'*so stupid of her*'; and a housemaid, who was later dismissed for not mending my mother's gloves properly; and a Swiss manservant, Rittler. He slept in a sort of cupboard opening out of the pantry. One of Rittler's duties was to row the boat on the river, and a special uniform was designed for him, for nautical service; I wish I knew what it was like!

Rittler was obviously charming; but alas, one night '*when he came home he had been drinking; he was not drunk, but still his breath was strong.*' And on this pretext he was dismissed, and a good place was found for him in America, where presumably drink did not matter. But he was really sent away because the women servants *would* fall in love with him. Apparently Nana was particularly drawn towards him, though he appears not to have been much interested in her. Poor Nana! Even now, after so many years,

The Hermit (Mrs. C.) coming out of the Hermitage. Here you may also see our dog, Sancho, wishing he were the Hermitage dog. He is standing in the road, not on the pavement, just to show how miserable he is.

it seems to me an extraordinary idea, to think of her as a young woman, capable of falling in love. She seemed so old and fixed in her place in the firmament. But this feeling of hers is probably the reason why I am quite sure that I can remember Rittler, though he left when I was only eighteen months old. After that we had only woman servants; but my mother regretted Rittler. '*I do think intelligence in servants adds to their value,*' she writes sadly. This was an advanced view to hold, in those days.

Next door to us, at the Hermitage, there lived a lady who had eight servants, a little dog, two horses, a carriage, a coachman and a footman. In the Middle Ages a hermit had lived on that spot to take the tolls for the bridge. Now the Hermitage stands there, a very large depressing Victorian house, built of white brick, with a slate roof and plate-glass windows, many of them barred against burglars. There, when I was small, the Hermit of the Hermitage was Mrs. P., afterwards Mrs. C., generally a rich widow, except during the two periods when she was a rich wife. She had stiff white hair, done up on top, little black eyes, and a face like a prune —a very proper prune. Dr. P. died when I was very small; he was a Fellow of St. John's, and I can just remember the choir of St. John's coming to sing carols under his window at Christmas time—in the middle of the night, as it seemed to me then.

After a decent interval Mr. C., a Fellow of Trinity, decided to ask for Mrs. P.'s hand. So he caused to be set up in the Roundabout —the Trinity Fellow's Garden—a little artificial monticule, and on top of it to be erected a small but elegant arbour in which he could propose to her. This he successfully did, and the arbour and the mount, known as 'Monte Cobbeo', stand there to this day to witness if I lie.

They used to give very grand dinner-parties, in all the glory of mahogany and silver and port; and after dinner Mr. C. would approach Mrs. C. in the drawing-room, and say: 'Now, my dear,

'Music hath charms.' Seen from my mother's bedroom window.

shall we let our friends hear our Duet?' He would then hand her to the piano, and they would perform together. Even after Mr. C.'s death (when I chiefly remember her) we could sometimes get a fascinating glimpse, from my mother's bedroom window, of Mrs.

# Ladies

C. playing on the (very) grand piano, with a brisk, prancing movement, just like that of her two overfed horses, when the coachman brought the carriage up to the front door. She went to the same evening concerts at the Guildhall that everyone attended, driving there alone in state with the coachman and footman; and passing on the way my mother, and sometimes me too, going down on foot. But though she always bowed graciously, and often spoke to us in the concert hall, she never once, in all the years we knew her, offered my mother a lift. However, she sent a covered plate of hot dinner every day to the lame and disfigured crossing-sweeper at the corner of the Backs, and that was far more important. When she died it was found that she had left him some money, and one of her maids married him and took care of him for the rest of his life! Though how she could bring herself to do so, I can't imagine. He had met with some accident, and was a dreadful sight; and besides could not speak plainly; he was one of the terrors of my youth, poor fellow. I believe Mrs. C. was always generous to the poor.

The only words I can remember her saying were a comparison between her two husbands: 'Yes, poor Francis liked his beef quite red and underdone, but Gerard would not eat it unless it was well cooked and brown.' A good way of remembering the difference between them.

There were not many people in Cambridge who had carriages, apart from the doctors, who drove about in broughams, in their top-hats and frock-coats. But Uncle Frank and Aunt Ellen had a donkey-cart, in which Aunt Ellen sometimes drove two donkeys tandem. One of these donkeys first came as a foal and, for a while, he used to run free beside the cart—showing how quiet the roads were in those days. Another friend had a very enormous kind of dogcart, in which she drove, in a masterly way, the horses she had bred herself. But for the most part people depended on flies—four-wheelers—until first the tricycle, then the safety bicycle, came

Going to the concert. Mrs. C.'s carriage passes us on the bridge.

in: and then bicycles gradually became the chief vehicles for ladies paying calls. They would even tuck up their trains and ride out to dinner on them. One summer evening my parents rode ten miles to dine at Six Mile Bottom; their evening clothes were carried in cases on the handlebars; for of course you couldn't possibly dine without dressing. Right up to 1914 one always made some kind of change

My mother had the first lady's tricycle in Cambridge. Our dog Sancho was horrified to think that anyone belonging to him should ride such an indecent thing.

of dress for dinner, even if one were alone; and for quite a small party, full dress was usual. But when my mother came to dress that evening she found that, though the bodice and train were there, the skirt had been left behind—dresses were in three pieces then. So she had to borrow a very inharmonious skirt from her hostess, who was much shorter and stouter than herself. They rode back by moonlight.

But if we had no carriage my great-aunt Mrs. Jebb (later Lady

Jebb) had one, and my mother drove out with her nearly every day. Springfield, where the Jebbs lived, stood across the road, behind the crossing-sweeper's corner; it was a dull, plate-glass-windowed, white-brick-and-slate Victorian house. But though it was even uglier than the Hermitage, it was a very different affair; quite as comfortable and much more amusing and less formal.

Aunt Cara was an exceedingly beautiful woman. Rembrandt's painting of 'Bathsheba' at the Louvre is a pretty good portrait of her. I once saw her in much the same costume, and she looked quite lovely. She had auburn hair—real auburn, not red—a charming Rubenesque complexion, and a deep rich voice, like red velvet. She was quite unselfconscious about her appearance—as you can afford to be if you are beautiful enough. I have seen her playing tennis in a ridiculous little black nose-bag, tied on with elastic, to keep the sunburn from her nose. Her amusing American turn of conversation, complete lack of inhibitions, and great personality, gave her a unique position in Cambridge society.

She had had a romantic history. She was born in 1840, Caroline Reynolds, the sister of my mother's mother. Her father was an English clergyman, who had emigrated to the States, round about 1825. At the age of sixteen she married Lieutenant Slemmer of the United States Army. Four years later, when in 1861 the Civil War seemed inevitable, he was sent to command the fortifications at Pensacola in Florida. One of the many legends about Aunt Cara concerns this time. She is said to have wept on President Lincoln's shoulder in order to obtain promotion for her husband, which she considered had been unjustly withheld. I began to try to draw this scene, and at once came to the conclusion that it was impossible to imagine Aunt Cara weeping on anyone's shoulder. I then learnt the true story. She went, with two brothers-in-law, to an arranged interview with the President; saying to herself, 'After all he's only a man like any other,' by which she meant that, of course, she could get him to do what she wanted. They found the President sitting at a writing table; at first the conversation was rather halting, but presently Aunt Cara, who was standing beside him, laid her hand lightly on his shoulder, as she put forward her plea. Mr. Lincoln smiled, and gently placed his hand on hers for a moment, and the ice was broken. She was successful, for among the *Lincoln Papers* is the following note in his own handwriting: '*List of Officers I wish to remember when I make appointments for Officers of the Regular Army,* [several names, and last of all]—Lieut. Slemmer—*his pretty wife says a Major or First Captain.*' Aunt Cara always said that Lincoln was the greatest man she ever met, so perhaps she had not found him quite so easy to manage as she had expected.

It was known at Pensacola that plans had been made by the Southern Militia to capture the navy yard there. There was much doubt as to whether the place should be defended, for there had been, as yet, no fighting. (This was before the attack on Fort Sumter.) '*A council of war was held in Captain Slemmer's house. . . . The discussion lasted a long time without any decision being reached; at last Mrs. Slemmer* [aged twenty] *could stand it no longer; and, with a flash of her quick manner, she said, "Well, if you men will not defend your country's flag, I will".*' This settled it. The garrison withdrew to Fort Pickens in the harbour and held it against several attacks; and so, by her action, the first shots of the war were fired. Incidentally, the North thus retained a naval base in the Gulf of Mexico, which was of some importance to them during the blockade of the Southern States.

There was another legend: that Mrs. Slemmer was a spy! She had been seen walking about on the mainland, a few days before the first skirmish. She was probably only shopping; but with Aunt Cara one never can feel quite sure. She was a very ardent partisan of the North.

Her husband eventually became a general, and died in 1868; her only child, a boy, had also died young. Aunt Cara then came to England to visit relations; and among others a first cousin, Mrs. Potts, who lived at Cambridge. There it is said that every marriageable man proposed to her; three in one day, including the Vice-Chancellor. I do not guarantee this; and yet, when years later, she visited the house (15 Fitzwilliam Street) where she had once stayed with Mrs. Potts, and the lady who lived there then, said to her: 'Lady Jebb, I believe you received three proposals in one evening in this room?' Aunt Cara merely replied: 'Oh no, that is absurd; one was in the garden.'

In 1874 she at last decided to marry Richard Jebb, and her house soon became a social centre. Her popularity gave her many openings for match-making—that delightful pursuit; but her views on affairs of the heart were always more practical than romantic. Her letters are very candid about this; she would try to allure a niece into paying her a visit, by promising her a meeting with a young man, whom she describes as *'a possible object of interest'*. *'And now he is such a very good match! His father is rich, has just been made a Baronet, Tom is the eldest son,'* etc., etc. In mere justice to her nieces, I must say that this sort of thing did not appeal to them at all. It was of assistance to her in match-making, that among her other gifts, she had a special instinct for knowing at first sight exactly what anyone's income might be. Money was very important to her and she thought a great deal about her investments. She managed all Uncle Dick's affairs, and gave excellent advice to others of the family.

She used to tell me strange stories about all the love-affairs of all the well-known people who had confided in her; they were all mixed up with hair-bracelets and graves and love-letters and other stage properties; but I did not listen to them very much, for I did not then believe that they were true; and I have unfortunately now forgotten them all. There was, however, probably some foundation of truth in most of them, for she could always draw confidences from a heart of stone. Or, at least, from a man's heart of stone. She was emphatically a man's woman, though she was always on good terms with women, too. I must admit that I often felt a certain temptation to invent dramatic circumstances when she tried to draw me out about my own affairs. I never did so, but I have sometimes wondered if others were less scrupulous.

It was no wonder people liked talking to her; her conversation was amusing, even witty; and she was well-read. There is a pleasant story of how she once set a Jebb niece to read *Paradise Lost* aloud to herself and her sister Aunt Polly, in order to improve Aunt Polly's mind. The poor old lady was terribly bored and was nearly asleep, when Aunt Cara woke her up, by saying sternly: 'Listen now, Polly; it's Satan speaking.'

Aunt Cara was not, I think, at all warm-hearted; but she was really kind and generous; and as she wished people to like her, and had a pretty shrewd idea of character, she managed to make up an excellent working substitute for warmth of feeling. Indeed, I have often wondered whether intelligent kindness, such as hers, is not of more value to the world at large, than warm-hearted blundering. Of course, her worldliness shocked me very much, as a child; but I was abominably serious and high-minded in those days.

In 1918 she decided that she would like to spend the rest of her life in America, away from the Horrid War; so she sold her house and much of her furniture, and went off without showing any regret at leaving my mother and all the friends with whom she had lived for the last forty years. My mother felt her loss very much indeed. Aunt Cara had her horse and dog and cat destroyed; I rather thought she had Melbourne the gardener put down, too; but I am told that he was reprieved at the last moment. Uncle Dick had fortunately died in 1905.

The Springfield household consisted of: first, Aunt Cara's Prime

Minister and confidant, the said Melbourne, the groom-gardener; a perfectly round little man, a 'reg'lar Norfolk dumpling', as he justly called himself. Next in the hierarchy came Zoë, the pretty, yellow mare; then Glen, the collie dog, given her by Mr. Carnegie; then Darius, the Persian cat; then the three maids, who stayed for ever; and last of all—or so we thought—poor Uncle Dick. I know that he was a scholar of international reputation, but to our childish minds he was a figure of extreme unimportance; a sort of harmless waif, who was kindly allowed to live in a corner of the library, so long as he kept quiet and gave no trouble. He used to slip furtively in and out, and never recognized us when he met us. Margaret was astonished when he said Good morning to her on the stairs one day, shortly before his death. I suppose he was terrified of

Melbourne assisting Aunt Cara to keep in touch with current events in Cambridge.

children. But other people besides ourselves must sometimes have thought Uncle Dick less important than he would have wished; for there has been handed down from his earlier days the well-known saying of Dr. Thompson (Master of Trinity from 1866 to 1886): 'The time which Mr. Jebb can spare from the adornment of his person, he devotes to the neglect of his duties.'

## Ladies

Nearly every morning my mother used to send me across to Springfield with a note or a message, to plan the campaign for the afternoon. I used to run across the early morning road and through the dewy, sweet-smelling garden, to the open front door; and go up the Axminster-carpeted stairs to find Aunt Cara comfortably

Paying calls. People, from left to right: Zoë, the pretty bay mare, Melbourne, me (very cross), Aunt Cara, my mother (behind the parasol), Glen the collie dog.

having breakfast in bed, and reading the newspaper, with Darius on the counterpane beside her. I did not like going there, because of the faint smell of Cat; but I don't know whether it was Cat which made me dislike going there, or going there which made me dislike Cat. Aunt Cara would give me an answer to the message, and then say: 'Go down and ask Kate to give you a piece of cake.' This made me indignant, because I was not a baby now, and I did not like being offered cake like that—although it was delicious cake. But even my indignation may have been caused by Cat.

Then after lunch, Melbourne would go out to Queens' Green, and catch Zoë and harness her to a kind of low, rather shabby, but elegantly built Victoria, squeeze himself into his navy-blue coat, put on his top-hat, take up Aunt Cara and my mother, and drive them off to the delightful duty of paying calls. As they bowled gaily along, Glen followed barking behind; and Melbourne drove with his head turned over his shoulder, for he took a principal part in the conversation. He knew all there was to know about the current events of the Cambridge world, and gave Aunt Cara much valuable information.

Occasionally I was forced into going out in the carriage with them. Heavens, how intolerably sulky I must have been, as, hatted and gloved, I clung unwillingly to the narrow front seat. It was necessary to hold on tight if one did not want to be shot out at the corners, and it made one feel sick, and was a supreme bore as well.

One of the important duties which ladies had to perform was going to London for the day to shop. They had to catch the 8.30 Great Northern train to King's Cross. In those days no one ever went to St. Pancras by the Great Eastern Railway if they could help it; and Liverpool Street was unknown to the genteel. The early start put a great strain on the whole household. Sometimes the Bull bus came to fetch my mother; it went round the town picking up such people as had bespoken its services. It cost sixpence, luggage and all. But sometimes the bus was booked up, and then a fly from the Bull yard was ordered to come at 8 o'clock. But when red-faced Ellis drove up to the door, my mother was nowhere near being ready. Once, when she was leaving to catch the boat-train for New

York, she was still in her nightdress when Ellis came; and she caught the train, too. If not actually in her nightdress when he came, she was always still in her bedroom; perfectly calm, though all the three maids, and Nana, and I, were running about to fetch things

Catching the train. Ellis is getting nervous, but my mother refuses to start until she has collected all the things she wants to take with her.

and to help her to dress; while my father stood at the foot of the stairs, watch in hand, looking worried, and calling up in his patient voice: 'Maud, you'll miss the train.' Of course she had not attempted breakfast, and I used to put slices of buttered toast on the seat of the cab for her. This was important, as her day's work was so absorbing, that she never had time for lunch, and used to come home in the evening quite famished and worn out. When she was in the fly I used to hand in through the window her boots and a button-hook, so that she could put them on as she went; while she gave me in exchange her slippers to take back.

Then, just as Ellis was gathering up the reins and chucking to the horse, she would call suddenly: 'Oh, wait a minute—there's that little dressing-table I was going to take for a wedding present to Mrs. X's daughter—it's in the attic, Isabel, just run and fetch it; and the silver teapot needs mending, will you get that, Alice, please; and Gwen, just run up on my washstand and get that empty bottle of cough-mixture. . . .' and so on, and so on. But at last, the dressing-table on the roof of the fly, and buttoning her boots and eating her toast, off she drove. We then went back and ate an enormous, leisurely, holiday breakfast, and a feeling of delicious peace descended on the house. But she never, never missed the train. I think she felt that it would not have been sporting to start in time; it would not have given the train a fair chance of getting away without her. How unlike the English side of my family!

In the evening Economy often made her come back from the station in the slow old tram, which went swinging and clanking along behind its one ancient horse. What with changing 'at the Roman Catholic' and waiting there for the other tram, she could well have walked home in the same time. *Racing the tram* was a Cambridge sport; a running child could beat it easily.

So often did we have to fetch things from upstairs for my mother, that *running up—or trotting up—on my washstand*, became a family phrase for doing an errand or a job. There always seemed to be a great many jobs to be done; and the thought of them reminds me of another activity of the Cambridge Ladies: Committees: lovely Committees. How they did enjoy them! There was a body called The Ladies' Discussion Society, of which my mother was President or Secretary or something. Anyhow, it entailed a great deal of adding up of accounts (chiefly done by us children); and of checking over and addressing of cards (also largely done by us); and of taking them round to their addresses by hand, to save the expense of the postage. This was entirely done by us. We strongly objected to this form of trotting up on my washstand. We did not see why we should save the Discussing Ladies' halfpennies by the unwilling sweat of our brows. So I am sorry to say, that when we had delivered a few of the nearest cards we used to sneak some halfpenny stamps out of the study and post the rest of them. Thus, in the end, my father paid for their discussions. My mother always had a regrettable weakness for saving halfpenny stamps.

She concentrated chiefly on the Ladies' Discussion Society, though she had some slight brushes with the 'Charitable' Organization, as she always called the Charity Organization. Her other chief mission was helping to run a private laundry. This gave her plenty of scope, especially as it had been mysteriously established (not by her) at a place where all the water had to be pumped up by hand, by a man with one arm. It was a pity, we thought, that laundries seemed to involve so much arithmetic. Hard on us; very hard.

Arithmetic was not one of my mother's strong points. Nor, as a matter of fact, was it one of mine either. But then, in my own affairs, I made short work of the natural malignity of numbers, by never doing any accounts at all. This made it all the more irritating to be obliged to do other people's sums for them. My mother, in imitation of my father, insisted on keeping accounts down to every halfpenny; but no one, least of all herself, ever understood them. I suppose that while my father was alive, he was able to identify and isolate the more important items from the jungle of undergrowth in which they were ambushed; and anyhow he did the adding and auditing himself. So that in those days we children only had the simpler matters of the Ladies' Committees to deal with. But after my father's death The Accounts became a constant menace to everyone of the family. How often have I not slipped quietly out of the room when I saw the moment approaching when I should be asked 'just to add up that page, please'. It was so hopeless and so useless. It was impossible to add up one page without being dragged into the complications of all the other pages of all the other account books, which were used indiscriminately for everything. The only system was that every item had to be written down somewhere— on any scrap of paper, or any page of any account book; and then, from time to time, everything must be rounded up and added together in one enormous sum. Fortunately no odious deductions were drawn from the resulting total, as quite often the Credits had got mixed up with the Debits, and they had all been added up together.

But I must in honesty add, that in later life, my mother succeeded in living in a large house on a relatively small income, and perhaps The Accounts helped her to do this in some mystic way which we cannot understand.

# CHAPTER VI

## *Propriety*

There was one profession to which I was very early apprenticed: that of being chaperon to courting couples. My mother often had friends and younger sisters staying with her; they were charming people; sociable, and foreign enough, being American, to be very attractive; and the chief excitement of her early life was the constant expectation that some of the Gentlemen, who were supposed to be 'very devoted' to them, would propose. I have since wondered how serious the supposed 'devotion' may have been; certainly none of those particular men married Americans. Though perhaps that was my fault; I must have been a very discouraging chaperon. But, at any rate, I am sure my mother was always thinking that an engagement might be announced at any moment.

Soon after her marriage my mother wrote to her sister about the sad state of things she found in Cambridge. *'It is hard for the girls here. . . . There is not a marrying man in Cambridge except Mr. C.; and I should not think he would be attractive to anyone now, though they say he used to be nice; but now he tries to look intense, and squeezes your hand a little, when he shakes hands; all of which is not exactly attractive in a man with gray hair. He hums all the time he is talking, and always goes back to twenty years ago; in fact he is what you might call prosy. . . . Oh, the poor English girls certainly have a hard time, excepting in Alice Balfour's class, where they are more like American girls. But the upper*

*middle class think they are acting rightly by over-protecting their daugh-
ters. . . . When Gwen grows up, it will be very hard to know how to treat
her. If I let her be as independant as a girl at home, people will say in
Cambridge she is fast.' And in another letter: 'M.F. [a girl of eighteen]
says that two undergraduates are going to give a dance in their rooms in*

The conscientious chaperon.

*college. They wrote to Mrs. F. asking if M. could go, and then said that
their rooms were so small, would she pardon them if they did not ask her—*
that Mrs. S. and Mrs. C. [two most correct Cambridge ladies] *had
consented to chaperon them. M. can't go because they will not let Mrs. C.
chaperon her. She says so many of the Cambridge matrons are furious. . . .
They say, "What right have young men to dictate to us?" It seems un-
utterably vulgar to me that girls, who are well brought up, and sons who*

99

*are well brought up, should not be allowed to associate, without every girl having her mother at her elbow, to see that no indecency is committed. The real truth is that the chaperons want the power in their own hands, and I believe, though they protest against it, they really enjoy the dances. . . . I hope that when Gwen grows up there will be a revolution in this respect, and I hope that she will help to bring one around. Why should not M. be allowed to go with her brother?'*

Now the odd thing about these letters is, that my mother obviously considered herself, and really was, more unconventional and wide-minded than the English ladies; and yet, later on, we young ones thought her distinctly more proper than they were. Perhaps the truth was that she was more puritanical, in an old-fashioned early-American way, while they were more concerned with gentility and appearances. The English ladies would not have been as shocked as she was, when she heard Spurgeon preach, and wrote: *'Some of his sentences were hardly refined, as, "*We need the Lord to back us*".'* [I suppose because this is a sporting phrase?] On the other hand, I am sure that none of them would have bicycled, as she did once, from one end of Cambridge to the other, dressed up as Father Christmas, beard and all. (Santa Claus she always called him.) But I think she was more particular than they were about such matters as bathing and undressing; and though parties were all right, she would never allow friendly couples to go anywhere alone together, no matter how old or respectable they might be.

That was where I came in; for by the time I can remember, things must have improved since the days, when Mr. C. was the only marriageable man in Cambridge. There always seemed to be plenty of bachelors about now, and I was often sent along to play gooseberry in the boat, or on some sightseeing expedition. Surely my mother must have been extra careful about boating? A couple were never allowed to go alone in a boat, even down the Backs; and she reproved one of her sisters for going out alone with *two* men for a very short time. Yet I know that an extremely correct lady gave permission for her daughter to go from Grantchester to Cambridge and back again, in a canoe with a young man. I am sure my mother would have been horrified at this.

All this matter of propriety seems to me quite fantastic, especially considering the ages and characters of the people to whom the rules were applied. When Uncle Frank was engaged to Aunt Ellen (his second wife), he was thirty-five, and she was twenty-seven, and a Fellow and lecturer at Newnham; and if any two people could be more respectable I would not like to know them. Yet, when Miss Clough, the principal of Newnham, had been away for a few weeks my grandmother wrote: '*Frank will be glad that Miss Clough has come back, so that he can call on Ellen again.*' He had not been able to go there at all while Miss Clough was away! She sat in the parlour with them herself; no one else would do as a chaperon. Of course, there could be no question of his going to Aunt Ellen's own sitting-room; nor obviously of her going to see him. One sometimes wonders how anyone was ever able to get engaged at all.

In her memoir, *What I Remember*, Mrs. Alfred Marshall tells a story, which she told me herself when she was very old; how she and Miss Marion Kennedy, both of them Newnham lecturers of nearly thirty, took rooms at a London hotel in order to attend the wedding of their friends Professor Henry Sidgwick and Miss Eleanor Balfour; and of how her horrified father, the rector, sent her young brother, a boy of fourteen, posting off in haste, to chaperon them. 'And when he came, we stayed on another night, and even went to a theatre with him!' she told me in triumphant amusement; and ended up: 'But I was in disgrace at home for some time after that.'

Now in both these cases the trouble was entirely over appearances. It would have been perfectly easy for Uncle Frank to meet Aunt Ellen in private somewhere; or for Mrs. Marshall to deceive her young brother, if any of them had been really bent on impropriety. But no one doubted their integrity for a moment; it was just the look of the thing that mattered. It is this which makes it so difficult for us nowadays to understand what all the fuss was about.

If pushed, the elders would probably have said: 'I have no doubt that it is quite all right for you, my dear; but it sets such a bad example to others'; or if they were really frank: 'to the lower classes'. There were many things we might not do, not because they were wrong in themselves, but 'because of the maids'. We might never sew or knit or play at cards at all on Sunday, not even Beggar-my-neighbour; and when we went out to play tennis, we used to make our rackets into brown-paper parcels, to avoid giving offence to the people in the street!

Surely 'the lower classes', who were so much more realistic than we were, must have known perfectly well that this was all eye-wash? But they were very tolerant; if rich people liked to behave in this strange way, that was their own affair. The rich were much less tolerant, and were apt to be self-righteous and interfering. But the poor protected themselves by an impenetrable secrecy. I don't believe that the middle classes of those days ever had the faintest idea of the real outlook of the poor. It was true enough that there were two nations in England then.

But if the Victorian views on propriety were strange, their views on morals were even more mysterious; though we did not hear much about all that, till we were grown-up and even married. However, there was a good deal of gossip among us young people, and we were often puzzled by what was reported of the grown-up attitude in such matters: even the attitude of such wide-minded, tolerant people as òur Darwin uncles and aunts.

Frances tells me that much later Aunt Etty once asked her whether X, an artist friend, had lived with Y before their marriage. '*I answered that I thought it very likely. Aunt Etty then said that she was sorry, but*

# Propriety

[Professor] *Albert Dicey* [a great friend of hers] *agreed with her, that one must uphold the moral standards, and therefore she could not give X a bed for the night, after his lecture at Dorking. She knew that I only told X that her spare-room was occupied, and it remains a mystery how that improved X's morals, or anyone else's either.*' You would think, that if a man married his mistress he would be doing the best he could, given the state of things, by 'making an honest woman of her'. But, not at all; it made it much worse. What *would* they have had the poor man do? I suppose the idea was, that such a marriage would be a travesty of a real one.

I do not find it much easier to understand Uncle Frank's attitude when Frances, after her marriage, went with Francis Cornford to see a well-known writer, who had just returned to live with his wife, after a serious interruption. Apparently his return made things no better, though it might have been thought, that he should have been commended and encouraged for his change of heart. But, no; Uncle Frank wrote that he was surprised that the Cornfords could go near the house.

Well, I can suppose that, *from his point of view*, it did seem rather unnecessary of the Cornfords to start a new acquaintance with a man who had behaved in an anti-social way; and the fact that he was an interesting and vital person ought not to make any difference. Of course there always have to be standards of some kind, if society is to go on at all. And if there are standards, something must be done to keep the standards up. *Cutting the sinners* was their sanction then; now we do not generally think that cutting is of very much use.

The truth was, that the gap between the standard and the reality —and there always must be some gap—was quite abnormally wide at that time, so that the standards were particularly false. One has only to think of the omissions in all the mid- and late-Victorian novels, to perceive the fantastic unreality of the outlook of decent people, from about 1850 to 1914. It is often hard to believe that these decent people were not being deliberately hypocritical, when they were so unwilling to face the facts; but very few of them were consciously shirking; they were merely taking on the views of the time, as it is natural enough for unthinking or inexperienced people to do. For nearly seventy years the English middle classes were locked up in a great fortress of unreality and pretence; and no one who has not been brought up inside the fortress can guess how thick the walls were, or how little of the sky outside could be seen through the loopholes.

But it remains very strange to me, that a man like my uncle, observant and experienced, a man who continually questioned everything in the physical world, should seem to accept, without question, the narrow and unrealistic moral values of his time.

To go back to my own experiences as a chaperon. Once I was sent in that capacity, on a whole-day expedition to Lincoln. Here I was quite aware that I (horrid little prig) took a greater interest in the cathedral than either of my charges; who incidentally, must both have been over thirty at the time. I imagine there must have been great hopes of engagement-producing opportunities on that expedition; for, from letters written by the lady many years later, it is pretty clear that her heart had been touched; but he, I am afraid, was something of a philanderer. At any rate, either I, or Lincoln Cathedral, were inauspicious, and he did not rise.

I suppose my mother must have thought that I should be less of a restraint than a grown-up companion would have been. But I doubt it. I think the lovers must have both feared and hated me; for surely they must have guessed how deeply I despised them. It seems to me now that, though I could not have said so at the time, I always knew exactly what they were after; whether it was a serious affair, or only a flirtation; and which of the two was the pursued

Curling her fringe.

and which the pursuer. Fortunately I was not, like a child I have heard of, tormented with doubts, as to what her duty would be, supposing the gentleman should suddenly kiss the lady. No such improper idea would ever have occurred to me; I merely fixed my eyes calmly on the couple, and observed the poor fools as coldly as a man of science might consider a pair of courting earwigs. I am not at all surprised that none of the romances put under my care came to anything.

There was one occasion which I remember very well. A young man came to call before the ladies were ready; they were all dressing upstairs; so I was sent down to the drawing-room to say that they would soon be ready. 'And talk to him nicely till I come,' said the lady of his heart, who was curling her fringe at the gas-burner in her bedroom. He was quite a nice young man, I thought; and, though bored at seeing me, he played with me fairly well for some time. I knew he was bored, but I thought that he might as well be useful while he waited. So we played at illnesses, and I lay on the sofa in the flowery summer drawing-room, full of green reflected lights; and he was the doctor and pretended to give me medicine out of a vase from the chimney-piece. But the vase had some dust in it, and it made me cough; and suddenly he could bear the suspense no longer, and he went away and stood by the fireplace with his elbow on the chimney, and had a little anguish, all by himself. I lay on the sofa and watched him, and realized quite well that he was in a state of insufferable agitation at the thought of seeing his lady. And it just seemed to me too absurd and silly for words.

Then the lady came rustling in, with her fringe nicely curled and a lovely embroidered muslin dress on; and I left them to it, and went away, back to a proper sensible life. But years later I recognized the sensation myself. I never can think how people can say they like being in love!

Here is my mother's considered opinion on courtship in England:

Love. How ridiculous.

# Propriety

*'June, 1887. My experience of English lovers is that if they mean anything, they come straight to the point and make it evident. But if not, they are as friendly as they can be, without the least idea of anything more.'* One longs to know how American lovers behaved?

The rules of propriety are supposed to have made life very complicated in the last century, but in practice, I can't say that I found nineteenth-century decency harder to manage than twentieth-century indecency. In fact, I always find it easier to pretend to be shocked, when I am not shocked, than to pretend not to be shocked when I am. So that, on the whole, I got on quite well in the 'nineties.

But some things were very queer. For instance, there were the river picnics. All summer, Sheep's Green and Coe Fen were pink with boys, as naked as God made them; for bathing drawers did not exist then; or, at least, not on Sheep's Green. You could see the pinkness, dancing about, quite plain, from the end of our Big Island. Now to go Up the River, the goal of all the best picnics, the boats had to go right by the bathing places, which lay on both sides of the narrow stream. These dangerous straits were taken in silence, and at full speed. The Gentlemen were set to the oars—in this context one obviously thinks of them as Gentlemen—and each Lady unfurled a parasol, and, like an ostrich, buried her head in it, and gazed earnestly into its silky depths, until the crisis was past, and the river was decent again.

Sometimes we children were sent off to fetch a compass round about the danger zone, and to be picked up by the boats further on; but sometimes we went in the boats with the grown-ups. And then I—but not Charles, which was so unfair—was given a parasol, and told to put it up, and not to look 'because it was horrid'. I obediently put up the parasol and carefully arranged it between myself and the ladies, so that I could see comfortably, without hurting their feelings. For I thought the bathing place one of the most beautiful sights in the world: the thin naked boys dancing about in the sun-

The ladies, God bless 'em.

light on the bright green grass; the splashing, sparkling river; the reckless high dives, when the slim bodies shot down through the air like angels coming down from heaven: it was splendid, glorious, noble; it wasn't horrid at all. It was the ladies who were horrid; but then, poor things, they always were even stupider than most other grown-ups.

I had not the faintest idea why they objected to passing the bathing sheds; though, with the fuss they made, it was really extraordinary that they never succeeded in putting ideas into my head. But they never did.

For I must here and now confess that I was completely and even scandalously uninterested in sex, until I was nearly grown-up. Shocking! Unnatural! you will say. Yes, certainly; I admit it; but then, think what a lot of trouble it saved. In fact, the only horrid curiosity I can remember, was a wish to know whether Keith at the dancing-class had anything in the way of trousers under his kilt; and that was really only an interest in costume.

All inconvenient questions I used to put to Nana when I was in my bath. She must have been very clever at baffling them, for when I asked why one had toes, she answered at once: 'Well, you wouldn't like your foot to end in a sharp bone, would you?' The form of her answer made me acquiesce; but on thinking it over afterwards, it seemed to me that I could have invented lots of other ways, besides toes, for ending off feet. For instance, a round soft flap. I rather favoured this—no toe-nails to cut—(which had been the original cause of my question). Or paddles like frogs' feet? And anyhow, if you came to think of it, *why not* a sharp bone? Would it really be so dreadful?

Another time I asked her what was the use of the interesting little button-hole in the middle of my tummy? 'That's where you were finished off,' she said. So I had a vision of God making a knot in the cotton, before he broke it off to begin on another baby.

The Boat Picnic. 'Youth on the prow and Pleasure at the helm.'

## Propriety

I don't know why this information made me think that babies (who apparently grew somehow inside) came out through this hole; but I did think so till I was nearly grown-up. And it still seems to me that it would be a much more sensible plan, than the complicated and painful exit arranged by the Management. But as time went on, I began to doubt the exactness of my deduction; and when I was seventeen or eighteen, I tried very hard, and quite unsuccessfully, to find out the truth about the matter from Chambers' Encyclopædia. You can have no idea, if you have not tried, how difficult it is to find out anything whatever from an encyclopædia, unless you know all about it already; and I did not even know what words to look up. Of course I would have died sooner than have asked anyone about it; and I never did, but the truth just gradually dripped through, like coffee through a percolator.

It is an interesting proof that *bustles* were still familiar to us, that when my mother was expecting another baby, my cousin Nora asked her nurse: 'Why does Aunt Maud wear a bustle in front?' This was only partly a very naughty joke on her part—though who would ever have expected such shocking flippancy from Nora? Quiet Nora, who always reminded me of a little, obstinate, grey Quaker donkey, so clever and sober and pretty. But this remark was also a sort of trailer, which she hoped might lead to more information on a subject, about which the grown-ups were being particularly mysterious and tantalizing. But it was no good; she drew a blank.

There were some problems which I never solved in all my youth. For instance, there was Gloucester's Natural Son, in *King Lear*. For if bad Edmund was a Natural Son, presumably Good Edgar must have been an Un-natural son; and what on earth could that be? Was Edgar's birth somehow miraculous? Like Christ's? Surely we must all be natural children, so ordinary as we all were? We couldn't *all* be un-natural? And yet being natural in the play was somehow wicked, and sinister and extraordinary.

## Propriety

David Copperfield was puzzling, too. He was a 'posthumous child' and was born with a 'caul'. The French dictionary, the only one I had, gave *posthumous*; *posthume*, which did not help me much; but for *caul* it gave *fillet*, and of course a *fillet* was a string bag. How very odd. Then someone gave me a present of *Esmond*; but my mother said I was not to read it, because parts of it were 'not very nice'. Of course I wanted to find out what was not nice about it; so, by a quibble, I decided that I might read all that I could manage without cutting the pages. With industry and perseverance this meant practically all of it, though the pages were not cut for many a long year. But I could never discover what was wrong with it.

But though my sex-life was so sadly simple, there were things which shocked, nay, positively disgusted me. For instance, I once saw, through the banisters at Down, one of my Darwin uncles give a friendly, conjugal kiss to my aunt, his wife. I rushed away in absolute horror from this unprecedented orgy. It seemed to me simply sickening, revolting, that this uncle—such a nice, quiet, decent sort of man, should be Fond of his wife: fond enough of her to kiss her in the hall! Even now I can't bring myself to tell you which uncle it was. I tried never, never to think about it again.

And then there was *Charley's Aunt*. This was the first real play we ever saw. It did not seem to me at all funny, only tremendous and exciting; and, at one point, most dangerously improper. I have never seen the play since then, but as I remember it, one of the young men dressed up as

The dangerous impropriety of Charley's Aunt.

Charley's Aunt, and ran across the stage, lifting up his petticoats, and *showing his trousers underneath.* No thing since then has ever shocked me so much.

Though, now I come to think of it, I ha dbeen shocked once before in the same sort of way. As a very small child I had been put to sleep in the room of an old lady, an American great-aunt on a visit. When I was in bed this elderly lady came up to dress for dinner. She wore

Sleeping with relations.

a bonnet with purple ostrich feathers, tied under her chin with broad ribbons; and a purple satin dress, very grand, with velvet bits about it, here and there. For some reason she began her toilet by taking off her skirt, and then came up to my cot dressed in her bonnet and bodice and feather-boa, but tailing off sadly lower down into a skimpy under-petticoat. I was absolutely appalled at the sight, and howled and shrieked and roared, till I had to be taken away and put to sleep somewhere else. I still think the costume was both sinister and indecent, but I admit that my memory of the poor lady has become hopelessly mixed up with the pictures of the Duchess in *Alice Through the Looking-glass.*

This was the aunt with whom my mother was travelling in Italy, when she got engaged to my father; and she seems to have been a perfect dragon of propriety. My mother writes from Nice at the end of 1883: '*Such a vial of wrath on my head I have not had for a long time. Oh, how I got it! Aunt Em made "one request, that while I am in her charge I am obliged to keep"; and that is "that I am not to shake hands with any gentleman. Ladies never do." I said, "If a gentleman holds his hand out, I am not going to put mine behind my back. I will not be rude. Aunt Cara told me in Cambridge what I should do, if a man held out his hand." "These are Cambridge manners," was her reply. If there had been any cause for the scolding I should have taken it* (maybe) *in good part, but there was not. I had treated Mr. H. like any other tennis player.'* The operative word in this passage is '*maybe*'; I cannot imagine my mother ever submitting tamely to such a rating. A tactless aunt, I think.

Much later, I was again most painfully scandalized by the lightness and impropriety of Margaret's behaviour. She was always extremely cheeky, a fault which requires much correction in a younger member of the family; but in spite of our firm, but kind remonstrances, she remained always incorrigibly uppish; even to the extent of sometimes pinching her elders, and once or twice actually biting them! Alas, she is still the same, though it is some time now since she last bit me.

Well, the occasion was this: we—Margaret and I—were being taken across London by one of the American aunts; and she chose to park us at the National Gallery, while she did some shopping near by. I should have liked the pictures very much if I had not been so terribly afraid that she might never come back to fetch us away. And then what would happen to us? Supposing no one ever came and at closing time we were still there? Should we be sent to prison? Or should we be left alone and starving in the gallery? Or should we be just turned out, alone, into those dreadful roaring London streets? Horrors, horrors, every way. . . .

But Margaret was not a bit afraid; she was cross and tired and bored, so she simply sat down on the floor of the big Italian room.

## Propriety

What could I do when a policeman came up (for there were police-men then in the National Gallery) but slink off into the next room, blushing to the end of my toes, and pretending that the impudent creature did not belong to me? Though the denial made me feel exactly like St. Peter himself.

The policeman told her to get up at once. At first she refused; but

'A Policeman's lot.'

on his reiterated command, she obeyed and went calmly into the next room and sat down on the floor there. He followed, and the scene was repeated several times, while I skulked about, watching through doorways. In fact 'the argument only ended with the visit', or rather with the return of the errant aunt. And I hope she was well scolded by the policeman for leaving us there alone.

# Propriety

One must always expect to suffer from the shamelessness of grown-up relations; it can't be helped, and is part of that curious thick-skinned obtuseness, which unfortunately seems to be an integral part of the grown-up character. But that a child, a contemporary, should humiliate me in this way, was unforgiveable; and I don't know if I have quite forgiven her even now.

The event I am now going to try to describe has nothing to do with the rest of this chapter, though it is inseparably connected in my mind with the old Victorian flirtations, which I used to supervise.

I think I was about six years old when it happened. It was on a Sunday afternoon in early summer. There had been people to luncheon, and now they were all sitting under the medlar tree on the Little Island. Presently I left them and came in and went up to the night-nursery—the long, big, old night-nursery, with the wavy floor, and the great window at the end, which looked right down on the river beneath. The medlar tree was just opposite on the other bank, and I could see bits of the ladies' summer dresses through the leaves, and hear their voices and those of the men, in a pattern of light and dark, with sometimes a laugh, all gay and self-conscious and sociable. The sun was shining and the river was flowing smoothly down, with the tiny noise that you could only hear if you listened for it

And then, with the sun shining, it began to rain. Not much, but a few big drops falling splash, splash, on the green lilac leaves. And suddenly the world stood still. It simply stopped, and I was quite alone and *outside*. I did not belong, I was separate, just looking on; *outside*.

With the next beat of my heart, the world went on again, and everything was quite usual and ordinary. Only I had been outside. This was the first time this happened to me, and I was much shaken and frightened, afterwards it happened often, and I grew used to it. But it was always terrifying and lonely, and seemed to point the contrast between ME and all those other friendly people, who sat there talking under the trees.

# CHAPTER VII

## *Aunt Etty*

Question: *Fussy people Darwins are,*
*Who's the fussiest by far?*
Answer: *Several aunts are far from calm,*
*But Aunt Etty takes the Palm.*
(From *Christmas Conundrums*, by Bernard.)

I have defined Ladies as people who did not do things themselves. Aunt Etty was most emphatically such a person. She
told me, when she was eighty-six, that she had never made a
pot of tea in her life; and that she had never in all her days
been out in the dark alone, not even in a cab; and I don't believe
she had ever travelled by train without a maid. She certainly always
took her maid with her when she went in a fly to the dentist's. She
asked me once to give her a bit of the dark meat of a chicken, because she had never tasted anything but the breast. I am sure that
she had never sewn on a button, and I should guess that she had
hardly ever even posted a letter herself. There were always people
to do these things for her. In fact, in some ways, she was very like a
royal person. Once she wrote when her maid, the patient and faithful Janet, was away for a day or two: '*I am very busy answering my
own bell.*' And I can well believe it, for Janet's work was no sinecure.
But, of course, while Janet was away, the housemaid was doing all
the real work; and Aunt Etty was only perhaps finding the postage

stamps for herself, or putting on her own shawl—the sort of things she rang for Janet to do, every five minutes all day long.

Aunt Etty was my father's elder sister Henrietta; and she had married Uncle Richard Litchfield, who worked on the legal side

Uncle Richard has been sent to bed, because Aunt Etty suspects him of having a cold. She is feeling very anxious about him. This is their Ruskin and Morris drawing-room at Kensington Square.

of the Ecclesiastical Commission. The Darwin brothers were always inclined to laugh at him; indeed there still survives the unkind saying of one of them, that 'Little Richards have long ears'. And, of course, they sometimes laughed at Aunt Etty, too! But *I* liked him very much, because he talked to me as if I were quite grown-up.

He was a nice funny little man, whose socks were always coming down; he had an egg-shaped waistcoat, and a fuzzy, waggly, whitey-brown beard, which was quite indistinguishable, both in colour and texture, from the Shetland shawl which Aunt Etty generally made him wear round his neck. For her business in life, her profession, was taking care of healths, her own and other people's.

She had been an invalid all her life; but I don't know what (if anything) had originally been the matter with her. I should guess, however, that she had really been delicate when young. Her tiny form, her little monkey hands, seemed to belong to a frail, but wiry, person. But I am quite sure that, with her iron will, she could have ignored and controlled her ill-health, both of the nerves and of the body, if only she had been set off in the right way when young.

The trouble was that in my grandparents' house it was a distinction and a mournful pleasure to be ill. This was partly because my grandfather was always ill, and his children adored him and were inclined to imitate him; and partly because it was so delightful to be pitied and nursed by my grandmother. She was a most remarkable woman, to outsiders appearing rather stern and alarming, and with great independence of mind. But she was also extremely tender-hearted, and I have sometimes thought that she must have been rather too sorry for her family when they were unwell. A little neglect or astringency might have done some of them a world of good. Hundreds of letters of Grandmamma's exist, and hundreds more of Aunt Etty's; and every single one of them, however humdrum, contains some characteristic and charming phrase; and every one of them also contains dangerously sympathetic references to the ill health of one, or of several, of the family. Many of their ailments must have been of nervous, or partly of nervous, origin; of course, there was real physical illness, too, though no one now will ever know how much, for a great deal of illness was left undiagnosed in those days. But of one thing I am quite certain: that the attitude of the whole Darwin family to sickness was most unwholesome. At Down, ill health was considered normal.

Every time I re-read *Emma* I see more clearly that we must be somehow related to the Knightleys of Donwell Abbey; both dear Mr. Knightley and Mr. John Knightley seem so familiar and cousinly. Surely no one, who had not Darwin or Wedgwood blood in their veins, could be as cross as Mr. John Knightley was, when he had to turn out to dine at the Weston's. 'The folly of not allowing people to be comfortable at home! And the folly of people's not staying comfortably at home when they can!'—it might be Uncle Frank himself speaking. But it is obvious, too, that there is some strain of the Woodhouses of Hartfield in us, of Mr. Woodhouse in particular. There was a kind of sympathetic gloating in the Darwin voices, when they said, for instance, to one of us children: 'And have you got a *bad* sore throat, my poor cat?' which filled me with horror and shame. It was exactly the voice in which Mr. Woodhouse must have spoken of 'Poor Miss Taylor'. But it had one good effect: it quite cured us of *enjoying* ill health. I denied having a sore throat at all if I possibly could.

I have been told that when Aunt Etty was thirteen the doctor recommended, after she had a 'low fever', that she should have breakfast in bed for a time. *She never got up to breakfast again in all her life.* I admit that I know none of the facts, but I cannot think it good mothering on the part of my grandmother to have allowed a child to slip into such habits.

The three of her children who were most affected by the cult of ill health, were Aunt Etty, Uncle Horace, and, later on, my father, George, though as a boy he was strong enough. But illness, real or imaginary (and there was certainly both), did not prevent my father and Uncle Horace from doing a great deal of work. Unfortunately Aunt Etty, being a lady, had no real work to do; she had not even any children to bring up. This was a terrible pity, for she had nothing on which to spend her unbounded affection and energy, except the management of her house and husband; and she could have ruled a kingdom with success. As it was, ill health became her profession and absorbing interest. But her interest was never tinged by self-pity, it was an abstract, almost scientific, interest; and our sympathy was not demanded. She kept her professional life in a separate compartment from her social life.

Aunt Etty ordering dinner in her patent anti-cold mask.

She was always going away to rest, in case she might be tired later on in the day, or even next day. She would send down to the cook to ask her to count the prune-stones left on her plate, as it was very important to know whether she had eaten three or four prunes for luncheon. She would make Janet put a silk handkerchief over her left foot as she lay in bed, because it was that amount colder than her right foot. And when there were colds about she often wore a kind of gas-mask of her own invention. It was an ordinary wire kitchen-strainer, stuffed with antiseptic cotton-wool, and tied on like a snout, with elastic over her ears. In this she would receive her visitors and discuss politics in a hollow voice out of her eucalyptus-scented seclusion, oblivious of the fact that they might be struggling with fits of laughter. She characteristically wrote to a proposed visitor: '*Don't come by the ten o'clock train, but by the 3.30, so as to give me time to put you off, if I am not well.*' In the year 1920, when she was seventy-seven, one of her little great-nieces happened to get chicken-pox in her house. Aunt Etty wrote to Charles at Cambridge, asking him to look in the Down family Bible to find out whether she had had the disease herself, as she did not want to catch it. He was not able to find the Bible at once—it was in a box at the bank—so she wrote again, very urgently. Upon which he had the satisfaction of replying by telegram: '*Yes, you had chicken-pox in August* 1845.' (All the illnesses and vaccinations are carefully recorded in the Down Bible, but it does not look as if it had been much used for anything else.)

Yet all that sort of thing did not affect her relationship with us. To us she only showed her immense interest in everything in the world, her vitality, her affection. We all laughed at her and we all adored her. And when there was anything to be decided or arranged she could always do it; especially, of course, if anyone were ill. To quote from a letter of hers: '*Anybody being ill is like champagne* [to me] *for the time being.*' In fact, she enjoyed her profession very much indeed.

I don't think that Uncle Richard had originally been ill, or hypo-chondriacal at all, but Aunt Etty had decided that he was extremely delicate; and he was very obliging about it. I believe that he thought it saved trouble to obey orders; as indeed it probably did. Yet Aunt Etty always managed to combine the proper Victorian respect for a man and a husband, with this obedience of his over merely material affairs. 'Uncle Richard says' or 'Uncle Richard thinks' were matters of serious importance.

At frequent intervals Janet used to bring poor Uncle Richard bowls of Benger's food—which we called 'Uncle Richard's porridge'. He always seemed surprised when this occurred, and a little saddened; but he set aside his book, pushed his spectacles up on to

his forehead, and ate it up like a man. If the window had to be
opened to air the room in cold weather, Aunt Etty covered him up

Airing the room. Aunt Etty is keeping guard over Uncle Richard during this dangerous
proceeding. She is holding a thermometer in her hand.

entirely with a dust sheet for fear of draughts; and he sat there as
patient as a statue, till he could be unveiled.

Number 31 Kensington Square, where they lived, was full of
Morris wallpapers, and Morris curtains, and blue china, and peacock

feathers, and Arundel prints, and all that sort of thing; for Uncle Richard had once been the typical cultured young man of his time. Darwins never cared enough about Art or Fashion, to be much interested in what was Right and Highbrow. When they bought an armchair they thought first of whether it would be comfortable; and next of whether it would wear well; and then, a long way afterwards, of whether they themselves happened to like the look of it. The result, though often dull, and sometimes unfortunate, was on the whole pleasing, because it was at any rate unpretentious. But Uncle Richard had adored Ruskin, and worshipped Morris, and had slept for years with a copy of *In Memoriam* under his pillow. He told me once how he and his friends used to wait outside the book shops in the early morning, when they heard that a new volume of Tennyson was to come out. He had read all Browning, too, and all Wordsworth, and Carlyle, in fact nearly everything contemporary; and he constantly re-read the Classics in their own classic tongues.

He was really fond of music and tried, with remarkably poor results, to make us sing. At concerts he indulged in a special kind of intellectual sandwich, by reading certain passages of Greek plays, while listening to certain pieces of music. A triumph of timing occurred once, when he was listening to the thunderstorm in the Pastoral Symphony, and reading the thunderstorm in *Oedipus at Colonus*, and a *real* thunderstorm took place! The concertina was his instrument, and, of course, he only played classical music on it. He also kept numbers of large dull photographs of all the things you go to look at in Italy, specially of the ones that Ruskin praised. They were all kept in green baize bags, carefully made with buttons and buttonholes and highly suitable for moths. I have often wondered: *why green baize?* But I think Ruskin must have recommended it.

In fact, Uncle Richard had done everything that an enlightened person, flourishing in the middle of the nineteenth century, ought to do; taught at the Working Men's College, organized great country walks, admired Nature, and all the rest of it.

When I remember him best he was always, between the cups of Benger's food, cutting bits out of newspapers and sticking them into scrapbooks, for he was making a dossier of the Dreyfus case.

Janet bringing poor Uncle Richard's porridge.

He used to tell me all about it, but as the case was then in a somewhat confused state—if indeed it was ever anything else—it is perhaps pardonable that I can only remember that there was a very wicked man, with the fascinating female name of Esther Hazy.

We used sometimes to stay at 31 Kensington Square, all among the London smuts (much thicker then than now); and we would sleep in the chintz-curtained beds, surrounded by the bright patterns and the Morris wallpapers; and enjoy the supreme delight of driving to a Gilbert and Sullivan in a hansom cab; though we really saw more of Aunt Etty at Down, where we spent most of the summer. The only disadvantage of going to stay with Aunt Etty was the end of the journey, which I dreaded. For, when we got to

Mrs. Bewick.

King's Cross, two or three cab-runners would attach themselves to us and would follow behind the four-wheeler, all the way to Kensington Square; hoping to get a tip for carrying our luggage upstairs. The great heavy trunks and portmanteaux of those days had to be carried by two men, but Aunt Etty would never let the touts into the house; she had always engaged beforehand a most Respectable Person, the Square-keeper, to help the cab-driver to carry up the boxes. My father would put his head out of the cab-window, and tell the runners that they would not be needed; but they followed us all the same, and were very angry when we got there and they were told to go away. Once one of them burst into tears, and my father, rather shamefacedly gave him a shilling after all. This was supposed to be very wrong—indiscriminate charity: helping those who begged, and not those who really needed help. I am sure that these runners made my father quite as miserable as they made me.

It was here, at No. 31, that I discovered Bewick, one afternoon while Aunt Etty was having her rest. I remember lying on the sofa between the dining-room windows with the peacock blue serge curtains, and wishing passionately that I could have been Mrs. Bewick. Of course, I should have liked still more to be Mrs. Rembrandt, but that seemed too tremendous even to imagine; whereas it did not seem impossibly outrageous to think of myself as Mrs. Bewick. She was English enough, and homely enough, anyhow. Surely, I thought, if I cooked his roast beef beautifully and mended his clothes and minded the children—surely he would, just sometimes, let me draw and engrave a little tailpiece for him. I wouldn't want to be known, I wouldn't sign it. Only just to be allowed to invent a little picture sometimes. O happy, happy Mrs. Bewick! thought I, as I kicked my heels on the blue sofa.

Of course I wanted still more, more than anything in the world, to be a man. Then I might be a really good painter. A woman had not much chance of that. I wanted so much to be a boy that I did not dare to think about it at all, for it made me feel quite desperate to know that it was impossible to be one. But I always dreamt I was a boy. If the truth must be told, still now, in my dreams at night, I am generally a young man!

It was here too, at Kensington Square, that I first knew the dreary pangs of jealousy. The occasion was The Jubilee Procession of 1897.

Aunt Etty had hired a room from which to see it; and as she was much afraid of the difficulty of getting there through the morning crowds, she characteristically made all the complicated arrangements necessary for sleeping there the night before. And Frances and Charles were to go, too, and *to sleep on the floor*! I was to go with my father, in the morning, to a very good seat at the Athenæum; but what was that compared to *sleeping on the floor*? I stood in the doorstep of No. 31 in an agony and watched them all drive away in a four-wheeler—Aunt Etty, and Uncle Richard, and the pre-Janet maid, and Frances, and Charles—with plenty of bags and bundles and hot-water bottles, you may be sure; and next day all the grandeur of the Athenæum was clouded by pain.

The old house at Kensington Square had a very strong flavour of its own. It was a peculiar kind of earthly paradise—earthly, not celestial. It was a tapestry, worked in rich, bright colours to a complex pattern, a Morris tapestry, not a medieval one. The food was delicious, the beds were soft, the rhythm ran smoothly, everyone was kind and good and true and happy; and it seemed as if evil could never come near.

Down, my grandmother's house, had a different flavour, much cooler and barer, less of the earth, less comfortable: a fresco in pale clear colours, a simpler, larger pattern. Aunt Etty was generally at Down when we went there, but she was only an incident there, though an important one, bringing a breath of her own warm atmosphere with her.

When Uncle Richard died Aunt Etty moved to a house near Gomshall in Surrey; and there she transformed a very ordinary villa into the same Earthly Paradise we had known in London; only now there was a garden and a wood to replace the mysterious charm of the old Kensington Square house, where Esmond's mistress and the lovely Beatrix might have lived.

The journey to Burrow's Hill was always a happy one. One drove in the bumpy four-wheeler up the deep narrow lane, past the saw-mill and the level-crossing, and turned steeply up the drive to the house. The door would be opened instantly by the beaming Frances, the parlourmaid; while deaf Nelly smiled a welcome from the stairs—Nelly, who ran about all day long with shining copper cans of very hot water; and in the kitchen Emily—who wore such a fascinating wig—would be preparing all the dishes I was known to like best: boiled chicken with white sauce, and coffee trifle so rich that really I could hardly eat it at all. And there would be Aunt Etty on the drawing-room sofa, in her red chuddar shawl and her little lace cap, with all her bags and books and papers around her; and I would see again her small, downy, soft-skinned face; and would know for certain, that here, at any rate, I was loved and welcomed by everyone. At home I was loved to be sure; but there I was always apt to get across the current; and though I knew that it was all my own fault, that did not seem to make it any easier. But here we were all godlings; benevolent, witty beings; heroes to Janet and Emily and all the dear everlasting maids; and though we knew very well how unheroic we really were, there was great reassurance in their affection.

All day long at Burrow's Hill one would be interrupted by Janet, coming every few minutes with messages from Aunt Etty; it made it difficult to settle down to any work. 'Could you please look up the date of the year of The Great Comet for Mrs. Litchfield.' 'Mrs. Litchfield says would you like lamb or soles best for lunch?' 'Mrs. Litchfield says, do you know how long is the quarantine for mumps?' And every morning came the message: 'Mrs. Litchfield would like to see you in her room at five minutes to eleven' (or five minutes past twelve, or some other exact time)—an interview which was always interesting. Even when, very occasionally, Aunt Etty gave one of us a gentle and reasoned remonstrance about some piece of bad behaviour, it made us feel all the more that we belonged to her; and it had the greater effect, from the obvious reluctance with which she spoke.

Under Uncle Richard's influence Aunt Etty had learnt, after her own fashion, to appreciate poetry and music. Unfortunately she had no ear for rhythm, and always applied the full measure of her drastic common sense to all the more imaginative passages of the poets. One would be called upon to read aloud, say, Wordworth's *Excursion* with her—Wordsworth was her religion—but one was never able to read more than two or three consecutive lines without stopping to discuss *exactly* what the words meant; or, alternatively, for her to give messages to Janet. One of her most engaging habits was to alter a phrase in a poem to suit herself, if she did not happen to approve of the poet's own version; and if she was not satisfied with her alteration, she would apply to Frances, Margaret, or even me, to improve it for her. I remember that Wordsworth's

*The wind comes to me from the fields of sleep*

did not please her. What does it mean anyhow? Sleep does not grow in fields. I said, why not try *fields of sheep*. This was not well received. There exist five or six versions of Browning's lines in *The Lost Mistress,*

*For each glance of the eye so bright and black*
*Though I keep with heart's endeavour,*
*Your voice, when you wish the snowdrops back,*
*Though it stay in my heart for ever!*

This won't do at all, because bright black eyes remind one so much of '*the bugles on old ladies' mantles*'. She tried changing the first line to '*eye so dark and bright*', and rhyming it with '*your voice wishing back winter's firelight*' or '*the snowdrops pure white*' and several other variants, none of which scan at all; and at last applied to Frances in despair. Frances changed '*bright and black*' to '*bright and clear'*, and rhymed it with *'snowdrops here'*; and all was well. There is a version of Wordworth's *Tintern Revisited,* entitled: *Tintern Revisited and Improved.* The Bard himself was not above amendment, but the alterations have unfortunately been lost.

Aunt Etty was a very fierce anti-Catholic. One evening, at Burrow's Hill, she attacked me on the subject. I was only about eighteen and no match for her vehemence, but I did my duty, and stood up to her as well as I could; and my friends could not have been more surprised than I was to find myself defending Catholicism.

She began: 'If you want a novel to hot you up against the Catholics, I've got a most shocking one here.'

*Me,* 'Well, I don't really need one just now, thank you; but what's it about?'

*Aunt Etty,* 'It's about a priest who rides so fast to give a man absolution before he dies, that he KILLS his horse under him. Isn't it *horrible!*'

*Me* (mildly), 'Well, I suppose they believe that absolution matters more than anything else.'

*Aunt Etty* (almost unable to speak with indignation), 'But doesn't the *Horse* matter? Doesn't *Cruelty* matter? How can they think,' etc., etc.

And so the battle was engaged. The whole evening the unequal contest raged, and I was thankful when, at ten o'clock, I was able to escort her up to bed, with all her luggage of hot-water bottles, and bags, and books, and shawls.

By that time I had a headache myself, and I was glad to go to bed too. I was lying peacefully reading, and beginning to feel a little calmer, when the door burst open and a tiny frail figure, in a red dressing-gown and a white shawl, appeared at the end of my bed. Fixing me with eyes burning out from the deep hollows under her shaggy brows, she began without preamble: 'I could SWALLOW the

'I could SWALLOW the Pope of Rome.'

Pope of Rome, but what I can NOT swallow is the Celibacy of the Clergy.' I think I must have become unconscious here, for I can remember no more of the interview.

Her indignation could be terrifying. Once, at Cannes, she burst into the midst of a crowd of louts who were kicking at a dog which had been run over; and, a tiny, furious figure, with blazing blue eyes, she terrified the policeman and the whole unsympathetic mob into obeying her orders in cowed submission.

Once she suddenly asked Charles at lunch how you should address the Archbishop of Canterbury in writing to him; this was in 1920, or thereabouts.

Charles said: 'I don't know; I suppose your Grace or something. But why do you want to write to him?' Aunt Etty said: 'Because he's been making a speech in the House of Lords, saying that the Bolshevics are doing inexpressibly horrible things in Russia. And when one of the other peers asked him what exactly they had been doing, he answered it was so dreadful that he couldn't possibly speak of it. Now, that's all wrong; there's nothing in the world that the Archbishop of Canterbury ought not to be able to say in the House of Lords, and I'm going to write and tell him so.' And I hope she did. This was like her realistic attitude to life. She

134

once said to me, about the Roman occupation of Britain—in her most downright tone: '*Don't tell me*' (I wasn't telling her), 'that all those Roman soldiers lived all that time in England and didn't leave a lot of Roman babies behind them. And a very good thing, too, I dare say.'

Margaret tells me how one spring, when Aunt Etty was quite old, she suddenly announced that she had never heard a nightingale sing, and must do so at once. But as the nightingale's turn did not come on till quite late, she would get ready for bed first. So, at 10.30, Margaret pushed her in her bath-chair up to the little wood at the end of the garden. She was in a special bird-listening costume of red dressing-gown, several shawls, scarves and rugs; a hot-water bottle and rubber boots; her hair was in a wispy pigtail, and she was without her teeth. (I am thankful to say that I never had an aunt who was afraid of seeming ridiculous.)

At the first sight of her the nightingale, who had been singing madly up till then, naturally left the stage; and with all a *prima donna's* proper feelings, entirely refused to sing any more. So Aunt Etty had to add 'not having heard a nightingale' to all the other things she had never done.

This little wood was also the scene of a form of sport, of which Aunt Etty can claim to be the inventor; and which certainly deserves to be more widely known. In our native woods there grows a kind of toadstool, called in the vernacular *The Stinkhorn*, though in Latin it bears a grosser name. The name is justified, for the fungus can be hunted by the scent alone; and this was Aunt Etty's great invention. Armed with a basket and a pointed stick, and wearing a special hunting cloak and gloves, she would sniff her way round the wood, pausing here and there, her nostrils twitching, when she caught a whiff of her prey; then at last, with a deadly pounce, she would fall upon her victim, and poke his putrid carcase into her basket. At the end of the day's sport, the catch was brought back and burnt in the deepest secrecy on the drawing-room fire, with the door locked; *because of the morals of the maids.* Perhaps now that there are no maids, this part of the ritual does not matter so much. Anyhow, it was the chase and not the morality which appealed to Aunt Etty. She used to excuse her ardour by saying: 'Some day there will be no more stinkhorns left in the wood,' but she would have been dreadfully disappointed if that had happened. How is it that this exhilarating and wholesome sport is so little known? There must be many owners of fine preserves of stinkhorns, who make no use of their privileges at all.

This wood always needed a great deal of discipline: a branch lopped here, a path widened, a tree felled there. Old Newton, the gardener, was once sent for to Aunt Etty's bedroom, and forced to lay his hoary head on the pillow beside her own, in order that he might see exactly which bough should be cut back to improve the view for her, as she lay in bed.

Stinkhorn hunter in full cry.

The thought of Newton reminds me that when she received the news of my engagement—which like all engagements was to be kept secret—she wrote to Frances: '*I have put Gwen's dear letter in an envelope labelled* Pigs, Newton; *so I think it will be quite safe, and no one will read it.*'

When she was tired by day, she used to take refuge in doing her accounts and seeing to her investments—(the mere thought of this relaxation makes me feel tired). At night, she often lay awake, struggling with the problem of why God allowed suffering. Like

## Aunt Etty

Man Friday, she asked: '*Why God no kill the Devil?*' And like Robinson Crusoe she found the question very difficult to answer. Crusoe himself was obliged to '*pretend not to hear*', till he was ready to explain that '*we are preserved to repent and be pardoned*'. Upon which Friday floored him again with: '*So you, I, devil, all wicked, all preserve, repent, God pardon all.*' Crusoe was again forced to '*divert the discourse*', till he could remember why God would not pardon the devil; he then gave poor Friday a set of very specious explanations; or so they seem to the unbeliever. Aunt Etty was far too honest to quibble, and never did satisfy herself with an answer; but when pushed too far, she would turn to a short list of subjects, about which she was annoyed. She kept these ready for use as counter-irritants, so that she could feel pleasantly indignant about them, when she was not able to sleep. During the 1914 War, the thought of Admiral Jellicoe's weak mouth was a very satisfactory standby; and the untrustworthiness of Winston Churchill at this time, or the immorality of H. G. Wells, often sent her comfortably off to sleep. I feel sure that she would have forgiven Churchill now, and would have been one of his strongest supporters; but I doubt if Wells would ever have been accepted.

Sometimes she would say to one of us: 'Now, you must be Churchill, or Wells, or the Pope of Rome [or anyone else who was out of favour]; and just you *try* to answer a few questions I shall put to you.' And then the most devastating questions would be fired off: 'How on earth did you expect to take the Dardanelles?' or 'You must surely agree that Adultery is Wrong?' or 'How can you think that Confession can strengthen anyone's sense of responsibility?' It was quite shattering. Often you were driven into a corner, and just had to admit that you (as the culprit) had made an unfortunate mistake; or that you hadn't exactly meant what you said in your books. There really seemed to be no possible defence at the time.

I must add that, hard as it may be to believe, every single word

137

of this chapter is true. Dear Aunt Etty, how easy it is to draw your absurdities, how difficult to show your lovableness; yet we were all your children, and coming to Burrow's Hill was always coming home.

Not that I want to stay at Burrow's Hill for very long. It is too comfortable, a little stifling; and really Janet does interrupt too often —one can't get anything done.

Aunt Bessy in the drawing-room at Down.

# CHAPTER VIII

# *Down*

I n one of my mother's early letters there is a sad heart-cry: 'We are going to Down. Oh, you can't imagine how dull these English country-houses are! There is nothing at all to do there.' Down—now spelt Downe—in Kent, was my grandfather's house. He—Charles Darwin—had died in 1882, three years before I was born, and after his death my grandmother spent the winters in Cambridge and only the summers at Down House, where we all went for long visits. Sometimes, too, she lent us the house for the winter or spring holidays, so we knew the place well.

I am afraid it *was* dull for my mother, and probably would have been dull to most people. There was hardly any local society at all There never had been many real friends in the neighbourhood; this was chiefly owing to my grandfather's ill health; but also partly because the Darwins did not fit very well into any particular pigeon-hole in the life around them, though they were on good terms with all their acquaintance. Social needs were supplied by congenial relations who came to stay. There were still plenty of relations staying in the house when I remember it; all kind and good and pleasant, but generally much older than my mother. There was very little talk about any of the things in which she was interested; only mild family jokes, and long quiet conversations about politics; or, more often, about facts and theories; interesting, if you were interested in general scientific ideas, but utterly boring to her. There were no

games, because no one wanted to play, except that Uncle Frank and
Bernard used sometimes to knock about golf-balls a little. It is true
that there was croquet on the lawn, but there was generally no one
to play with, except Aunt Bessy or us children, which can't have
been very amusing for her. I remember the exasperation of a game

Down House. A little game of croquet. Note my mother's style of play.

of croquet, where no one would play seriously; even my mother
playing with one hand, while she held Billy upside down under the
other arm, because he kept on running away. There was no riding
or shooting or anything of that kind; nothing to do but to go for
long walks in the steep valleys and great lonely woods, and to get
your boots stuck in huge balls of red clay, as you crossed the heavy

plough-lands. 'A congeries of muddy lanes', Aunt Etty said scorn-fully of the country round; but I thought, and still think, it beauti-ful. The villages and farms all stand on the plateau of high cultivated chalk-and-clay downland, and not in the deep waterless valleys which intersect it.

But we Darwins never found it dull there, for we loved every moment of life in the country; and we all, old and young alike, were apt to fly away out of doors and windows, at the first sound of the front-door bell. 'Visitors! Danger!' would be the cry. I truly admire my mother for enduring so good-humouredly the long country holidays we spent at Down or in Yorkshire; for she did not care for the country for itself; people were her real interest. Pros-pects did not please her very much, but Man was far from being vile.

But to us, everything at Down was perfect. That was an axiom. And by us I mean, not only the children, but all the uncles and aunts who belonged there. Uncle Horace was once heard to say in a surprised voice: 'No, I don't really like salvias very much, *though they did grow at Down*.' The implication, to us, would have been obvious. Of course all the flowers that grew at Down were beautiful; and different from all other flowers. Everything there was different. And better.

For instance, the path in front of the veranda was made of large round water-worn pebbles, from some sea beach. They were not loose, but stuck down tight in moss and sand, and were black and shiny, as if they had been polished. I adored those pebbles. I mean literally, *adored*; worshipped. This passion made me feel quite sick sometimes. And it was adoration that I felt for the foxgloves at Down, and for the stiff red clay out of the Sandwalk clay-pit; and for the beautiful white paint on the nursery floor. This kind of feel-ing hits you in the stomach, and in the ends of your fingers, and it is probably the most important thing in life. Long after I have forgotten all my human loves, I shall still remember the smell of a gooseberry leaf, or the feel of the wet grass on my bare feet; or the pebbles in the path. In the long run it is this feeling that makes life worth living, this which is the driving force behind the artist's need to create.

Of course, there were things to worship everywhere. I can remember feeling quite desperate with love for the blisters in the dark red paint on the nursery window-sills at Cambridge, but at Down there were more things to worship than anywhere else in the world.

The magic began from the moment when John, the coachman, met us at Orpington station with the wagonette, and we drove off through the tunnel under the railway, all shrieking shrilly, to make the echo answer. We drove four miles, through the deep narrow lanes, where the trees met overhead, and there was a damp smell from the high earth banks on each side. The lanes were so narrow that it was often hard to pass a cart without stopping at a wider place. Then came the village, and the wagonette rumbled round three sides of the churchyard which surrounds the humble little old flint church, before turning up past the blacksmith's shop and the pond, and reaching Down House. And as soon as the door was opened, we smelt again the unmistakable cool, empty, country smell of the house, and we rushed all over the big, under-furnished rooms in an ecstasy of joy. They reflected the barer way of life of the early nineteenth century, rather than the crowded, fussy mid-Victorian period. The furnishing was ugly in a way, but it was dignified and plain.

I have said that the nursery at Down had a white painted floor; it had green venetian blinds, too, and a great old mulberry tree grew right up against the windows outside. The shadows of the leaves used to shift about on the white floor, and you could hear the plop of the ripe mulberries as they fell to the ground, and the blackbirds sang there in the early mornings. They lived permanently in the tree in the fruit season. I used to get out of bed to listen

The mulberry tree by the nursery window.

to them before anyone else was awake. Under the window was the pump, which squeaked in the hot afternoons when they pumped up the drinking water for the house. The well was supposed to be 365 feet deep. In the passage by the nursery door hung the rope which pulled the great bell in the roof; it was rung for meals, very loud and majestic. And on the landing hung a swinging rope with a crossbar, on which we did all kinds of gymnastics.

We had sponge-cakes and honeycomb for tea when we arrived; we never had honeycomb at home. We only came down to lunch here, but we preferred nursery meals anyhow; they were shorter and the conversation was more interesting. Lunch downstairs always seemed to consist of Shepherd's Pie and rich, creamy-brown Rice Pudding and Prunes; not that we minded that. Only I hope that the grown-ups had more interesting things for dinner.

After nursery breakfast we always began by paying a round of calls on the people who were having breakfast in bed. First of all we went to see Grandmamma and her little fox-terrier Dicky. Grandmamma was now a very old lady; she was over eighty before I can remember her; and she always went out in a bath-chair. I liked her very much indeed. We used to play on her bed with little tin pots and pans, called Pottikins and Pannikins; and then she gave us bits of liquorice out of her work-basket, cut up with her work-scissors. I don't think the work-basket was ever used for anything but liquorice, which she kept for her cough. Indeed I have the basket itself still, and it contains nothing but some half-finished book-markers, worked in cross-stitch by my uncles Leonard and Horace—her little boys—in the 'fifties of the last century.

It was interesting to watch old Mathison, her maid, a most dignified Highland lady, put Grandmamma's cap on for her over her still brown hair—tobacco-coloured hair, like my father's. First there was a black silk lining cap; then a white lawn cap, with beautiful crimped and frilled edges and long lawn strings; and then, if she were going out, yet another black hood over that. Mathison always spoke to her in the third person: 'Does Mrs. Darwin need a shawl?' Grandmamma used to tell us how *her* children wore linen shifts (a new word to me) and not woolly 'combies' as we did; and that she used to have to cut out the postage-stamps with scissors, because perforated edges had not been invented when she was young. And she told us how, at her boarding-school on Paddington Green, she had been sent for as the best piano player to play to George IV's Mrs. Fitz Herbert, when she came to visit the school. And how she had written a little reading book for the Sunday-schoolchildren at Maer, in Staffordshire, where she lived as a girl, and her brothers had laughed at her because in it she had spelt plum-pie *plumb-pie*.

After all the other calls we finished up with Aunt Etty, the nicest visit of all. Here we first drew the curtains all round her four-post bed, so that it was quite

Grandmamma in the drawing-room at Down. The chimneypiece was just like that in the picture of Alice going through the Looking Glass. There was the same squiggly gold clock under a glass shade, and there were sweet-smelling cedar-wood spills in the vases. Grandmamma holds her peggy-work.

dark inside; and then, having pulled them back again, we took off our shoes and all got into bed with her, while she read us a chapter of the current book. She used to complain that our Darwin feet were all stone cold, but we were quite unconscious of the fact.

Aunt Etty was the best reader-aloud I have ever known. She

could alter bits which she did not consider suitable, skip whole pages and episodes, and join up the narrative again with an invisible seam; or turn an unhappy ending into a happy one, without anyone being able to guess at the liberties she had taken with her author. But she always took the precaution of keeping the book hidden away between times. After her death I found a book she had once read to us: *Don John* by Jean Ingelow. The story is about two changelings, a bad boy and a good one. By a series of accidents, nobody quite knows which boy belongs to which family. In the end it is proved that the good boy is the son of the bad parents, and *vice versa*. This was more than Aunt Etty's eugenic conscience could bear; and in the cause of the truth that moral tendencies are inherited like other characteristics, she changed the entire sense of the book, so that the good boy should be descended from the good parents and the bad from the bad; and none of us ever discovered the fraud (though we were oldish when this occurred) till, thirty years later, when I happened to find the book again.

Lovely books she read us, all on this system: *The Wide Wide World*, with all the religion and the deaths from consumption left out, and all the farm life and good country food left in; *Masterman Ready*, with that ass Mr. Seagrave mitigated, and dear old Ready not killed by the savages; *The Little Duke* with horrid little Carloman spared to grow more virtuous still; *Settlers at Home*, with the baby not allowed to die; *The Children of the New Forest*; *The Runaway*; *The Princess and the Goblin*, and many more.

Aunt Bessy used to read aloud to us, too, not with such mastery, but still very pleasantly. She used to prepare her readings beforehand, marking the places where the skips were to be. She was my father's younger sister; unmarried, very stout and nervous, and apt to fumble her fingers when agitated. She was not good at practical things it must be confessed; and she could not have managed her own life without a little help and direction now and then; but she was shrewd enough in her own way, and a very good judge of character. She showed great daring in being sometimes rather sceptical about Aunt Etty's ill health; for Aunt Etty always maintained her position as the older and cleverer sister, and the married woman. It was amusing to see the way in which the relations between the sisters remained the same to the end of their lives: Aunt Etty rather superior and impatient; and Aunt Bessy submissive, but a little resentful and critical.

Aunt Bessy 'gathering the nosegays'.

Even as children we knew instinctively that Aunt Bessy needed our help and affection, for The Family was really her only interest. She was one of those pathetic people who seem only able to enjoy things through others. If she took you to a play, she was always glancing at your face to see what you were feeling about it; yet she would give a perfectly sound criticism of the play afterwards, and it would be quite her own, and not a bit second-hand. When she went for a walk she was always hoping to find 'a little secret path' (as she called it in her inherited Wedgwood tongue); because she had once explored such a path with someone who had enjoyed it so much, that she had been able to share in their delight. But she was so warm-hearted and dependent on affection, that we found it easy enough to love her.

I used to go with her at Down to '*gather the nosegays*' for the house; down the long pebbled walk between the tall syringa and lilac bushes all wet with dew, to the kitchen garden, where the roses were imprisoned behind high box borders, near the empty greenhouses, where my grandfather had once worked. We took the wooden trug full of flowers, which smelt sweeter than any other flowers in the world, back to the house, and arranged them in water on a green iron table, in the Old Study, where the *Origin of Species* had been written.

Aunt Bessy did not do very much else that was useful in those pleasant leisurely days at Down; she read a good deal, in French as well as in English, and went for little walks, and wrote letters; and I expect she had some small philanthropic jobs. When she lived at Cambridge later on, I know that she did a great deal for the old people at the workhouse. She used to read *Little Lord Fauntleroy* over and over again to the old women there, because they never wanted any other book. But at Down she seemed only to sit about on the veranda with the other ladies, reading and talking; and what they talked about I don't know, for I never listened to such dullnesses. No doubt the other ladies had employments of their own at home; but every one then seemed to exist very comfortably without anything particular to do.

Grandmamma and Aunt Bessy had only one form of 'work', in those days, when every lady had a piece of *'company work'* in hand. We called it *Peggywork*. They made long strips of knitting in thick wool, by pulling the wool over the pegs of a wooden frame; and the maids sewed the strips together into rugs afterwards. They were made in queer Victorian colours, which one would not see now: stripes of a musty terra-cotta along with dark red; or sage green and spinach green together; or two shades of peacock blue. It was easy work, much easier than real knitting, and stupid fingers could do it. Grandmamma's fingers were all twisted up with rheumatism; and Aunt Bessy's had always been very clumsy indeed. She could never find her way into her pocket to get out her handkerchief—though certainly it was not always easy to find a pocket hidden in the gathers at the back of your skirt; and she used to get into a regular fuss when she had to put her arms into the sleeves of her coat.

# Down

She had always been sheltered by Grandmamma, and after Grandmamma's death she became a good deal more independent. There are two pictures of her which remain in my mind, both of this later time, when she had a house of her own in Cambridge. Just after my father's death we went round to see Aunt Bessy, knowing her to be alone. She had not expected us, and was lying down on her bed. As we went in, she sat suddenly up in bed and threw her arms out wide, as if she wanted to embrace us all, with a magnificent gesture of her great clumsy, cumbrous body. It was like a figure by Giotto or Donatello, in the strength and splendour of the movement, and in the unself-conscious passion of the feeling.

Aunt Bessy was extremely loyal to her friends. Among these was a certain Miss S., who was rather apt to impart information to us, in a voice that went up in a pedagogic manner, at the end of each sentence. After one of our Christmas plays Margaret, flown with her success as an actress, invented a short monologue, in which she *did* Miss S. being instructive. We considered this one of the funniest things that ever was heard; and one morning, when we were calling on Aunt Bessy, Frances suddenly suggested that Aunt Bessy herself might be amused by it. So, rather against the better judgment of the rest of us, Margaret began her performance, but she had not gone far, before Aunt Bessy drew herself up and said, with great dignity: 'Miss S. is my oldest friend.' It was quite dreadful; we collapsed completely, apologized, and all went home in tears, simply shattered by remorse.

There was another ludicrous occasion when I can remember admiring Aunt Bessy's dignity. We had been for a picnic to the Fleam Dyke, and the wagonette had been left near a dingy little cottage on the main Newmarket road. As Aunt Bessy and I were walking back to the carriage, we stopped to speak to a ragged, rough-looking woman who was leaning on the fence of her yard. She told us, among other things, that a golden chariot had been buried in the barrow near by, '*at the time of The Wars*'; and after a few more words, she said, with some hesitation, but obviously offering us the greatest courtesy in her power: 'I don't know if you'd like to see it, but the Sow is just pigging; she's had seven already.' It is impossible to imagine anyone less suitable than Aunt Bessy to receive such an offer; however, though terribly flustered, she managed to thank the woman with apparent gratitude, and to excuse us from accepting the treat, by the necessity of starting home at once. *I* should rather have liked to see the show!

These very low-class, country-slum people used to give me the horrors. In that same cottage garden I saw, another time, a man crawling on all-fours, because he had drunk up all the money which had been given him to buy a wooden leg after an accident. I believe my father helped him to get a leg, but I don't know that things went much better even then. This was a class ignored by the story-books; there might be drunken and degenerate people in the towns, but in the country there were only the Good Poor in rose-embowered cottages.

But I found even the Good Poor terrifying when I was small. There was fat old bedridden Betsy at Down, whom it was 'kind' to go to see. She had been laundress there for many years, and my Grandmother had pensioned her off with a cottage and ten shillings a week. This was a handsome sum, if you consider that twenty years later the Old Age Pension started at five shillings a week, and no cottage. But I did not think it a very nice cottage, though it was quite good by the standards of the time. It was round behind the stables, in a mysterious unknown land beyond the pigsties; two little rooms, with a door into the lane as well as the door into the yard. The lane door had been fastened up, and the bed had been put right across it, and across the tiny window, so that Betsy could see everything that went along the lane; which was precious little. The daylight showed all round the edge of the closed door, and the floor was made of worn bricks; but there was a home-made rag mat on it, which I admired. Betsy was so fat that she made a great hump in the bed, and her fingers were all swollen up. An even more sinister old woman from the Workhouse was kept there by my grandmother to take care of her. I dreaded them both.

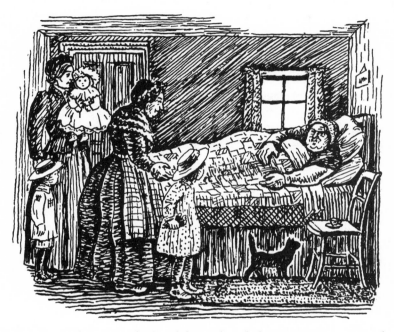

Visiting the Good Poor. People, from left to right: Charles, Nana, Margaret, Horrid Old Woman, me, Tommy the cat, Poor Old Betsy in bed.

But we liked the servants at Down very much. Harriet was head housemaid then, beautiful Harriet, with her rich voice and lovely laugh and strong Kentish accent. She knew she was beautiful, I am sure, for she wore a black velvet ribbon round her neck, like any duchess. I used to follow her about and see the cook's room, and the maids' room, a huge one, where three or four girls slept together. Once I received a shock on seeing the men's room, a long dark attic, with a board floor, and three beds, and hardly anything else at all. Here John the coachman, and Price the butler, and the footman all slept together. It did not seem very comfortable, I thought, though it was very clean. Mrs. Brummidge was the cook; I don't see what else she could have been called, the name suited her so perfectly; for she was exactly like a cook. You felt at once that she cooked everything in the best possible English way—and very good that can be—but that there would be no nonsense about any new-fangled foreigneering dishes.

There was no bathroom at Down, nor any hot water, except in the kitchen, but there were plenty of housemaids to run about with the big brown-painted bath-cans. And just as everything else at Down was perfect, so there too was the most beautiful, secret, romantic lavatory, that ever was known; at the end of a long passage and up several steps. It had the only window which looked out over the orchard, and was always full of a dim green light. You looked down into the tops of the apple trees; and when I read *Romeo and Juliet* (which was the first Shakespeare I read for myself) the line: 'That tips with silver all these fruit-tree tops', always made me think of that window. But the place of all others, where the essence of the whole house was concentrated, was in the cupboard under the stairs, by the garden door. It was full of ancient tennis rackets, smaller than those we use now; and parasols and croquet mallets, and it was there that the exquisite, special smell of the house was strongest.

There was another door into the garden—into the orchard— through the New Study. The New Study had been left just as it was when my grandfather died, to be shown to occasional sightseers, and often the shutters would be left shut all day. If we wanted to go out that way we used to dash across it at full speed, for it was rather an awful place, faintly holy and sinister, like a church. There were many mysterious things on the tables and shelves, including a baby in a bottle; or at least something in alcohol, which I took to be a baby. But sometimes when the house was full the room would be humanized by being used for a dressing-room by one of my uncles; and then there would be a round bath of cold water there.

The faint flavour of the ghost of my grandfather hung in a friendly way about the whole place, house, garden and all. Of course, we always felt embarrassed if our grandfather were mentioned, just as we did if God were spoken of. In fact, he was obviously in the same category as God and Father Christmas. Only, with our grandfather, we also felt, modestly, that we ought to disclaim any virtue of our own in having produced him. Of course it was very much to our credit, really, to own such a grandfather; but one mustn't be proud, or show off about it; so we blushed and were embarrassed and changed the subject. It was probably the same wish not to seem presumptuous, which gave my uncles the odd habit of never claiming him as their own father, in conversation with each other. They always said: '*Your* father said so-and-so'; to which the other uncle often answered: 'Well he was *your* father, too.' Sometimes stupid people even made jokes about our being descended from monkeys! This annoyed us very much. We thought it in bad taste.

In so far as I conceived of my grandfather at all, I thought of him as a kind of synopsis of his five sons, my uncles; with the same warm family voice, the same love of children and dogs; and the same gently humorous charm and transparent honesty and absence of any sort of pretension. His beard made him different, of course, for none of the uncles had long beards, or white beards. Also Aunt Etty said that he had been taller than any of them; and, when he was well, gayer, more spontaneous and enthusiastic than they were.

There was more reserve about my grandmother, because she was a Wedgwood. My father explained to me once, that my grandfather was rather different from his children, because he was only half a Wedgwood, while they had a double dose of Wedgwood blood in them, owing to the two Darwin-Wedgwood marriages in two successive generations. 'You've none of you ever seen a Darwin who wasn't mostly Wedgwood,' he said, rather sadly, as of a dying strain. He can hardly have known any pure Darwin himself, as his grandfather Robert, the last unmitigated Darwin of the line, died when he was only three.

The whole place was full of stories about my uncles as children—innocent stories, whose chief value is to show how very unlike Darwin family life was to the received idea of Victorian upbringing, with its beatings and unintelligent discipline. A good sample is the tale of how Uncle Lenny was found jumping up and down on the springs of the new sofa, an exercise which had been forbidden. His father said: 'Oh, Lenny, Lenny!' to which Lenny replied: 'I think you had better go out of the room.'

But there had always been a tradition of sympathetic education in our family. There still exists a diary, written in 1797–9, about the management of children, by my great-grandfather Josiah Wedgwood II (1769–1843), son of Josiah I, the potter. Josiah II was a young man when he wrote these notes about the upbringing of his very young children, and he was clearly influenced by Rousseau and Godwin, and was experimenting with some of their theories; but, unlike his preceptors, he had plenty of common sense, and was never above admitting that he might have done wrong in certain cases. He was the very opposite of a crank, which makes his notes the more interesting. In later life his children and nephews and friends all considered him 'the wisest of men' and trusted him completely. He was the uncle who advised my grandfather to accept the offer of a post on the *Beagle*, and to make his great voyage.

# Down

His views are quite startlingly modern, and show a knowledge of psychology, which would surprise those who think of it as a modern science. He holds very strongly that children should be left free, as far as possible. 'I think one can scarcely recollect with sufficient force that every act of interference and direction does harm, and nothing can excuse it, but the necessity of preventing a greater injury to the child;'—a statement which he qualifies in his sensible way, by adding that, of course, this does not mean that 'the commands and caprices' of the children should be obeyed. The new governess finds it rather difficult to understand this part of his doctrine, for she has been forbidden to scold, or preach to, or punish the children; they are not even to be made to feel disgust at filth! And she is 'to refrain from constant and overweening attention' to them; and to keep 'her own independence'. But he has to explain to her several times that she is not meant to obey *them*. As for teaching, his precepts are:

'Nothing well done, but by inclination.'
'Art of Education is leading inclination.'

There cannot have been many well-to-do gentlemen of that time who actually themselves superintended the putting to bed of their three-year-old sons. He tells a rather pathetic story of how little Jos cried at being washed and how, acting on the correct principles, he told the nursemaid not to scold him, but to go away and leave him all wet. I believe little Jos would far rather have been scolded! Some of the children's conversations are recorded: there is something very odd about overhearing one's baby ancestors talking in bed at night, a hundred and fifty years ago. Their talk is so like that of modern children, that one can feel quite certain that Josiah wrote down the actual words they used, as he stood listening behind the door.

They do not seem to have been taught anything about religion

Down

till a little cousin came to stay, from whom 'they learnt much about God'. 'They applied to Marianne to know why God would not let Adam and Eve eat the apple of that tree? Their instructress replied: "I suppose God wanted it himself." ' This little Jos, Josiah Wedgwood III, was my grandmother's eldest brother; he married Caroline Darwin, my grandfather's sister; and they were the grandparents of Ralph Vaughan Williams, the composer.

Of course, Josiah's theories wore off in time; but a very free humane system of education grew out of them, in which children were treated as human beings from the first; and the upbringing at Down must have been much the same.

Sometimes it almost seems as if life at Down must have been too happy, the relations between parents and children too perfect; for the uncles in all their lives never seemed quite to get away from that early Elysium, or quite to belong to the ordinary horrid world.

Uncle William told a story, in his speech at the Darwin Centenary, which showed the relationship between their father and his grown-up sons; and it also illustrates my grandfather's very rare anger, only aroused by cruelty. In 1865, Eyre, Governor of Jamaica, had repressed a rebellion of the negroes there with considerable brutality. For this he was tried, but an influential party took up his defence. Uncle William said: 'One day at Down I made some flippant and derogatory remarks about the committee which was prosecuting Eyre. My father instantly turned on me in a fury of indignation, and told me I had better go back to Southampton [from whence he had just come]. The next morning at seven o'clock he came to my bedside and said how sorry he was that he had been so angry, and that he had not been able to sleep, and with a few kind words he left me.'

Of all places at Down, the Sandwalk seemed most to belong to my grandfather. It was a path running round a little wood which

156

he had planted himself; and it always seemed to be a very long way from the house. You went right to the furthest end of the kitchen garden, and then through a wooden door in the high hedge, which quite cut you off from human society. Here a fenced path ran along between two great lonely meadows, till you came to the wood. The path ran straight down the outside of the wood—the *Light Side*—till it came to a summer-house at the far end; it was very lonely

The beech tree by day.

there; to this day you cannot see a single building anywhere, only woods and valleys. In the summer-house faint chalk drawings of dragoons could still be made out; they had been drawn by my father and Uncle Frank as children. That made it romantic; but also, once, when mercifully my father was there, there was a drunken tramp in the summer-house, and that made it dreadful.

The *Light Side* was ominous and solitary enough, but at the summer-house the path turned back and made a loop down the *Dark Side*, a mossy path, all among the trees; and that was truly terrifying. There were two or three great old trees beside the path, too, which were all right if some grown-up person were there, but much too impressive if one were alone. The Hollow Ash was mysterious enough; but the enormous beech, which we called the Elephant Tree, was quite awful. It had something like the head of a monstrous beast growing out of the trunk, where a branch had been cut off. I tried to think it merely grotesque and rather funny, in the daytime; but if I were alone near it, or sometimes in bed at night, the face grew and grew until it became the mask of a kind of brutish ogre, huge, evil and prehistoric; a face which chased me down long dark passages and never quite caught me; a kind of preDisney horror. Altogether the Sandwalk was a dangerous place if you were alone.

One day Charles boasted that he had been all round the Sand-walk quite by himself; so naturally, as an elder sister, I had got to do so too. I took Billy in the pram for company, and set off bravely enough; but my heart sank into my boots when the kitchen garden door banged behind me and shut me off from the civilized world. However, by whistling and singing and talking brightly to Billy, I got safely down the Light Side, and there was no tramp in the summer-house. But when I turned back down the Dark Side, the strangest rustlings and whis-perings began to flit about all over the wood. I held my head up and walked along briskly, but the sighings and shiverings followed me as I went; and someone seemed to be

The beech tree by night.

saying something over and over again, something that I could not quite hear. There was a strange creaking noise, too, and certainly footsteps following along behind me. I walked faster and faster until I was fairly running; and then absolutely galloping; the pram swayed madly from side to side, but by a miracle did not upset. At last, the hot breath of the pursuer on my very neck, I reached the blessed garden door; and after a short but most dangerous struggle, managed to wrench it open, got through alive, and fairly slammed it after me. I never told anyone of the perils I had passed through. I was not proud of this adventure.

All the same, when there were grown-ups about to make it safe, I loved the Sandwalk; I used to crawl on all fours through the undergrowth for the whole length of the wood, worshipping every leaf and bramble as I went. In the very middle there was the secret clay-pit, where we grubbed up the red clay, and rolled it in our handkerchiefs, and tried to make little pots to bake on the bars of the nursery grate; which were not a success. And, under protection, I would even dare to climb right down inside the hollow ash. There is something extraordinarily moving about a hollow tree.

There were other frightening places at Down besides the Sandwalk; there was the Poison House. This was a tumbledown shed which had once been a gazebo; a regular witches' hovel, overgrown with ivy. It was hidden in a thicket and we used to go to look at it with awe and admiration; but we never dared to go inside it. I don't know why there was supposed to be poison there, any more than I know why, at Down, there was supposed to be a Bottomless Hole at the top of the second floor staircase, where it was rather dark. You could not exactly *see* the hole, but you had to go very carefully round it.

Every day at Down my father used to take us for the most romantic walks, telling us stories about the places as we went: up the steep hill to Cudham Church; or to look for orchids at Orchis Bank, or along a legendary smuggler's track, or to the Big Woods where Uncle William had been lost as a child. The sudden valleys, the red, red earth full of strangely shaped flints, the great lonely woods, the sense of remoteness, made it different from any other place we knew. We were only sixteen miles from London Bridge, and yet it was so quiet that if a cart came down our lane we all rushed to look over the orchard wall to see it go by. Sometimes we went with Nana to the village to watch the smith shoeing the cart-horses; or to call on the old woman who made pillow-lace, with little bobbins on her threads. And sometimes we went to the Shop.

I remember going to the Shop on Bernard's fourteenth birthday to buy a penny stick of chocolate for his birthday present. I have a

The birthday presents. Frances, me and Bernard.

perfectly clear picture of him, when we went into the drawing-room to give him our presents, lying with his long Etonian legs on the sofa, in a negligent, grown-up attitude. I was five, so I gave the chocolate first; Frances was four and a half, and she gave him a red flannel doll's cap, about two inches long, which she had made herself. He thanked her warmly and put it on top of his head at once, which we thought extremely witty. We loved and admired him very much, and we did not mind, even if he did switch our legs rather too hard when he played at school with us, because it was such fun to play with him. We were proud to fag for him, when he lay on the lawn under the mulberry tree and he sent us to fetch gooseberries and apples for him. We knocked the early Kentish Beauties down for him with the croquet mallets; they were pale pink and green, juicy and fresh-tasting, and they used to fall down on the grassy grave of Polly, my grandfather's old dog, who had been buried under the Kentish Beauty tree.

On the lawn were two great yew trees, and the swing hung between them; I adored their magic, open-ended, scarlet berries; and at the top of the lawn stood a Spanish chestnut, which sometimes had chestnuts almost big enough to eat; under this tree was the mysterious Earthworm stone, which had been put there by my grandfather, with an apparatus to record how fast the earth-worm castings would cover it up. In front of the veranda stood the sundial, about which Aunt Bessy's friend Miss S. used to be particularly instructive; and there grew the salvias, whose blue flowers we used to suck for the honey that is in them. Grandmamma would look out of the upstairs window and smile and shake her finger at us if she saw us picking them.

When I was eleven Grandmamma died and it all came to an end. Now the place belongs to the British Association. They have tried to keep the grounds just as they were; and even though Down is now called Downe, and London has crawled much nearer, it still seems as quiet and remote in the garden as ever it was.

CHAPTER IX

# Ghosts and Horrors

The only ghost I ever saw was at Down, and it was a rabbit. All the best beds at Down were great four-posters, with ceilings and curtains of stiff shiny chintz hanging all round them. One night, when I was sleeping in a little bed beside my mother's big one, I saw, I most certainly saw, a rabbit come out on the top of the canopy and run all along it and disappear at the far end. They never would believe me about this, which was unkind of them, for the tops of beds were always dangerous places.

In our own house at Cambridge, there were no four-posters—my mother did not approve of them—and bed-curtains were becoming vestigial; but still, all proper grown-up beds had muslin curtains hanging from small round canopies, which were fixed to hooks in the ceilings. That was where the tigers lived. I never actually saw one myself, but that only made it the more frightening. This was one of the reasons why I never liked sleeping in my mother's room. Fortunately, ordinary beds for children no longer had any curtains at all, so that the night-nursery was quite safe. The tigers can't have been very comfortable on the canopies, which were only about a yard across, but that was their own business. One really must not start being sentimental about tigers.

Anyhow, I had very little sense of relative size in those days. I remember a fierce argument with Charles, in which I maintained that Dobbin, our rocking horse, was as big as a real cart-horse.

The Habitat of the British Tiger (*Felis Tigris Britannicus*). Note the protective colouring of the stripes. This species is now almost extinct, owing to the progressive abandonment of the use of bed-canopies; just as the draining of marshes has diminished the number of malarial mosquitoes. These tigers used to suffer very much from the occupational disease of *Canopy Cramp*.

# Ghosts and Horrors

Dobbin was about three foot high. And I was always afraid of being sucked down the bath-hole when the water ran away with that dreadful scrautching noise.

One of the chief advantages of going to boarding school was that there I slept in a room with other girls; and surely neither tigers, ghosts, nightmares nor burglars would dare to come into a room stuffed so full of people? Whereas my lonely bedroom at home was often quite stiff with horrors. Once, when I was about fifteen, I spent a whole night of panic lying awake listening to a strange muffled knocking on the wall. It was not till the next day that it occurred to me that it might have been the beating of my own heart. Another time, when my parents were away, I am ashamed to say that the footsteps and whispering in the garden under my window grew so alarming that I actually telephoned to the Police. Who came and said it was Cats. Cats! It would be cats; they knew I didn't like them, the devils.

My room was always full of dreams. The worst one was Joan of Arc. She came one windy night in full armour, and galloped up and down the passage outside my bedroom, stopping sometimes to shake and bang at my door and vow that she would kill me when she got in. Fortunately the door held and I woke before she broke it down; but the clanking of her armour and the fury of her feet have given me a permanent dislike to her. If you once dream about a person, the taste of your dream, bad or good, will cling to him or her for the rest of your life.

I suppose it was because one so often saw fallen and ill-used horses in those days, that I came to identify myself with them. It is still a great relief to me that one so seldom sees them now; even though this is only because there are so few horses to see. And that is really a sad business, for surely horses, like men, would rather exist than not exist at all, in spite of all the drawbacks of living.

At any rate, I often dreamt I was a horse, and I know exactly

164

what it feels like to be one. I even know what it feels like to be able to twitch the skin on my shoulder, and shudder away a fly. Once I dreamt that I was a young yellow mare, and I was trying to hide behind a gorse bush from a very wicked bull. My yellow legs were so long that it was difficult to keep them folded up, and I was afraid that spots of my hide would shine out through the holes in the bush; but I woke before the bull got me. Bulls, of course, were always frightening; chiefly because of the bull in *Holiday House*, which chased Lord Rockville in a wood. It seemed so unnatural of a bull to be in a wood. But bulls in dreams were far more frightening than real bulls.

Once I dreamt a regular ghost story. I thought that Mrs. Phillips, our housekeeper, came to my father and said: 'I think I ought to tell you, sir, that there is a wolf in the laundry.' My father said 'Nonsense', but we all went down to the laundry and looked over the top of the half-door. It was late and rather dark, but we could see a creature there, running up and down, and hear him snarling. My father said: 'I think it's only a dog, but he seems very fierce; leave him there for to-night, and I will get the police in the morning.' Then there was a gap in my dream and I thought I had gone to bed and to sleep, still vaguely knowing that there was a restless animal shut up not far away. Then I dreamt that I woke suddenly, with an unspeakable shock, to the consciousness that someone was lying in bed beside me. I put my hand out and touched the soft naked shoulder of a woman; and a cold, gentle, little woman's voice said: 'I have not been in bed for a hundred years.' My heart stood absolutely still with fear, for I knew with complete certainty that this was the spirit of a werewolf woman, which had been inhabiting the body of the wolf in the laundry; and that she had now come to try to take possession of me. She lay beside me in the bed, a little, soft-skinned, small-boned, fair-haired creature, and talked to me very quietly, and told me all about her life; and my blood ran cold with horror at her every word. It was a hundred years since she had been a woman, and had been used to slip away from her husband's side, and run about at night in a wolf's form, killing lambs and hens, and smelling the wild smells of the woods. 'Feel the scars,' she said, and she guided my hand to the dry scars on her back, where the wolves had bitten her in play. Her husband had tried to keep her in at night, by 'the magic of iron' beside her bed, and 'by the holy power of salt'; but when he had failed and failed again, he had finally killed her, 'more than a hundred years ago'. Never since then had she been able to take possession of a human soul, or known human comfort or food or firelight. 'But now', she said, 'You . . .' and she took my left hand and began to draw it across towards herself, very slowly and softly, but quite irresistibly; and I knew that if she got it right across and laid my hand on her heart, I should be hers for ever; and her wolf-soul would take possession of my body. I could neither move nor speak, and my hand was being pulled further and further across her; when suddenly I was able to make the sign of the cross with my right hand; and I woke trembling and sweating to see the blessed dawn coming in at the window.

The personality of the woman was still so strong in the room that though I was broad awake, I did not feel safe for an hour or two longer; nor could I escape from the sense of her presence for several days. It has always been a mystery to me that I should have saved myself by making the sign of the cross. I had hardly ever seen it done; nor, in my waking life, would it ever have occurred to me to sign myself. I suppose it came out of some story. I have often wished that I could see Lady Macbeth acted as a character like my werewolf woman; it would surely be more impressive than your great ranting hoydens. That gentle quiet voice would make the cruel words sound more unnatural, the small still figure would look more ruthless and implacable than any Lady Macbeth I have ever seen.

My dreams were always rather melodramatic, though mostly in a more agreeable way. I was generally a boy, swimming rivers with a dagger in my mouth, or riding for my life with a message, or

The dreadful boys and the poor white hen.

shooting my way out of a fray; in fact, I led at night a sort of Henty existence of most pleasurably exciting adventures. And so I still do, thank God.

# Ghosts and Horrors

But by day I was not nearly so brave as I was at night. The rough gangs of boys who used to rove about Castle End were quite enough to terrify me. To reach our grandmother's or uncles' houses in the Huntingdon Road, we had to pass through a corner of Castle End, called Mount Pleasant. (I used to mix this name up with Mont Blanc, Blanc Mange, Mont Blange, etc.) At the top of a steep green bank stood a short row of tumbledown cottages, inhabited by most *un*pleasant people. The place was quiet, there were only gardens with very high palings, on the lower side of the road, so there was little hope of help if we were attacked. We tried to rush through quickly, if possible when the boys were at school; for if they could, they threw stones at us; and I was knocked off my bicycle and my hair was pulled. Once when we were being snowballed, Bernard suddenly appeared, and rushed at the insurgent populace like a V.C., and said, 'Damn you, go away,' in a very heroic manner, and the rioters fled to their purlieus in a panic.

Even when we went with Nana and the pram we were sometimes stoned; and we saw unpleasant things: a drunken man, or a child being beaten. The sight I remember with most horror was a little group of dreadful boys near the pump and horse trough at the corner of Shelly Row. They were wringing the neck of a white hen; and a smaller boy stood apart, sobbing pitifully. I suppose it was his hen. Nana hurried us by. As we grew older, the danger from the boys grew less, and gradually ceased altogether. I suppose there may still be such gangs about, terrifying to the children, but imperceptible to the grown-up people; but I hope I am right in thinking that their activities are not quite so public as they used to be then.

The Poor always frightened me very much. There was a most evil Blind Man, with a beard, who sat in a little hole in the railings, which seemed to be specially made for beggars, opposite the Bull Hotel of those days. Beggars sometimes sit there still. He always had a dog, but it was never the same dog for long. We thought perhaps he murdered his dogs? I have only now realized that the reason why Blind Pew in *Treasure Island* frightened me so extremely, was that I gave him the face of our own Blind Man. The lame crossing-sweeper at the corner of the Backs had a terrible mutilated face. I tried never to see him, though his crossing was so near our house that it was difficult to avoid doing so sometimes.

One saw drunken men or really horrible tramps much more often in those days, especially on Castle Hill, or down the New-

The Blind Man.

market Road; but the worst people I ever saw were in London. It was when I was first at the Slade School. We were all working one afternoon in the Big Life Room, when the most blood-curdling screams of Murder! Murder! Help! Help! began to come up through the high windows. We could not see out at all on that side of the building. The cries went on and on, and at last another girl and I ran out, just as we were, in our pinafores, to find out if we could help anyone. We had to go an immense way round to reach the place, right across the wide courtyard of University College, and out of the gate; and then round two sides of its great

169

enclosure, till we reached a shabby street where we had never been before. At last, out of breath, we found an archway giving entrance to a yard which ran along under the Slade School windows. It was a foul place, closed at the far end; in every hovel the door was open, and there were groups of women and children sitting on the ground, picking over heaps of dreadful rags. It seemed to me that all the women, even the young ones, had black eyes and no teeth. By that time the screaming had ceased, but we asked a one-eyed hag what had been happening. 'Ow, she was drunk,' she said, "er 'usband was beating 'er. You can't do no good to 'er. You'd better go 'ome, dearie.' A little group of filthy, battered women had gathered round us, and we felt that this was true. We went back to work very silent and crestfallen. I suppose there were many such backwaters then, in among the respectable streets; but this was the only time I ever saw such a God-forsaken hole.

I cannot exaggerate the terror to me of driving across London alone in a four-wheeler, even after I was quite grown-up, and even in the daytime. And in the evening, the thought of having to get home afterwards, quite spoilt the pleasure of a theatre. Of course, one could not go in a hansom without a Man. Generally there *was* a man to take one home; and then going jingling and cantering along, with the wind in one's face, was delicious. But one could never quite count on it; sometimes one was just put into a smelly old four-wheeler; to be driven round and round London to a 'den of iniquity' (whatever that might be) for what seemed like hours, before one suddenly found oneself at Uncle William's front door.

One evening, in Cambridge, I saw something really frightening, and I never told anyone anything about it. When I was about eighteen I used to play second flute in the little C.U.M.S. orchestra of those days. I did not play well and was always afraid of coming in on the wrong beat after counting 153 empty bars. However, Mr. Dent and Clive Carey, who were the conductors, were very kind to me, and I dare say I did not do very much harm. One evening the friend, who generally went with me, did not turn up. I was not supposed to go out alone after dinner, but I thought that silly, and anyhow if they didn't know, they wouldn't mind. So I went off alone, rather nervously. Well, I was coming quietly home again by myself just about ten o'clock, and there was nobody at all to be seen, as I turned into the narrow darkness of Silver Street. I was just

What had happened? I shall never know.

abreast of the little public-house, the Anchor, which stands at the town end of the bridge, when suddenly a small gang of rather disreputable undergraduates came running quickly towards me from the other side of the river.

They were carrying, flat out, the body of a woman who seemed to be dead.

Drowned in the river? That was my first thought. And then at once all kinds of possibilities rushed into my mind. Murdered? Or captured for some nameless purpose? Something horrible and vague and improper? It did not occur to me that she might be drunk. Men got drunk; women didn't. Anyhow, the men were in desperate haste and looked frightened and guilty, in their smashed-in caps and tattered gowns. They took no notice of me, but dashed across the Bridge and huddled quickly into the safety of the Anchor. Two or three more men, who were behind, came running up—one was carrying the girl's hat—and followed the others into the public-house and banged the door behind them. And then everything was quite quiet and ordinary again; as if death and melodrama had never been there at all.

I went slowly on, wondering what on earth I ought to do. Surely someone ought to find out what had been happening? There was something so evil about the whole affair. Ought I to tell my father? But I could hardly endure the thought of speaking to him about it. Perhaps it was something improper as well as wicked? And that would make him even more uncomfortable than it would make me—intolerably embarrassing to us both, to know that the other knew of it. Of course, in those days it would have been inconceivable to me that any respectable woman should go into a public-house on any occasion whatever; far less a young girl like me. A public-house was a mysterious sinister haunt, full of Bad Women, where decent working men might occasionally go for a glass of beer (though it would be better if they didn't); but where a Gentleman would only go (*a*) if he were Fast, or (*b*) if he were showing off and pretending to be Fast, or (*c*) if he were on a walking tour. I had never been into the bar of any public-house till some time in the 'twenties, and then I felt very shy and out of place. But naturally my father could have gone there on an errand of inquiry.

Undecided I went on home and went into the study. It was the usual domestic scene. My father was working with his shoes off as always, and his feet in their dark red socks in the fender. He looked up at my entrance and waited, in his kind patient way, for things to settle down again, before going on with his long neat rows of little figures and symbols. My mother was sitting there, too, surrounded by heaps of papers: advertisements, old bills, letters, newspapers, flotsam and jetsam, most of which would have been better in the waste-paper basket. It was all very quiet and humdrum, and I burst into the familiar room, feeling like a bomb so highly charged with horror and emotion that I should blow the whole house up if I exploded.

My mother said: 'Gwenny dear, just add up the milkman's book, will you, please? I can't make it come right.' They had noticed nothing at all. These old people! They never did notice anything, so blind and deaf and insensitive as they were. The most appalling, the most shattering things, could happen under their very noses, and they would know nothing about them. It was perfectly easy to hide anything from them, from Love to a bad cold and cough. In fact, if you wanted them to know something, you absolutely had to shout it at them, and even then they probably would not grasp it. When I wanted to tell my father that I was engaged to be married, I had to follow him up and down the meadow for nearly an hour—he was absorbed in shooting with a bow on the Lammas Land—before I could bring myself to interrupt him. He had never noticed that I was trying to attract his attention, till I spoke; and then he reproached me for not having done so sooner!

So I quite coldly decided to mind my own business and to say nothing about what I had seen. I knew I was being cowardly, and that this was wrong, but I did not regret my decision. Though I would still like to know what had really been happening that night?

But anyhow, that was one great comfort: that it was perfectly easy to hide one's feelings from the old people. They never knew about any of the things I have written in this chapter. I simply could not have endured the touch of their stupid, kind sympathetic fingers on my private soul.

Yes, it was a great comfort, how easy it was to be secret.

# CHAPTER X

## *The Five Uncles*

O ne year, at the Christmas party, all the five uncles were there; and among uncles I include my father. A father is only a specialized kind of uncle anyhow.

Uncle William, Uncle George, Uncle Frank, Uncle Leonard and Uncle Horace; a solid block of uncles, each more ador-able than the other. There was a great family likeness among them; and when I was quite small, the chief difference between them, to my short-sighted eyes, was that three of them had short beards, and the other two only rudimentary whiskers. At a little distance I even found it difficult to tell the three bearded ones apart—and they included my own father! For they all had the same kind of presence; the same flavour, and the same family voice—a warm, flexible, very moving voice; the same beautiful hands, and, of course, the same permanently chilly feet.

So that year we five nieces, with affectionate impudence, acted a short scene, in which we each took the part of one of our uncles.

The plot was simple: we came into the room one by one, making some characteristic remark; then, each in turn, took off our shoes and sat down to warm our feet at an imaginary fire. Margaret, as Uncle William, stumped into the room (he had a wooden leg), whistling under her breath his theme tune: '*Girls and Boys come out to Play*', and produced *one* sock out of her pocket to warm at the fire; I, as my father, made some mild complaint about the crowing of the cocks, which waked him so early of a morning. I cannot remember what Uncle Lenny and Uncle Horace did; but Ruth, as Uncle Frank, captured the show. She came in humming an air of Handel's; the real Uncle Frank was kneeling up on a chair, and then moving about near the chimney-place; and Ruth began imitating every movement he made as he watched us. And for quite a long time he had not the faintest idea that he was being copied; and kept on saying, 'Who *is* she acting? What *is* she doing?' Till at last we all laughed so much at them both that the scene came to an end.

### UNCLE WILLIAM

They really were the most unself-conscious people that ever lived, those five uncles; but Uncle William was the most unself-conscious of them all. He hardly knew that he had a self at all. There is a story about him at my grandfather's funeral at Westminster Abbey. He was sitting in the front seat as eldest son and chief mourner, and he felt a draught on his already bald head; so he put his black gloves to balance on the top of his skull, and sat like that all through the service with the eyes of the nation upon him.

He was as sound as a bell in body and soul—the only one of the five sons entirely free from hypochondria. In fact, he was as nearly made of pure gold as anyone on this earth can be; and I am really afraid of writing what I feel about him, in case I might sound like Queen Victoria writing about the Prince Consort. You had only to see his fresh pink cheeks, his clear blue eyes under the shaggy eyebrows, his white hair and strong chin, to know what sort of a man he was. Uncle Frank said once: 'You could eat a mutton chop off William's face,' because he looked so clean and wholesome.

His life, like himself, was very simple. He became partner in a bank at Southampton, and married Sara Sedgwick, a member of a cultivated New England family. She was the sister-in-law of Professor Charles Eliot Norton, of Cambridge, Massachusetts; the friend of William and Henry James, and of many well-known Englishmen.

They had no children, and we did not know them very well till we spent a Christmas with them, once when my mother was ill. Then Nana took us all four to stay at their house at Basset, on the outskirts of Southampton. It was a very large, and really hideous, Victorian villa, with lawns and a carriage-sweep and a monkey-puzzle tree and plate-glass windows; painfully tidy, psychologically clean, rigidly perfect in organization. 'Mrs. Darwin is very particular,' the maids used to say; and it was a triumph of understatement. There was no shouting up the backstairs here; you rang the bell and the footman came. What terrible little hooligans we must have seemed there! They were well off and lived in style and comfort; but it was neither for the style nor the comfort that Aunt Sara really cared. Her religion was Duty, and it was her duty to her position and her class to live like that. It was Right, for instance, for people of her kind to keep a carriage and horses. This is not a manner of speaking; she truly felt it a Duty.

As for Uncle William, of course he liked comfort up to a point, but he would have been perfectly happy living in any way that was suitable for a gentleman. But Aunt Sara decided what was proper for them; for she understood about that sort of thing better than he did.

I liked Aunt Sara very much, in spite of her rigidity, her conventions, her particularity. She was intelligent and fine-grained, and above all, she could laugh. I liked her lined, sallow, tragic face; and I somehow caught a glimpse of the strand of heroism which underlay it all. I liked the taste of the steel in her. She would certainly have died for her faith; and her faith did not seem much odder to me than any other faith. All faiths were queer; the point was, would you die for them?

177

## The Five Uncles

One evening that Christmas, she told us the story of Voltaire's intervention in the case of the Protestant, Jean Calas, with an ardour of admiration, which quite carried us away. I once overheard my mother say: 'Sara talks so well; all the gentlemen like talking to her.' Another evening she read us Cowper's *Epitaph on a Hare*; and when she read:

> *A Turkey carpet was his lawn,*
> *Whereon he loved to bound,*
> *To skip and gambol like a fawn,*
> *And swing his rump around . . .*

the irrepressible Margaret immediately asked: 'What's a rump?' She was hurriedly suppressed; but afterwards Aunt Sara lay in wait for her, caught her alone, and said in a hushed voice: 'I think I ought to tell you that the rump is the *back* part of an animal, but it is a word you must never, never use.' And even at that age Margaret felt what an effort Aunt Sara had had to make, to speak of such a matter. But it was her duty, and so, of course, she did it.

During the time we were at Basset the Black Week of the South African War occurred. Everyone seemed very cross and gloomy, but no one told us what was happening, as they would have done at home. We were, however, taken down to the docks to see Lord Roberts embarking for South Africa. We saw a ship and some soldiers, but we did not see Lord Roberts, because the Carriage had to go home, or the Horses might have been tired.

You, who know only motors, have no idea of the responsibility The Horses were in those days. They could hardly do anything, they got tired so quickly. At least carriage horses did. Cab horses were different, of course. Aunt Sara always had to walk up the smallest hill behind her own carriage; and when she had driven exactly ten miles she used to get out and send it home; and transfer herself into a cab to finish her shopping. Of course, the cab-horse might have done more than ten miles, but that was not her business. It was like the Boy Scout who did his good deed for the day by taking the mouse out of the trap and giving it to the cat. Sometimes I used to think it would almost have been easier to put The Horses into the carriage and push them ourselves.

It was the same with the servants: dinner must not be a minute late or they would be Upset. I have never quite been able to forgive the cook, who Aunt Sara thought might have been upset, if dinner had been put off for five minutes, the night the Mummers came. Her worry about it quite spoilt and cut short the only sight we shall ever have of real natural Christmas mummers, singing their native notes, in the suburbs of Southampton in 1899! But Aunt Sara said the dinner would spoil. We begged and prayed most urgently, and as a very special favour we were allowed to see some of the play before we were hustled into the dining-room.

As the front door was opened, the men came walking straight into the hall, in single file, looking neither to right nor to left, and speaking their lines as they came, in a sort of half-chant. Then some of them stood in a group on one side, and whoever was on the stage, so to speak, walked up and down—three steps up and three steps down—as he said his part; and when he had done he retired into the standing group, and the next man came out to speak. The only lines I can remember are:

> *Here come I little Jumping Jack,*
> *With my wife and family on my back.*

This was a little man with a basket of dolls on his back. Sometimes they fought lovely stylized duels; one, two, three bangs each, with their wooden swords, and then the loser fell down dead, and the Devil came with a bottle of medicine and brought him to life again. And now it occurs to me even as I write: was it perhaps the Devil who was wrong? and not the Cook's fault at all? Did Aunt

179

Sara think it vulgar and unsuitable for children? It is possible; but when we told our parents about it, they only laughed and said: 'Sara is so particular, she couldn't bear to have dinner a minute late if the end of the world were coming.'

The only other event was that Uncle William took us to see Sir Neville Chamberlain, an old general who had lost several fingers in the Indian Mutiny; and in coming back in the dark we got lost in making a short cut through a wood, and Uncle William plunged about among the briars and the rabbit-holes and got rather cross. He was nice when he was cross like that; vigorous and refreshing.

Also Aunt Sara unfortunately thought it her duty to give a children's party to entertain her little nephews and nieces. This was Hell, particularly to me, because I looked so very miserable that a kind sort of colonel felt he had a mission to cheer me up, and *would* keep on dancing with me. I did so wish he would leave me alone. We were dreadfully disappointed in our Christmas presents, too; for Aunt Sara gave a mirror to me and a blue satin handkerchief sachet to Margaret; dull, useless objects, when we had so much wanted story-books.

Some time after this visit Uncle William broke his leg out hunting and was obliged to have it amputated; so that in our memories he always stumps about with a stick, and only warms one foot at the fire, instead of two like all the other uncles. But after a time, when he got a wooden leg that fitted him, he became fairly active again. Then Aunt Sara died, and soon afterwards Uncle William retired from the bank and took a house in London, next door to Number 12 Egerton Place, where Uncle Lenny and Mildred lived. They were tall gloomy houses, furnished in the most proper late-Victorian and Edwardian style, with everything really good and lasting, though often quite surprisingly ugly. Indeed, everything was so solid that most of the things we had from his house after his death, are still nearly as good as new. Aunt Ida herself (!) took one of Uncle William's silk under-vests, and had it made into the most beautiful evening blouse for Ruth.

After moving to London Uncle William gradually flowered into a second youth and became, what he always ought to have been, a really first-class uncle. I suppose that after Aunt Sara's death he turned to various half-forgotten interests to fill his loneliness; he had always read a good deal, but now he read more widely than ever. He read everything: all the classic works in all the languages he had ever known, or not quite forgotten: Latin, Greek, French, German, Italian; a bit of each every day; and when he was late for dinner, it was always because he was 'just finishing a paragraph'. He was very shy about it, and would be caught hiding Homer under a pile of papers, and have to be gently coaxed out into the open to talk about him. 'Fine fellow, old Homer,' he would say; or 'Fine fellow, old Go-eethe.' He went to plays and exhibitions, and sometimes bought pictures, when I fancy he was fleeced by the dealers. He was passionately fond of architecture, too; I remember that when he had seen Selby Abbey for the first time, on his way north to Durham, he felt obliged to motor all the way back next day, to see it again—a long way for those early motors. He took to going to concerts; and even sometimes, if he thought he was alone in the house, he would sneak into his little used drawing-room and try to pick out bits of

Uncle William at a picture gallery.
'Fine fellow, old Rembrandt.'

Beethoven's symphonies on the pianoforte. 'Fine fellow, old Beet-oven,' he would say.

You will notice that I talk quite naturally of a *pianoforte* when I am thinking of that generation, because it was always called so by them. They all said *Ingine* for Engine, and *Chimist* for Chemist and *Yumour* for Humour; they called a dress a *gown*, and a bunch of flowers a *nosegay*, and medicine *physic*; and Uncle William always said *Hunderd* for hundred. 'I would go a hunderd miles to see a really fine tree'—I can hear him saying; and once he did, too.

To the end of his life he was a little ashamed of never quite knowing what was proper and what was not. He certainly sometimes lent me books which were rather surprising to my youthful mind. I suppose Aunt Sara had always undertaken this branch of criticism for him. He startled me once by saying :'I wonder when leasehold marriages will come in?' I was still so young that it had never occurred to me that all marriages were not permanent; so I said, in an appalled voice: 'Do you really think they will?' 'Well, it looks like it, doesn't it?' he said.

Another time, as he was watching the dowdy Newnham students of those days passing our house, he said sadly: 'Why do those young women always wear dung-coloured coats?' For he dearly liked to see a pretty girl well turned out. If he were out walking with me, leaning on my arm, as he usually did, and a pretty girl came by, he would stop dead, turn round, stare, and say loudly: 'Good looking young woman that.' She must certainly have heard him; however, any girl must have been pleased by such hearty approval. Once, when he had been entranced by the singing of a duet by two girls, who both happened to have rather prominent teeth, he said, 'Miss X sings like a bird, but little Miss Thingummy sings like an angel fine powerful teeth they both have'—without any pause between the sentences.

At Egerton Place he used to keep all the books which were

suspected of not being quite fit for the *jeune fille*, in a large book-case in the bathroom; and there on the walls hung photographs of nude works of art by such people as Michelangelo, or Praxiteles. But one did not feel much inclined to study the Venus of Milo, or to settle down to *Tristram Shandy*, or *Madame Bovary* in that bathroom, it was too alarming a place. The enormous mahogany-sided bath was approached by two steps, and had a sort of grotto containing a shower-bath at one end; this was lined with as many different stops as the organ in King's Chapel. And it was as difficult to control as it would be for an amateur to play that organ. Piercing jets of boiling, or ice-cold, water came roaring at one from the most unexpected angles, and hit one in the tenderest spots. Only Uncle William was not afraid of the monster; but he had perfect physical courage.

Presently he bought a Motor Car! A White Steam Car, which he named Betsey. In this we had wonderful fun in the holidays—for he generally now spent the holidays with us. Sometimes we drove what seemed immense distances then—over thirty miles! Once we drove from a place on the borders of Wales to London in three days, sleeping at Hereford and Oxford on the way; a tremendous effort; we were quite exhausted. The car was always breaking down and having to be given drinks of water with a teacup out of the nearest ditch. Sometimes it blew up and spattered us with orange spray out of the boiler; and at any steep hill it was no better than Aunt Sara's Horses; it stopped, and we all had to get out and push behind; while someone carried a large stone to scotch the wheel, when we were out of breath.

Mr. Hoskins, the Chauffeur, was a gruff sort of character; like Straker in *Man and Superman*, he always knew everything without being told. We rather liked him, but I am afraid he had the length of Uncle William's foot; as indeed all the servants had. They must have had an agreeable time of it, unless they quarrelled too much among themselves over the loot. Betsey had to be painted every year, and it took two months every time; but Mr. Hoskins insisted that it must be done; he needed a holiday, I suppose.

Dear Uncle William, how sweet he looked in his tasselled night-cap, when he shyly received company in bed, if he were unwell; how enchanting he was when he stumped over to the sideboard to fetch a bottle, and stumped back again, hugging it and muttering affectionately, 'Dear old Gin.' (Query: What would Aunt Sara have said to that? But I think she would have laughed.) How angelic he looked on the pony on which he sometimes rode after he lost his leg; how shamefacedly he would arrive at Christmas with 'a few odds and ends'—(an enormous box of good things from Fortnum and Mason's); and how certain he was to say, every night at half-past ten 'Let me see; how goes the Enemy? I think it is time for B-E-D.'

### UNCLE GEORGE

When we acted the uncles that Christmas we thought afterwards that my father had been just a little hurt by my too light-hearted reference to his troubles with the cocks that crow in the morn. For he took his ill health seriously, and in many ways was very like Aunt Etty. When he felt unwell he always walked about with a shawl over his shoulders; this was a regular sign of feeling 'seedy' with all the uncles and aunts (Aunt Etty wore one permanently); but it was exceedingly easy to divert him at those times; you could do wonders with a little affection and a question about something which interested him. I could not talk science to him as Charles could; but I could ask him what *party per pale* meant, or who was John of Gaunt's third wife? And he would react at once, and soon would be talking away quite gaily in spite of his discomforts.

Anything historical or heraldic would do, for he was the most romantic man alive. Heraldry had been the unforgotten passion of his boyhood; history and languages remained his chief interests all his life; outside science, of course. Though I should not be surprised to learn that even his scientific interests had had a romantic origin; at any rate, what can be more romantic than the tides or the moon?

He loved travelling, and always wanted to see absolutely everything in any country he visited; to learn the history and to speak the language and talk to everyone he met. Besides the ordinary European languages, he was always playing about with odd dialects —Provençal, Platt Deutsch, Romanche, Icelandic; and he liked to get all the technical terms of any craft right, and to find out the pedigrees of the words. I am sure that he never played real tennis— the classic game—without enjoying the ancient names of the parts of the court: the *Grille,* the *Dedans,* the *Tambour*; or without remembering the first act of *Henry V.* In the same way, when he took up archery, he loved using the right terms: the *nock* of the arrow, the *bracer* on the wrist, and so on. And all the time, whether he were playing tennis or pacing the Lammas Land to measure how far he had shot, he was, half-consciously, being himself a character in medieval history; and when he was playing with throwing-sticks or boomerangs, he was being an Australian blackfellow. He always wore a little flint and steel on his watch-chain. How he would have loved it if he had ever found occasion to make a real fire with them!

The books he read to us were all in the romantic vein: Shakespeare's Histories, Chaucer, Percy's Reliques, Scott's novels. He adored a Roman road or a prehistoric fort, and no one enjoyed a good dungeon, or a fine set of battlements, more than he did. To him the north was always more romantic than the south; so nearly every summer we went to Yorkshire for part of the holidays, and as we crossed the railway bridge over the Trent he would say, with great satisfaction: '*Now* we're in the North of England.' There our poor mother was dreadfully bored, but the first taste of the iron-cold air, the first glimpse of the dry-stone walls, went to our heads like wine. What fun it was, walking with him through the driving rain and mist, over hills and walls and bogs, while he told us stories about the Stone Age inhabitants of the moors.

With all this side of him I was very much in touch. It used to make me feel quite ill to think that I should never, never see Chaucer or Queen Elizabeth, or Rembrandt, or John Hampden, or whoever was the hero of the moment. I would have given years of my life to spend a day in another century, to see what it was like, and I would still give quite a lot to do so. Once I was overcome by the sad end of a story-book, and was found sobbing in the nursery, saying for all explanation: 'Robin Hood's dead! Robin Hood's dead!' My mother could not help laughing a little, but my father quite understood.

He was much more alert than the other brothers, more active, quicker in his movements and in his reactions; quickly fond of people, fond of the servants and tradesmen; really caring about their chilblains or their sick mothers; considerate of everyone. When our dog, old Sancho, had to be shot, it was he who comforted the broken-hearted Margaret. And yet he was oddly clumsy at times, not always tactful. This was caused by his simplicity, not by selfishness—he was completely unselfish; but he was not quick at noticing people's expressions, and was apt to take things at their surface value. If you said you were well, he would believe it quite simply; and if someone said he was glad to see him, it would never occur to him to doubt it. Warm and open, his spirits were quickly up and quickly down. In his *up* moods you might sometimes have thought him vain; he was so proud of his knowledge of languages, so naïvely delighted by the honours he received. How pleased he was when he was made President of the British Association, for its South African visit in 1905; how he enjoyed being made a Knight of the Bath, with its romantic associations. But it was all a transparent, almost childish, surprise at his own success; and one could prick it in an instant, if one were cruel enough to try. He was more a man of the world than the other brothers, if you could possibly call any of them men of the world at all.

As a girl I was apt to consider my elders strangely innocent. Perhaps they really were, though my father was certainly not quite so simple as I thought him then. I remember my intense astonishment when, at a dinner-party, Virginia Stephen made a slightly double-edged joke, and my father *understood* it! And turned away, shocked! This was, no doubt, chiefly because the joke was made by a young woman; for men's and women's worlds were more sharply divided then, than they are nowadays. But my surprise and his disgust are very significant, both of our time and of our family; for it was a mild enough joke; nowadays not even the very young would think it unsuitable for their parents to be able to understand it. I thought it natural enough that an advanced person like me should understand the joke, but it seemed to me really improper that he should. I remember, too, that he was disgusted by Stendhal's *Le Rouge et le Noir*, when I lent it to him; though I am still surprised that he did not appreciate the romantic fire which lies beneath Julien Sorel's somewhat unscrupulous methods of getting on in the world.

With his nerves always as taut as fiddle strings, it was really extraordinary that my father should be the most patient man alive. He was a little sad sometimes, a little worried; but never sad *at* you; just plain sad. And never, never, never cross. Indeed Aunt Cara had written of him in early days: 'He has an absolutely perfect temper,' and it remained true of him to the end of his life.

We used to rush in and out of the study, when he was working, to get 'frog-paper'—half-sheets of paper for drawing on, which he kept for us, under a green china frog—and he would just wait, with his 'Stylograph' pen in the air, looking disturbed but friendly, till we had banged the door and he could get back to the 'Pear-shaped

Figure of Equilibrium' again. My mother, too, always sat in the study, rustling and scrattling about in her heaps of papers, and sometimes talking to us or the servants in whispers, which can't have been very soothing. I am afraid he had very little peace in the study; but though he sometimes looked rather distraught, he never gave us the slightest hint that he would like to be quiet. Indeed, he was so affectionate, that it is quite possible that he did really prefer the human warmth of the interruptions to the coldness of solitude.

## UNCLE FRANK

Uncle Frank was the most charming of the brothers, always excepting Uncle William. He was the musician, the writer, the artist, in a family which might well have been called benevolently Philistine. Overtly, explicitly, they would have admitted that they knew nothing at all about music, very little about art, and not a great deal even about Literature, though they all loved reading. They were apt to regard the arts as the inessential ornaments of Life; unimportant matters. But this is a superficial view of them: in their scientific work they showed many of the characteristics of the creative artist: the sense of style, of proportion; the passionate love of their subject; and, above all, the complete integrity and the willingness to take infinite trouble to perfect any piece of work. Some of them found style difficult, but they did at least know that it mattered.

But they were sometimes very blind about things which lay outside their own particular world. There were whole realms of thought about which they were entirely ignorant; and yet they, who questioned every scientific statement, would sometimes be content to accept the most superficial views on those other matters. For instance, they had no feeling at all for philosophy or religion. They accepted the Christian ethics, and would have liked to be ordinary Christians themselves, if they could have believed in the dogmas. In fact, they might well be called *Christian Parasites* (which is what most of us are, in reality). They were tolerant of the religions of others; only all religions seemed equally strange to them; and the rites and ceremonies were just curious survivals of magic and paganism: mumbo-jumbo.

Neither had they any idea of the complications of psychology. They found it difficult to conceive of a mixture of motives; or of a man who says one thing and means another; or of a person who is sometimes honest and sometimes dishonest; because they were so completely single-hearted themselves.

So, being what they were, it was rather wide-minded of my father and Uncle Frank to take part in some of the early psychical experiments conducted by Mr. F. W. H. Myers and Professor Henry Sidgwick. Uncle Frank and Mr. Myers were actually each holding an ankle of the medium Eusapia Palladino, when she made the movements which led to her exposure. This was unfortunate, for it shook the uncles' faith in all the subsequent investigations of the Society for Psychical Research. They had probably not much wanted to believe in these manifestations anyhow, but had thought that it would be only fair to give the experiments a trial; but I have the impression that they were rather relieved to discover that the medium was a fraud. Certainly spiritualism went against the grain with them. Once Mr. Myers touched Uncle Frank and said: 'Frank, let me *feel* you: a man who really does not WANT immortality.' And Uncle Frank answered: 'Well, Myers, I don't like myself very much as I am, and I really could not bear the thought of going on for ever.'

But though there were many things to which they were blind, things in art and literature which they could not perceive at all, at any rate they hardly ever liked anything that was bad. This is perhaps a negative virtue, but such as it is, it was theirs; and, on the whole, they had good taste. Even when their vision was imperfect, they always had the grace of honesty, and there was something engaging in the candour with which they said what they thought, about things which they did not understand in the least. There was Grandmamma's remark about Tennyson's play *Queen Mary*: 'It's not nearly so tiresome as Shakespeare' —and Aunt Bessy's that '*Henry IV* would be such a good play without Falstaff'—both of which delight me.

But Uncle Frank, at any rate, had a good deal of the artist in him. He loved music, and played by turns the flute, oboe, bassoon, recorder and pipe-and-tabor. He had a fine sense of style, and a light touch in writing—he wrote two charming books of essays—and his very personal turns of speech and of humour were enchanting. He certainly set the tone in which both Bernard and Frances have always thought and written. He wrote heavenly verses in the Poetry Game; he made lovely drawings in the Picture Game; but the old

The cab had been ordered for 12.20; it was now nearly 12.15, so Uncle Frank said bitterly: 'I have now given up all hope of catching the train.' And after all, he had to wait 35 minutes at the station.

jokes are now too fragile to bear the public light of day. A few sayings remain: of a social lie he was to tell: 'I will do my best, but though I am a willing, yet I am not a ready liar.' Of a dull book: 'I have tried to read it by repeated charges at the point of the bayonet, but I have failed.' To a host, who told him that if he insisted on starting at once, he would have to wait an hour at the station: 'I would rather wait *anywhere* but here.'

Uncle Frank was always apt to suffer from fits of depression. This was his form of the family hypochondria; but it had no doubt been accentuated by the shock from which he never recovered: the death of his young wife, Amy Ruck, at the birth of her first child, Bernard (later to be the golfer and writer). Certainly, after this, he continually expected the worst about everything; though, from various stories of his childhood I have the impression that he had always been of a melancholy temperament. It was natural enough that he should have a horror of childbirth and illness, but his melancholy went deeper than that. He was difficult to cheer in his moods of heaviness; he seemed to have no spring of hope in him. Sometimes it even seemed doubtful whether it was good for him to play golf, it reduced him to such despondency; nearly every day he came home saying that 'nobody had ever played so badly before!'

Uncle Frank was the only one of the brothers who was a naturalist. My father or Uncle Horace would notice the ripple-marks in the sea-sand, or the way in which the deep pot-holes in a worn road were formed; or they would notice that an obsolete wooden plough was still in use; but neither of them—none of them except Uncle Frank—noticed 'birds and beasts and flowers'; though Uncle William knew something of geology. But Uncle Frank was a real field naturalist, making botany his chief study, but knowing a great deal about birds as well. He became his father's assistant at Down, and his father said once, when they were collaborating on a paper: 'Frank works *too* hard, he'll never get on.' In a way this was true; he would work for ever on a subject, but he had little ambition, and hardly cared at all for the honours that came to him. After his father's death he returned to Cambridge and worked at the Botany School on the physiology of plants. He was at various times lecturer and reader there, but when once the chair of Botany was vacant, he refused to stand for the Professorship, for which he would have been a strong candidate, saying that a younger man needed it more than he did. This was characteristic both of his lack of ambition and of his consideration for others. He was President of the British Association in Dublin in 1908; but he will probably be best remembered for his edition of the *Life and Letters* of his father.

Uncle Frank married again in 1883, when Bernard was seven. His wife was Ellen Crofts, Fellow and lecturer in English literature at Newnham. Their only child was Frances, seven months younger than I am. She married Professor F. M. Cornford, who later became Professor of Ancient Philosophy at Cambridge, and who translated Plato.

After my grandfather's death, Grandmamma spent the winters in Cambridge, at the Grove, a large house on the Huntingdon Road. It was surrounded by great park-like meadows, and here both Uncle Frank and Uncle Horace built themselves houses: *Wychfield* and *The Orchard*. It was a lovely place, where the children and Grandmamma's cows and carriage-horses, and Frances's donkeys all wandered about under the trees. When Grandmamma died the Grove was sold; and Aunt Bessy moved to a smaller house in Cambridge; and then the children felt very much injured at having to be content with their own large gardens instead of roving about over the whole domain; and they were particularly insulted by having to go out into the common, vulgar road to get from one house to the other. They stood in a row on the fence and solemnly cursed the new owners.

It is odd how little I remember Aunt Ellen, though I was eighteen when she died. Perhaps she did not care much for children, or know how to make friends with them? Anyhow, much as I enjoyed going to Wychfield, I always felt that I went there rather as fodder for Frances than as a person in my own right. It seemed to be difficult to Aunt Ellen to be warm and open to the ordinary lowbrow inhabitants of the world; for she was reserved; her sympathies were deep, but narrow.

But I liked her very much, and admired her daring in cutting short her rough black hair—an unconventional thing to do in those days. She always looked picturesque and charming; with her straight eyebrows and square whitey-brown face, especially as I remember her best in a Victorian pink gown with large red bows all down the front.

And then, how impressive the cigarettes were! I can't remember seeing any other women smoke, except her friends Jane Harrison and Alice Dew Smith, sitting in wicker chairs in the delightful untidy veranda at Wychfield. They used to play games there: making rhymes about their friends, or comparing them to animals or plants or puddings. The veranda was full of pretty things, all among the golf-clubs and tennis rackets; Persian rugs and gay cushions, and even the dogs' drinking bowls were of queer Italian pottery. There were always dogs hanging about: Whisk, the clever Aberdeen, and stupid old Pat, the Irish terrier, who was always being exploited by Whisk. They were quite as important as the people. One year the dogs sent Christmas presents to Frances, with Bernard's rhymed labels on them:

*Little Whisk*      *Little Pat*
*Sends you thisk.*    *Sends you that.*

Aunt Ellen and her friends seemed to me wonderfully up-to-date and literary. She used to read Stevenson and Henley to us, which was the height of modernity then. I believe she had a real feeling for literature; yet there was always something about it that made me a little uncomfortable. Was it possibly rather precious? For instance, she did not care for Dickens. This must have been a barrier between her and Bernard, who was always a Dickens expert.

# The Five Uncles

The house was full of lovely things, but that was Uncle Frank's doing. Aunt Ellen's own taste in art had more of the vogue of the moment. There was just a trace of greenery-yallery and Japanese fans about her own rooms; and the nursery was rather pitch-piney and bleak. In the drawing-room hung a large engraving after a painting by Fred Walker, 'The Harvest Moon', in which a rustic character with a scythe and several maidens wended their classical ways across the face of the full moon. You could almost date the marriage from that picture alone, it was so often given as a wedding present about 1883. I knew two other of the best academic houses in Cambridge where it was the chief adornment of the drawing-room. There was a small cast of the 'Venus of Milo'; and all about the house there hung large photographs of the Best Pictures: the 'Sistine Madonna', of course (all proper drawing-rooms had *her*; we had her ourselves, even larger, at home); and Watts's 'Hope', and 'Love and Death'; and in Frances's room, an adorable row of Carpaccio babies brought back from Italy. Even in those cultivated circles the French Impressionists had not yet been heard of; though J. F. Millet had got through. Aunt Etty had a photograph of 'The Angelus', but it was hung in a second-class spare bedroom.

Aunt Ellen was not a happy person, though I don't know what was wrong. Possibly she suffered from being too closely surrounded by Darwins. She ought to have been an early member of the Anti-Darwin League, a society recently founded by people who have inadvertently married Darwins. Certainly her cry was often: 'Don't tell Henrietta I'm ill; *promise* not to tell her.' 'Don't tell Ida; I know I've done wrong again.' But that is not explanation enough. Long after her death Jane Harrison said to me: 'I could not be sorry when Ellen died, because she was so unhappy; though I don't know why. She loved her husband and child, and had everything she wanted in the world.' Was it a temperamental melancholy; had she a real distaste for life? Was it a reflection of Uncle Frank's broken spirit? Or did she need work, a career, a religion? Probably she didn't know herself.

When he was quite old, Uncle Frank fell in love again; and married Florence, the strange and beautiful widow of Professor F. W. Maitland, the historian; but that is another story, and does not come into this one.

### UNCLE LENNY

Question: *Which of all the Darwin brothers*
*Eats still faster than the others?*
Answer: *Spite of Mildred's watchful eyes,*
*Uncle Lenny takes the prize.*
(From *Christmas Conundrums,* by Bernard)

Uncle Lenny was Major Darwin, R.E., but anyone less military it would be hard to imagine; even his moustache looked benevolent and civilian; and his round face, with its rudimentary whiskers, was kind, patient and amused. We used to wonder what had made him go into the army, till he told me that he had done so 'because he was afraid of being afraid'; not a reason a coward would give. Probably, too, with his usual humility, he considered the army suitable, because he thought himself less intelligent than the other brothers. He was a slow developer, but he went on growing all his life. When he was a very old man he was more interested in the future of the world than in the past; which is rare in the old.

He was at Woolwich and Chatham with Lord Kitchener, and said once that he was not much of a believer in the value of examinations: 'Why, in one examination I came out top and Kitchener was ploughed.' And, 'We really never thought then that *Kitchener* would do anything, which just shows. . . .'

Uncle Lenny did all kinds of scientific odd jobs in his twenty years in the Royal Engineers: observing eclipses, or teaching chemistry or photography, or working on the topography of Africa. He did very little routine military work, and the only time he saw active service was at Malta, when he was leading a file of men down a narrow high-walled lane, and they met an infuriated cow. After a moment of painful indecision, he was obliged to give the order for an ignominious retreat.

He had only inherited the family hypochondria in a mild degree, but in 1890 he resigned from the Army for the rather unconvincing reason that 'his health was not very good'. His life then became fuller than ever, with many different interests. He was in Parliament for three years, in consequence of which we all believed firmly, that 'poor Uncle Lenny never went to bed'. But he was far too even-minded to be successful in politics. He became President of the Royal Geographical Society, and then of the Eugenic Society; and so at last, when he was over sixty, he found that he was doing work which he felt to be of importance.

I can only remember his first wife, Aunt Bee—Elizabeth Fraser—as an extra loud rustling silk petticoat coming along the nursery passage at Down, in the days when the more you rustled the grander you were; or as a bell-shaped modish silhouette against a window. Nana said, 'Aunt Bee doesn't care for children.' I believe she was gay and sociable as well as elegant; but it must have been hard to be lively at Number 12 Egerton Place, as I remember it. This was their house, just off the Brompton Road; and Aunt Bee seemed to have furnished it entirely out of the purchases she had made on a tour round the world: carved Oriental furniture, all of it quite black, except a few brass trays. It *was* a dark and dismal house. When, after Aunt Bee's death, Uncle Lenny married Mildred, nothing was altered there at all; and Mildred, with her fresh, light grey clothes and golden hair, looked very odd in Aunt Bee's setting. Once, as a girl, I went to a dinner-party during Mildred's reign at No. 12, and I must reluctantly state that it was the dullest I ever endured, but I am sure it was chiefly the fault of the furniture. Nobody could possibly have sparkled in that sombre setting.

Mildred kept her own cheerful furniture for the house they built on Ashdown Forest. That was really their home: Cripps's Corner, on the very edge of the forest, with the half-wild fields running down between the woods in front, to the little brook at the bottom; and the great view, out over the Weald to the South Downs, twenty-five miles away. They had been quite unable to control the architect, who got the bit between his teeth, and designed the house chiefly to please himself. He insisted on putting in heavily leaded, small-paned, pseudo-Gothic windows, through which it was quite impossible to see one of the loveliest views in England (a study of the minds of architects would be a psychological curiosity). However, I dare say that they did not put up much of a fight against him, for I can well imagine Mildred saying, with kindly tolerance: 'Yes, the windows are dreadful, but they make the young man so happy, Poor Darling.' When Uncle Lenny showed the new house to Uncle Horace, he said: 'Well, Horace, I suppose you think these windows are not only ugly but immoral.' And Uncle Horace said: 'Yes, that is exactly it.' Which shows that they had the right principles in design, when they chose to think about it.

It is there, at Cripps's Corner, that we always think of Uncle Lenny and Mildred; at the end of the road, at the end of their lives, living in happy and uneventful solitude, three miles from the nearest village.

My mother used to say that in some ways Aunt Bee was better for Uncle Lenny than dear Mildred: more stimulating and less damping to any enterprise. It is true that Mildred was inclined to think that nearly every activity was very rash, and more likely to do harm than good; and Uncle Lenny was far too judicious to need soft-pedalling; but they were so happy together, that it is quite impossible to think that anything could have been more perfect than their marriage. It used to be delightful to be welcomed at Cripps's Corner by Mildred, with real sympathy in her voice for the dangers and exhaustion we had suffered during the two-hour train journey from London. 'You *Poor Lamb*, how *tired* you must be after that *Horrid* Journey.' One might have been arriving from Timbuctoo.

We had always known and loved Mildred Massingberd, because she was our cousin before she was our aunt. It is difficult to draw the very queer character that Mildred was, and yet to show her charm. Everything one writes about her seems so grim and puritanic, and yet she was one of the most lovable people I ever knew. She was one of those strange beings who really *enjoy* discomfort, and who always remind me of the sheep in the French proverb: '*Le mouton aime la misère.*' She would have lived happily for ever on tea and bread-and-butter, with a cold bath every morning, and a backless wooden stool to sit on. 'It doesn't matter if she's a good cook, so long as she's a good woman,' she said once, as she engaged a cook. She did, accidentally, once have a good cook; but the cooking soon deteriorated sadly from a lack of encouragement which amounted almost to Cruelty-to-Cooks.

Once when some children were staying at Cripps's Corner, Mildred gave them ginger-nuts for their elevenses—she loved to spoil children—and Uncle Lenny always had one, too. On the last day of the visit, she said: 'There, Leonard, that's your last ginger-nut; you won't get any more.' The children were dreadfully upset, and came privately to their mother to ask: '*Why* can't poor Uncle Lenny have any more biscuits?' Of course this was a joke of hers; but, for all that, she really cared so little for bodily joys, that she could not understand how small pleasantnesses like ginger-nuts can add up together to make life solid and good.

Yet she was always ministering to the weaker brethren about her, and moreover doing it without making them feel ashamed of their grossness. There was none of that guilty feeling of being a cannibal, which good vegetarians always manage to give you. Not at all: 'They do so like these things, poor Darlings,' she seemed to be saying, as she tenderly and amusedly provided us with coffee, or hotwater bottles, or any other of the harmless comforts of the flesh.

But NOT with drink; a line was drawn there, for Mildred was a fanatical teetotaller; and took in, believe it or not, a periodical called *The Journal of Inebriety*. However, she allowed Uncle Lenny to have a tot of whiskey every night 'as medicine'; but he had to drink it in one gulp, while she kept her eyes averted from the horrid sight. He was then given a charcoal biscuit to take the taste away. He used to tease her gently about alcohol, and she loved the teasing!

She hated all innovations, and for a long time she would allow no electric light or telephone in their isolated house; and the motor car, which they finally kept, must have had a miserable life of it, owing to a lack of that motherly love which motors need, like all other animals.

She had a deep distrust of art in all its forms, but particularly of music. She wrote to Margaret: '*I wonder why so many literary and artistic people have so little power of leading good and helpful lives? It is sad indeed to be born with the artistic temperament. I do hope your Richard won't succumb to it, but I feel anxious about the clarionet and piano.*'

We used to have fierce arguments on this subject, and Uncle Lenny used to shock me when, in talking about Eugenics, he maintained that a money standard was the *only possible* criterion in deciding which human stocks should be encouraged to breed; though he admitted that this test was not a perfect one: 'A man who can earn and keep money shows that he has the qualities essential to survival.' I said that money had little importance for such people as artists, philosophers, inventors, gypsies. It would be an irreparable loss to the human race if those valuable strains were to be bred out altogether. It depressed me deeply to think of everybody living in tidy little suburban villas, earning and keeping money—*what for*? But Uncle Lenny could not see this at all. He had very little use for artists; and gypsies were generally dirty and dishonest. During one of these conversations Mildred, in her horror of the Arts, was driven into the definite statement, that a man who successfully held a small job in a post office was worth more than the greatest artist in the world! And Uncle Lenny sat there, listening and amused; but in substantial agreement with her.

I must add, however, that when the Ashdown Forest Conservators wanted to shut up a half-crazed old cave-man, who had lived all his life as a kind of outlaw on the forest, Uncle Lenny told them that they should have caught him fifty years ago; if they shut him up now he would certainly die; so they left the poor old fellow free. But Uncle Lenny was rather apologetic about his action, as it was against all his best principles.

In her own way, Mildred was an ardent feminist, and often deplored matrimony for her friends as a most rash and unnecessary venture; though she held that women should be kind to men, and not expect too much of them, 'because they are such helpless things, Poor Lambs'. Once, when she was ill, I begged her to see a doctor. She answered: 'What's the good of my getting the doctor? I don't know what's the matter with me, so I can't tell him what to do, and that is the only thing that is any use with doctors. But, of course, he's only a *Man*.' Later on they had a woman doctor, whom she did trust.

I remember a letter of congratulation to a girl on her marriage; it ran something like this: '*My dear X. I must tell you how much I admire your courage in getting married. I can't myself understand this enthusiasm for matrimony, as women are so much happier single; still it does sometimes turn out quite well;*' (etc. etc.; accompanied by a large cheque). If, after some such incident one pointed out that she and Uncle Lenny appeared to be very happy, she would only say

that of course that was quite different, and that they were exception-
ally fortunate. She used to boast: 'Of course I have no sense of
humour' (which was quite untrue), and then would take much
pleasure in guying her own idiosyncrasies; and yet she meant what
she said, too.

She had a large circle who were known as 'Mildred's Poories',
to whom she was endlessly attentive. They were mostly elderly
women:

> *Who can't be said to coruscate,*
> *Who are not quite as fair as houris,*
> *The deaf, the dull, the desolate,*
> *The too immortal race of Poories . . .'*

as Bernard described them in a poem, written for Uncle Lenny's
ninetieth birthday. I think of Mildred sitting up very straight—she
never leant against the back of a chair—sewing flannelette nightgowns for the poorest of the Poories; garments which I am afraid
the most miserable of paupers would not now condescend to die in;
but which I am sure she would thankfully have worn herself.

After about 1905 Mildred's clothes never altered again, and
throughout all the wild vicissitudes of fashion, she went on wearing
her long narrow skirts, high-necked blouses, large straw hats and
narrow-footed boots. But, in her own curious aristocratic way, I
believe she took a good deal of trouble about her unfashionable
attire, and was conscious that she had been, and still was, good-
looking. Aunt Etty once wrote, after some function of Uncle
Lenny's, that 'being dressed like a Duchess' suited Mildred, and it
was true.

Everything Mildred said and did delighted and amused Uncle
Lenny, even when she refused him ginger biscuits! He was often
amused at himself, too, and would tell us many gentle stories to his
own detriment. Once, when he was presiding at a solemn commit-

tee meeting, he was roused from contemplation by a voice saying: 'Do you find that soothing, Major Darwin?' and became aware that he was slowly and rhythmically rubbing his nose from one end to the other of the large sheet of pink blotting-paper which lay before him. He was not quite so unself-conscious as Uncle William, or he could not have told that story about himself.

Sometimes, when one was walking with him in his solitary garden at Cripps's Corner, he would look carefully all round him, and if there was no one at all in sight (and there never was anyone within miles), he would tell one in a lowered voice about some relation who had been dead for about sixty years, and who used occasionally to drink.

Or he would tell one of his three celebrated improper stories. The one I liked best was about a lady who got locked into the lavatory on a Sunday morning; so her brother-in-law, a clergyman, sat on a chair up against the door and read the morning service aloud to her from outside. The other two stories were not quite up to this level of impropriety. It was sometimes very difficult to imagine Uncle Lenny in the army!

He was extraordinarily humble about himself. He told me several times: 'I remember all the silly and bad things I ever did; all the times I was unkind or tactless or made a fool of myself; every one of them. I wish I didn't. It makes me so unhappy even now. I wish I could remember the good things, if there were any.' There was one painful story of which I cannot remember the details: about how he had been asked for advice, and had given it; and how for forty years now he had been harassed by the thought that he might have given the wrong advice.

But he remembered with the most touching satisfaction how a man, not an intimate friend, came to him in great distress, saying that his wife had left him, and what ought he to do? Uncle Lenny felt very doubtful, but at last said: 'Do you know where your wife has gone?' 'Yes, I know where she is.' 'Then I think you had better go after her and try to bring her back.' The advice was taken with success, and the couple lived happily together ever afterwards; and years later the man thanked Uncle Lenny for his good counsel. Another verse of Bernard's poem comes to my mind; of how Uncle Lenny was

> *Serenely kind and humbly wise,*
> *Whom each may tell the thing that's hidden*
> *And always ready to advise*
> *And ne'er to give advice unbidden.*

This was quite true.

### UNCLE HORACE

A fact about Uncle Horace, which set him in a most amiable light, was that he had the greatest difficulty in learning to spell well enough to pass the Little Go. My grandfather did not spell very well either; all through the *Beagle Journal* he spelt *broad* BROARD, and *yacht* YATCH—a sympathetic weakness. It was understood by us children, that Uncle Horace and Mr. Dew Smith had started a sort of concern called *The Shop*, where they made clocks and machines and things; and where we hoped that poor spelling would not matter much. Nowadays it is called *The Cambridge Scientific Instrument Company*, and is not unknown; but then it was in a very small way, and was just *The Shop*, and was considered by my father as rather a doubtful commercial venture. Long afterwards Uncle Lenny said: 'Of all my brothers, Horace was the one whom I should have thought the least likely to make a success in life.' Yet he made a great success as a scientific engineer. But in those days they used to say: 'Of course Horace is brilliant with machines, but will he really be able to make the business *go*? And his health is so bad, too. . . .'

# The Five Uncles

For Uncle Horace and my father were the two brothers who really had weak health. Uncle Horace was the youngest surviving child of the family, and had been delicate and backward as a boy. Doubtless my grandmother had coddled him a good deal, and he may have been over-protected by his brothers, who were very fond of him. However, he was far too affectionate and unselfish to be spoilt; but, though he grew up able to work, and to work hard, he always retained traces of the invalid's outlook, and of the old blissful dependence on his mother. When he was ill, he did not worry over details as my father and Aunt Etty did; but he did enjoy the extra affection he received at those times. Here is a scrap of a letter from Grandmamma, written in 1889, after a visit to Horace, who was recovering from an illness: '*I have seen the dear old man. He looks so sweet and so handsome, with his pale clear complexion, and his hair and beard so dark. . . . His poor hands are very transparent.*' This last phrase brings her vividly before me. '*His poor hands*' (there was nothing the matter with his hands), the expression somehow shows the quality of her dangerous interest in ill health.

In 1893, after years of ill health, he was at last successfully operated on by Sir Frederick Treves for *typhlitis*, as appendicitis was then called. This was one of the early operations, and was then considered very risky. Soon after this, in the Jubilee Year, he was made Mayor of Cambridge, and had a furred gown and a gold chain; so it looked as if both his health and his spelling had improved. We children thought it grand that he should be Mayor; but at the same time we felt that it was very kind and condescending of him to consort with the Town on equal terms like that! The University and the Town kept themselves to themselves in those days; Uncle Horace tried hard to bring them closer together.

However, his chief title to fame was that he used to amuse us by standing on a chair in the dining-room, holding a tin of treacle, and demonstrating that syrup always fell in a perfectly straight line, from the spoon in his high-held hand, into a saucer on the floor. After a time, the exceptions that proved the truth of the laws of gravity became rather frequent, to the detriment of the carpet; and then Aunt Ida decided that he must conduct his operations in the veranda in future. After that, the experiments demonstrated the effect of the wind on treacle, more often than anything else.

Uncle Horace had not taken kindly to the classical and literary sides of his education; but he had a certain directness of perception, and delicacy of touch, which were very attractive. Aunt Etty writes of him, when he was twenty-four: '*I've taken to being more in love than usual with Jemmy* [Horace]. *I think he has such a charming nature, so fresh and unspotted by the world; and his very absence of culture, gives him a certain originality which is refreshing.*' I felt this myself, but his absorption in his dear machines always remained a barrier to me, for they are not at all in my line; though I liked to watch the affection in his face and the tender movements of his beautiful sensitive hands as he touched them.

Also I did not know Uncle Horace as well as the other uncles because he and his family often spent the holidays at Aunt Ida's home at Abinger, so that he was not often at Down with us. (As Aunt Etty's Janet put it once so well: 'Mr. Rorace and Mrs. Sidar rar rat Tabinger Rall.')

But chiefly I did not get to know him because, warm, tender-hearted, sympathetic as he was, he rather tended to disappear behind the clear-cut distinction of Aunt Ida. She was the daughter of Lord Farrer, who was connected in rather complicated ways with our family. She must have been enchanting when young; so fine-spun and rare, with her sloping shoulders and shining Victorian perfection. Uncle Lenny had been attracted first; but when she accepted Uncle Horace there was great opposition from her family; or, at least from that part of her family, who were our own relations! Uncle Horace, they said, had very poor health, no proper profession, or likelihood of earning a decent living, and not much culture; really none of those Darwin young men were anything like good enough for Ida. So there was a terrible to-do, and everyone obeyed the advice given by a family poet on a like occasion some fifty years earlier:

> *Write a letter, write a letter;*
> *Good advice will make us better;*
> *Father, mother, sister, brother,*
> *Let us all advise each other.*

But, of course, the young people carried it through in the teeth of the clashing aunts; it is however interesting to consider the low esteem in which our revered uncles were once held.

So they were married and built the Orchard, and had three children: Erasmus, who was four years older than me, and who was killed at the Battle of Ypres in 1915; and Ruth, who is two years older than me, and is now Mrs. Rees Thomas; and Nora, who is of my own age, and who married Alan Barlow.

I did not really get to know Aunt Ida very well in my childhood; but when I was older I knew her and loved her exceedingly, and I never could enough appreciate the fineness of her quality and the sensibility of her perceptions. But, as a child, I only dimly felt all this, for as children we were all a little afraid of her. We felt that we were rough and rude, and it seemed impossible to live up to her standards. She never said anything critical, she was always kind, but we somehow felt that our hats or our legs or our manners were wrong (and so they were, particularly our manners). And what was worse, we never knew exactly how they were wrong, or what we could do about it.

There was always a feeling at the Orchard of things which had better not be said; though why not, or what they were, was beyond our imagination. Mystery seemed to veil everything there; but I

206

don't believe there was really any mystery at all. Aunt Ida would say: 'I am sorry that the children can't come to tea on Tuesday,' and it would seem as if there must be some portentous and secret reason why they could not come. And then, later, we would discover by accident that they had only had to go to the dentist, or do something else equally humdrum. I remember, almost with a shiver, how we heard from Aunt Ida that a favourite nursery-maid of theirs was going to leave. What could she have done? What could she possibly have done? for Aunt Ida to say in *that* voice: 'Rose is going away.' I believe she was only leaving to be married.

Frances and I used to gossip together and say that Ruth and Nora liked being mysterious, too. They would say: 'I'm going to see A Person,' where we would have said: 'I'm going to see Miss Greene'; or 'I've got Something to do' where we would have said, 'I've got to write a French Composition to-day.'

On thinking over this queer atmosphere at the Orchard, I believe that the mystery partly emanated from Aunt Ida's intense desire for privacy; and partly from her over-sensitive response to life. She saw the world with very clear eyes, and sometimes it was more than she could bear. There are many things in the world which are brutal and shocking, but most of us are coarse-grained enough to be able to think: 'Oh well, things *are* like that, and there is nothing I can do about it, so why worry?' and then we muffle up the facts and never see them naked again. But Aunt Ida could not do this; she never let her vision become thickened and fogged, as most people do. That was what was so wonderful about her. Only some things were too terrible for her to look at, or to tell.

Once you were through the barriers, you were accepted as a friend for ever; and talking to her was always a joy and a refreshment; she understood so much, she was so fine-grained and sensitive. But her artist's nature was always driving her on to aim at perfection in everything, and so she could never herself attain satisfaction. In manners and in morals; in rising up and in lying down; in the roasting of the chicken, and in the trimming of Nora's garden hat; everything had to be perfectly done in the only right way. This made life difficult at times—a little slackness is a comfortable thing; but she did reach some fulfilment in the finish and charm of her house, and in all the lovely things she had found and put there; and above all in her garden, her secret poet's garden, where the blackbirds sang all day long in the mossy apple trees, and where every flower was a new discovery. There she had really made an image of Paradise such as only herself could have conceived.

It is extraordinary how different the interiors of these five houses were. You had only to put your nose inside the front doors to smell their diversity: Uncle William's, correct, hideous, in the very best late-Victorian style; only his books and his writing-table reflecting anything of his personality; our house, untidy, undistinguished— (I am afraid that fiend Economy had taken a hand in the choice of some of the furniture)—yet somehow friendly and comfortable enough; Uncle Frank's, charming and solid and simple and gay, everywhere characteristic of his instinctive taste; Uncle Lenny's the strangest mixture of the unassimilated ideas of his two wives, yet very pleasant wherever Mildred had got the upper hand; Uncle Horace's—though one thought of it as Aunt Ida's—almost too full of detail; but beautiful, not grand—and every tiny corner of it loved and finished and exquisite.

When I read over what I had written about these five brothers, I felt that it might seem that I had made them too good, too nice, too single-hearted to be true. But it *was* true, for in a way that was what was wrong with them. I always used to feel that they needed protecting and cherishing, for they never seemed to me to have quite grown up. No doubt my attitude to them arose partly from the arrogance of my youth, and my children probably feel the same about me now; but still, when I think of my uncles beside some of their friends, they seem to me to show a sort of innocent lack of imagination, which was exceptional. They were quite unable to understand the minds of the poor, the wicked, or the religious.

My grandfather said once: 'I have five sons, and I have never had to worry about any one of them, except about their health.' Well, that is not quite right. One ought to have to worry sometimes about young people, because they ought to be growing out in new ways and experimenting for themselves. But my grandfather was so tolerant of their separate individualities, so broad-minded, that there was no need for his sons to break away from him; and they lived all their lives under his shadow, with the background of the happiest possible home behind them. Of course, that world, which now seems to us to have been so stable and prosperous, seemed eventful enough to them then; and they had certainly done their full share of work in it, and had had plenty of personal difficulties; all the same, it is probable that the reason for this feeling of mine about them lies partly in the relative smoothness of their lives, but yet more in the straightforwardness and simplicity of their characters.

At any rate, I know that I always felt older than they were. Not nearly so good, or so brave, or so kind, or so wise. Just older.

My grandfather on his horse Tommy. From a photograph.

# CHAPTER XI

## *Religion*

The first religious experience that I can remember is getting under the nursery table to pray that the dancing mistress might be dead before we got to the Dancing Class. I was about half-way through the exasperating business which dancing class entailed: being changed right down to my skin, and washed and brushed, and having the comfortable dirt taken out of my fingernails. Margaret was sitting on the table, while Nana made her hair into long sausage-curls, with a wet brush round her finger. We thought the sausages very ugly, but Nana admired them, and we all loved Nana so much that we would do anything she liked. So Margaret bore it as well as she could, and only gave a little snarl when a drop of cold water fell on her bare neck. Charles was carefully washing his hands without any soap, the usual expression of philosophic calm on his round face. I think that he sometimes washed without any water either, for I well remember the smooth and permanent pale grey texture of his fingers.

When I was about half-dressed, as I said, in my white flannel petticoat to be exact, I considered my costume suitable, and I got under the table for religious seclusion, and took up an attitude modelled on Sir Joshua Reynolds' 'Infant Samuel kneeling in Prayer', as the correct position for divine transactions. We knew the Infant Samuel very well, from the picture-card game of National Gallery, which we often played.

It was not that I had any grudge against that particular dancing mistress, who was called, I think, Miss Ratcliffe. Of course, all dancing mistresses were affected jades. Hamlet's words perfectly described them, when I read them later on: '*You jig, you amble, you*

The first prayer. 'Please, God, let Miss Ratcliffe be dead before we get to Dancing Class.

*lisp and nickname God's creatures and make your wantonness your ignorance.*' But that would not have mattered to me if only they had kept their jigging and ambling to themselves and left me in peace. But as it was, we were forced to go, and I really could think of no other weapon of self-defence except prayer. Not that I believed in that much; still, perhaps it was worth trying.

# Religion

But, of course, prayer did not succeed. Prayers, at least *my* prayers, never did. So far as I can remember, none of the dancing mistresses from whom I suffered, ever had so much as a cold in the head in all the time I knew them. There they always were, that scourge of the human race; and we always had to go through the whole degrading ritual, from the first March Past with its elegant bows to Miss Ratcliffe, right down to the bitter end of the waltz or the lancers.

I have sometimes wondered what would have been my reaction if the dancing mistress had fallen down dead, as I came into the classroom. I suppose I should have felt rather guilty; but after all it would have been God's doing, not mine; and that He should have done such a thing at my request would have destroyed my respect for Him, for once and all.

For the only virtue God had, to my mind, was that of impartiality; and so prayer itself seemed to me to be an immoral proceeding. It was as if you were trying to bribe the Judge. My idea of prayer was: 'Please God, if you will let there be Chocolate Pudding for lunch, I will be very good to-day.' I am now told that this is not the right idea of prayer, but it was mine then. Well, now: could it be right that God should suddenly put Chocolate Pudding into the head of the cook, when she had intended to make Marmalade Pudding, which I hated, but which other people liked? No, it would be exceedingly unjust. In fact, it would be a shabby thing for me to try to do a deal for myself in that way; and most unfair of God to agree to my terms. But, anyhow, He never did; God simply never did what I asked Him; so that on the whole I thought Him incorruptible, which was just as well. There remained the possibility that prayer might work as magic. But even as magic it never succeeded. It was altogether a bad idea. After that, prayer became synonymous for me with giving up hope; if ever I prayed again, it was only in a final frenzy of despair, and was the first step towards resignation at not getting what I wanted.

# Religion

God had a smooth oval face, with no hair and no beard and no ears. I imagine that He was not descended, as most Gods are, from Father Christmas, but rather from the Sun Insurance Office sign. Even now this hairless, earless, egg-shaped face, which I have drawn, gives me a sort of holy feeling in my stomach. He sat up in the night sky like that, sending out Good Things with one hand, and Bad Things with the other hand. This was somehow connected with not letting your right hand know what your left hand was doing. There were probably an equal number of Good Things and Bad Things, and they were probably sent out with fair impartiality; at least, I was willing to give God the benefit of the doubt about it—though certainly it did seem as if the Bad Things had a strong tendency to go to the Good people; and vice versa. For from my earliest childhood I knew very well that Being Good did not pay. It was just a thing that you might—or might not—like for its own sake; and the verse about the wicked flourishing like the green bay tree, was one of the few texts that went home to me with a click. God was not good and kind; at best, he was indifferent and the world was beautiful but quite pitiless.

God.

And yet, deep down in the furthest depths of my mind, I must still have wished to believe in the Justice of God; for during the war I suddenly noticed, with surprise, that I was half-consciously comforting myself with the thought that Hitler and his gang would get what they deserved after their deaths, and that the innocent people they had tortured would all receive prizes in the next world! In fact, I still half believed in an exceedingly primitive kind of Heaven and

213

Hell. How difficult it is to perceive in oneself the remains of early superstitions.

Prayer was not the only idea of the grown-ups which seemed to me wrong in itself. They had a complete set of values for Badness and Goodness, which I will call System A; and this only partly co-incided with my own private set of values: System B. I was always troubled by the confusion of trying to reconcile the two incompatible codes. System A and System B overlapped and agreed in disapproving of dishonesty, cruelty and cowardliness; but otherwise they had little in common; and there might often be very different points of view about what constituted dishonesty or cowardliness. For instance, when I had been obliged to steal some sugar, I felt that it made it perfectly honest if I put my head through the drawing-room door and shouted: 'I've taken three lumps of sugar out of the pantry,' and then ran away. My conscience was quite clear after that, and it did not prevent me from doing it again. This is the principle of Confession. I should have minded very much if I had felt myself to be dishonest; but I did not mind if they scolded me for disobedience. Obedience, though important in System A, had no place at all in System B.

Of course all kinds of goodness, in both systems, were hampered by being, by definition, something which you did not want to do. If you did want to do it, then it wasn't goodness. Thus being kind to a person you liked didn't count at all, because you wanted to do it; and being kind to a person you didn't like (like Poor Old Betsy at Down) was no use either; because—as I thought then—the person always knew perfectly well that you disliked them, and so of course the kindness could not please them. So kindness was no use anyway. Nor were other efforts at Goodness more successful. For one thing Goodness never made me feel nice afterwards; I must be abnormal, for the reputed afterglow of virtue simply did not occur. Goodness-against-the-grain simply made me feel mean, hypocritical and servile; so that Goodness only resulted in a weight on my conscience; a weight often heavier than if I had been Bad on purpose; and nearly as heavy, as if I had been Bad by accident.

For the most muddling thing of all was that the Badnesses you did *by accident* were what made you feel most guilty. Of course, this was all wrong by System A. The grown-ups pretended that it it was what you did *on purpose* that mattered. This was, and is, quite untrue. No one ever really regrets doing a Badness on purpose. For instance, if you were rude or disobedient to Miss X, a governess you rightly despised, you felt rather pleased with yourself afterwards; or if you paddled without asking leave, anyhow you had had the paddling, and no one could ever take it away from you again.

But if you were unkind or rude by mistake to someone you loved—Ah, then you just wished you were dead. The story of Aunt Bessy and Margaret's impersonation of Miss S. is a case in point. We had truly intended to amuse and please Aunt Bessy and when she was hurt, we were shattered by remorse. Once when Nana was ill in hospital, and my mother wanted to take me to see her, I refused to go, in all innocence. I could not bear the idea of seeing her changed, and sick, and surrounded by strangers. What could I say to her in public? We could only look at each other from far off, so what was the use of going? If I could possibly have believed that she would have liked to see me, I would willingly have gone; but that never occurred to me at all. This is the sort of thing one is sorry for afterwards, just because one did not do it on purpose.

My own code of virtue, System B, took this strange fact into account, but the grown-ups' System A was not realistic enough to do so. Yet if they would only be honest, even old people would admit that when they forget an appointment or are cross on purpose, they don't feel sorry at all; whereas, if they did the same things by accident, they would feel thoroughly guilty. Can it be called anything but Remorse, the anguish which pierces your breast when you discover that you have thrown away your return ticket, or lost your latchkey, by your own carelessness?

Anyhow, whether by accident or on purpose, by being Good or by being Bad, System A or System B, I always had a weight on my conscience of many pounds—if conscience weight is measured in pounds? Guiltiness was a permanent condition, like rheumatism; and one just had to learn to disregard it, and to carry on under it, as best one could. Huckleberry Finn has the last word on conscience—and I was as conscious-ridden as poor Huck himself.

*'It don't make no difference whether you do right or wrong, a person's conscience ain't got no sense, and just goes for him anyway. If I had a yaller dog that didn't know more than a person's conscience, I would pison him. It takes up more room than all the rest of a person's insides, and yet ain't no good, nohow.'*

This is most terribly TRUE.

There was another way in which the grown-ups were far from candid. This was about yet a third code of values: System C, or *Ladies and Gentlemen*. We were taught very carefully and with great insistence how gentlemen behaved. 'Gentlemen don't tell lies; Ladies don't pick their noses; Gentlemen never avoid paying their bus fares; Ladies are always polite to servants; Gentlemen never show they are afraid; No Lady would wear a hat like that; Gentlemen are always generous with money, don't hit smaller boys; never read other people's letters;' and so on and so forth; a mixture of morals and manners, which seemed to me a much more real and practical rule to live by, than the Goodness and Badness of System A. It was definite and easy to understand; and it was not holy and infected with piety; so that, whatever happened, it had no effect on the conscience afterwards. In this it was quite unlike Systems A and B. By System C, you were sorry if you did something wrong on purpose, but no sorrier if you did it by accident; and in neither case were you left with a load of sacrilegious guilt on your mind. I can't account for this, but it is a fact.

To be sure, there was a side of System C which seemed rather silly: for instance, when they made such a fuss because you walked out of the room in front of Mrs B.; or when public schoolboys—(not my brothers)—talked so much about bounders, and about the things no gentleman could possibly do; but in our family we really saw very little of the worst kind of snobbishness of System C, so that on the whole it seemed to me right—even fine—in its emphasis on disinterestedness and honour, and especially in its detachment from money values. 'He's very poor, but he *is* such a gentleman.' 'Of course you might make a lot of money that way, but it's not the sort of thing one could possibly do.'

But the grown-ups were not candid in being unwilling to admit that Code C was quite as important as Code A. They believed in it profoundly; much more passionately than in Code A (though they did not know this); and yet they would not say so openly, or let you say so either. This was partly because Being a Gentleman was already beginning to be considered snobbish and undemocratic; but still more because they felt so deeply about it that they really did not like speaking of it. You were scolded if you said that someone 'was not quite a gentleman', because it was vulgar to say so, *though not to think so*. In fact, it was exactly what they themselves had meticulously taught us to think. I will try to be braver and more realistic than they were; and so, in spite of overwhelming current opinion, and with the certainty of being thought snobbish, I will say, straight out, that System C was on the whole a good code, and that being a gentleman was, at its best, a fine thing.

Of course the code was not perfect; it had both the advantages and the disadvantages of being a rule it was quite possible to live up to; unlike System A, which gloried in aiming impossibly high. But the best kind of System C incorporated a good deal of the

Christian ethics of System A; and it was this C-with-a-dash-of-A, which was the fundamental rule which guided the best people I knew as a child. My own code was B-with-a-dash-of-C.

My chief Badnesses were furies. I used to get into really frightful states of red-hot, impotent rage, at being made to do such things as go to Dancing Class, or Parties, or Church (in that order of dislike); or at having to wear stockings in the summer, or gloves, or (later on) stays, or any clothes which were too smart, or too tight, or too hot. I did not mind how shabby they were. Or at having to eat vegetables; or learning to sew, or having Bible lessons. I admit now that some of these things were advisable, or even necessary; and I am sure that they must have tried to make me understand this, but they never succeeded, and these things all seemed to me completely unreasonable and unfair. The rages exhausted and frightened me, and I knew I was quite wrong by the grown-up Standard A; while even by my own Standard B, it was a useless, hopeless expense of spirit. Charles used to tell me how silly I was; of course the grown-ups were wrong, but it wasn't worth while to put myself into such a state about something I couldn't help. Yet all the time I felt that I was not more in the wrong than the wicked animal in the rhyme:

> *Cet animal est bien méchant,*
> *Quand on l'attaque, il se défend.*

But to finish up about prayer. I can also remember my mother telling me that the Cruel Turks were killing the Poor Armenians; and that the Archbishop of Canterbury, or Mr. Gladstone—or perhaps both of them—said we were all to pray for them, and that I was to remember to pray, too. I thought: 'Much good that will do them,' and 'That's just the sort of thing they *would* say;' and I had not the faintest intention of doing anything so silly. This must have been in the summer of 1894, for it was just before Billy was born.

Pretty soon after that, when we were both between nine and ten years old, Frances took me to a very private place under the wooden bridge on the Little Island, and told me there, in confidence, that it was not at all the thing nowadays to believe in Christianity any more. It simply wasn't done. I felt at once that this was what I had always thought, though I had not been quite able to express it. I admired Frances tremendously; she seemed to live in an up-to-date, sophisticated world, where Art and Literature were taken seriously. Her mother had short hair, and even *smoked cigarettes*; so that anything Frances said was sure to be right. Her information was a great relief to me; a real comfort. From that very night I gave up saying my prayers. I remember, that evening, catching a glimpse, through the doorway, of Charles kneeling by his bed and thinking: 'Poor boy, he's only seven; I won't disturb his mind just yet.' But, knowing my own incapacity for holding my tongue, I am certain that I told him all about it next day; and I don't suppose his mind was at all disturbed. He had probably known it all along.

I am sure that Frances was quite sincere when she preached to me under the bridge, but soon afterwards she began to be troubled by Doubt. She had never been christened, and various story-books now made her wonder if this could be quite safe. *We* had all been christened, and Frances had sometimes made us feel decidedly inferior on that account—provincial and behind the times. Now, gradually, she began to suffer torments of fear in case her parents might be wrong about Christianity. To her, her parents were perfect in wisdom, and the mere idea that they could be wrong was very dreadful. Now I could read *The Daisy Chain*, or *The Wide Wide World*, and just take the religion as the queer habits of those sort of people, exactly as if I were reading a story about Mohammedans or Chinese. But Frances took it all very seriously;

Frances (left) converting me under the bridge.

and was sadly upset when Ellen Montgomery, in *The Wide Wide World,* was told that she ought to love Christ more than her own mother. I didn't turn a hair at that sort of nonsense. Frances had always enjoyed pretending to believe in superstitions, even when she didn't. Believing what you can't believe is a kind of exercise which some people like. Others don't. I don't. This is however the religious temperament, and it got Frances in the end.

I must be more cynical than Frances by nature, for I am sure that I never thought my parents perfect in wisdom; nor any other grown-up people either, for the matter of that. But then I clearly have not got the right feeling about parents. During the last war a young French airman told me, that when he was trying to escape from occupied France across Spain, he was taken by the Spanish police, and was obliged to destroy all his papers in great haste. 'Et figurez-vous, Madame,' he said, dropping his voice to the lowest depths of blood-curdling horror, 'que j'ai dᵘ manger la photo de ma mère!' I hope I registered the right brand of consternation at this appalling confession, for if he had perceived what I really felt he would have thought me most indelicate.

It was unfortunate that my mother insisted on giving us Bible lessons herself, for they bored us dreadfully, and there was always trouble about them. She had little gift for teaching; but I do not now think that she was insincere about it, though I am afraid I thought so then. The fact was that she was far simpler in her views on religion that I would then have thought possible in anyone grown-up. She was a warm-hearted, innocently pleasure-loving person who, to the end of her life, enjoyed the things of this world in a fresh and youthful way, which was very attractive, though we superior children sometimes found it rather exasperating. She loved engagements and weddings and babies and food and games and dress and riddles and auction sales; and above all she simply adored parties and picnics and sprees of any kind. But she also truly wished to be good and to do right, and so she took us to church and taught us about religion, just as she had been taught herself when she was young. For the vestiges of her early-American puritanism still clung about her; rather oddly combined with the axiom that what my father thought was always right; however the demands of logic never troubled her at any time. She was not a bit worldly, like Aunt Cara, but she had not got a religious nature, and religion, as taught by her, made no sense at all to us. Perhaps it wouldn't anyhow, but we should have respected it more if we had been taught by someone with a natural feeling for spiritual matters. As it was, it was hopeless.

There was a certain grey Sunday-school book which seemed to us beyond bearing; and so, after a good deal of plotting and counter-plotting, we hid it in a very good place, between the rafters and the ceiling of the attic. It fell down into the hollow of the wall, and we thought we were safe. But after a time suspicion fell on us, and there was a dreadful fuss. We were sent up before the highest tribunal, and at last obliged to confess. Then my father took the fire-tongs and led a very solemn procession upstairs, and there was a ceremonial fishing in the wall with the tongs. Unfortunately the book was hooked and landed; and we were immediately given a lesson out of it. This we received very meekly, for we were much impressed by my father's intervention. After that the book tactfully disappeared of its own accord, and we never saw it again; I suppose my father had recommended its eclipse. It would have been better if he had intervened more often in our affairs—he hardly ever did—for things went very smoothly when he took a hand; and we grew reasonable and calm.

There were always difficulties about going to church, too, because it was such a supreme bore. It was not quite as bad as dancing class, though in the same category, because it only required passive endurance, not active participation. Still it made us very cross to have to spend all that time keeping still and thinking about nothing at all; especially when there were so many thousands of things we were simply dying to do at home. Boredom to me was an active torment, not a passive one, and I just raged and seethed with impatience, all through the service, waiting for the moment when I could rush home, tear off my horrible hat and gloves, and get on with whatever I had been doing, when I had been shanghaied by the Press Gang (my mother). I remember once how the congregation stared at me when I leapt enthusiastically to my feet at the sound of a premature '*And Now*' from the parson; and how miserably I sank back into my place as he went droning on again. I believe my poor mother felt that if only she could get us into church, some of the meaning of it might sink into us unconsciously; but I don't see how it could, with anyone in my usual church-going mood of white-hot indignation.

College chapels usually have the Litany instead of a sermon; this seemed to me the lowest layer of the dust-and-ashes of boredom and misery. I never listened to any part of the service except the Psalms; I liked them because I always liked poetry. For the same reason I did not like the hymns. I lived through the Litany by thinking what horrid words *Vouchsafe* and *Beseech* were, and wondering if they meant something frightfully improper; or by hoping that the pigeons would get inside the roof again.

For it was to King's College Chapel that we were usually taken; and that was another trouble: I couldn't bear the music there! I don't expect anyone to understand about this, but I simply hated the unfair, juicy way in which the organ notes oozed round inside the roof, and sapped your vitals, and made you want to cry about nothing at all. I liked my music dry, not wet, in those days, just as I still do. Dr. Mann was organist then, and I dare say that he was rather soulful; at any rate, I have never yet been able to dissociate music at King's Chapel from the kind of emotional appeal which I find most antipathetic of all.

Nor were other churches more congenial to me. For one thing, I was quite Oliver-Cromwellian in my distaste for all kinds of ritual and ceremony. They told you that God was a Spirit; that seemed to me a good idea, and I understood it and liked it; and then

The topmost floor of the Granary. A place of refuge on a Sunday morning.

they spoilt it altogether by doing all sorts of mumbo-jumbo, which could not possibly have anything to do with a God who was a spirit. This shocked me unspeakably; for I was very high-minded and pure in those days; not to say arrogant. I was really far more anti-clerical than anti-religious; I might conceivably have made quite a decent Quaker.

As it was, I went to church cross, and got crosser all the time; I grew to distrust the very church bells, and honestly believed that nine-tenths of the congregation were hypocrites, and the remaining tenth, sentimental fools. My only excuse is that I really did not know anyone of a religious temperament whom I could love and admire; and occasional pious governesses made it much worse.

We did not go to church every Sunday, so there was always a chance of escape, and presently we discovered a good retreat. Directly after Sunday breakfast, before any pronouncement had been made, we disappeared discreetly down to the end of the garden, where the old granary stood, as yet unmodernized. This tall old empty warehouse stood with its foundations in the river; there was a cellar, full of old wood and rubbish, not much above water-level; and above that there were four floors, each a large, low, dark empty room, where corn had once been stored. In the middle of each floor was a square hole, and a ladder leading up to the floor above. So if you climbed up from the cellar and pulled up all four ladders after you as you went, you were cut off from the world by five ladderless storeys and you could quite reasonably pretend not to hear people calling from the garden below. We took lumps of sugar and hunks of bread with us, and sat on the floor in the top loft, under the roof, till all danger of church was over. The roof was beginning to fall in, and the ivy grew through the latticed window-holes, and pigeons lived up there and cooed deliciously. It was a mysterious, happy place, far from the world and full of new ideas, and it did me a great deal more good than ever church did. I still often dream of it, and then I am always just on the point of making strange and wonderful discoveries.

Though I found all kinds of churches very indigestible, I was curious about Christianity; and when I was about twelve I set out to read the whole Bible through from end to end; and I did get all the way from Genesis to the Acts, before I got bogged down in the incomprehensibility of St. Paul. And later still, when I was fourteen or fifteen, I had a sort of private religious revival, and read the Gospels thoroughly and took in as much as I was capable of receiving. This was all done in the most shamefaced secrecy and solitude; for to speak openly of religious matters would have been terribly embarrassing. How we blushed and squirmed when a certain governess thought that we ought to say grace! And I always turned my eyes modestly away from the indecency of a calendar of texts which hung on my mother's bedroom door.

I took the Christian precepts to heart too, and tried to carry them out, quite literally. 'Do unto others, as you would that they should do unto you': it seemed right and fair. So I gave the kitchen-maid a copy of Milton's *Poems* for a Christmas present, because I wanted it so much myself. She thanked me most politely, but I somehow felt it was not quite a success (poor kitchen-maid!). And I can remember saying helpfully to a new-made widow, aged about thirty-five: 'Never mind, you'll soon be dead, too,' because I thought that I should want to die if I had lost my husband. I recall very clearly the startled expression of one of her blue eyes, looking at me over the edge of her pocket-handkerchief. I always supposed that my feelings were exactly like other people's; it was much later before I noticed, with surprise, that they weren't. I found people very puzzling. I used to sit and watch their impassive faces, and wonder what they were thinking about.

So I grew to be sixteen, and went away to boarding-school; and on the first Sunday there all the big girls, very old and powerful, got round me in a ring and began asking me questions. 'Don't you *really* believe in Adam and Eve, Gwen?' 'How do you think you were made then?' 'Do you think we are all kind of monkeys?'

# Religion

'Don't you believe in the Flood?' And so on and so forth. It was quite frightful; it was like being in the midst of a herd of bullocks, all staring at you, and coming closer and closer with their shining horns. Only they weren't bullocks, but very important top-girls, all with their hair fashionably puffed out over their eyes—which made them look still more like bullocks—and with very smart blouses and tight waist-belts and brooches in their ties. I was fat and awkward and ill-dressed and wore spectacles and my hair was not puffed out at all; and worst of all, I was a NEW GIRL. Still, one can die but once; and I wasn't going to let them see how frightened I was. So I dug in my heels and scrunched my hands together, and answered: 'No, I don't,' stoutly, to all their questions; and they were most delightfully horrified and shocked.

Therefore, when we went off in a crocodile to church next Sunday, I determined to testify to my faith. And when they all knelt down to pray on first going in, I sat up straight and didn't kneel; and when they all turned to the east for the Creed, I didn't turn; and when they bowed, I didn't bow; and when they mumbled the Lord's Prayer, I didn't mumble; and I felt like a real martyr. To my surprise, no one said anything to me about this; I imagine that the mistresses must have given the girls a hint to hold their tongues, which was clever of them. This somewhat deflated me; but I could not retreat from the position I had taken up, and all the time I was at school I kept up my silent protest; though, after a time, being a non-conformist became rather a bore. When they asked me to be confirmed, I just said, politely but firmly: 'No, thank you.'

Then there was a catastrophe. I was put into a Scripture class taught by a curate. The lessons were all about æons, which intrigued me exceedingly; but I was never to know what they were, because in the second lesson the curate saw me drawing in my notebook, and went to the headmistress and said that I was not reverent; and she decided that I had better leave the class. I felt this most unfair, and it hurt my feelings, for I always drew in my notebooks and it did not mean that I was not attending. And I did so much want to know about those æons, and now I never should.

The girls' ideas of religion, and even the mistresses' ideas of reverence, were a complete mystery to me. For instance, on the night before a hockey match we always had 'Onward Christian Soldiers' for the hymn at Prayers. It was sung *fortissimo*, and was supposed to ginger us up to martial prowess next day; indeed great importance was attached to the *brio* with which it was sung. This shocked and disgusted me very much indeed; and it made me doubt their sincerity in other ways. I was a very serious person then, and I conceived of religion as a high and spiritual affair, and did not like seeing it made ridiculous, even if I were not a believer myself.

This hymn-singing seemed to me just as silly as the port wine they gave us before the match; indeed 'Onward Christian Soldiers' and port wine are still inextricably mixed together in my mind. We had our usual enormous dinner at 1.30; and as the match was at 2.15 we used to get all ready first, even to strapping our hockey-pads on to our legs before we set to work to consume vast platefuls of pea-soup, great chunks of roast beef and vegetables, and slabs of suet pudding and jam. Then each of the team was solemnly given a glassful of sweet and sticky port, and we rushed straight from the table out to the hockey-field. I found the port extremely nasty and difficult to swallow; and everyone complained that it made them feel sick; still, it was an honour to get it, so we drank it gratefully. But if we won the match—and we generally did win—it must have been that the spiritual uplift imparted to us by 'Onward Christian Soldiers' was able to overcome even the acute discomfort of the mixture in our insides.

I got into hot water once again, most innocently. One wet Sunday we did not go to church, but the headmistress read us the morning service, and I had to read the first lesson. I was told to look it up;

and there was a choice of two lessons in the list. So I took the first one, without even looking at the other, though it happened to be some rather well-known bit. My lesson was all about a Harlot walking down a street, and all the men looking at her in an unsuitable manner. At least, that is how I remember it; but I cannot identify the passage without reading the whole Bible through. I didn't exactly know what a harlot was, but as I read I felt there was something uncomfortable in the air around me. Afterwards I was sent for to the headmistress, and she asked, why on earth I had read that chapter? I said: 'Because it was the lesson for the day.' And as it really was, and as it was out of the Bible, there was nothing she could do about it. But I am sure she suspected me, with my bad record, of trying to sabotage the Church of England.

Afterwards an intelligent Scripture mistress came, and I learnt with interest all about David, and read Browning's *Saul* with her; and that term I won the Scripture prize in the examination. This naturally annoyed the girls a good deal, and I thought that even the mistresses looked a little odd about it. Still, if religion consisted in an appreciation of Browning and a knowledge of the habits of jerboas (for which I got good marks)—I could do that. I think I could even have done æons, if I had had the chance.

But I think there must be more to it than that.

# CHAPTER XII

## *Sport*

My mother was one of the most intrepid women who ever existed. No illness or pain ever drew a murmur from her, and she always seemed to believe that no disasters could conceivably happen to any of her children. She had a most convenient theory that we could not possibly be drowned in the river which surrounded and divided our garden; in fact, that the waters of the Cam were hardly even wet; and as we never were drowned, this was an excellent idea. But why we were not drowned, I can't imagine. We fell in pretty often, and the river is almost everywhere deep enough to drown a child, and in places very deep. Later on in life she used to make our blood run cold by insisting on taking three or four very small grandchildren (our children) out in the boat alone, herself rowing. She was an old lady then, and she could not possibly have saved even one drowning child; but unless we were there in person to defend our offspring, she would carry off her delighted victims from under the very noses of the reluctant and responsible nurses. Nothing except *force majeure* ever prevented her from doing what she had a mind to do; and we ourselves had to fight like tigresses at bay to keep our children on dry land. But, of course, none of them ever got drowned either. Sometimes we almost wished they had; it was the only thing that could have *learnt* her.

Pirates. Charles and I are in the boat under the granary wall. Margaret and Sancho have been marooned on a desert island in the distance. In the boat can be seen the keg of rum indispensable to piracy.

# Sport

So we were all able to swim early, and grew up knowing how to manage boats by instinct: row-boats and canoes; but not punts, for there were then none on the Cam. We had the best games of pirates in an old square, flat-bottomed boat, which the gardener used when he was cutting the weeds in the river; it always needed baling, and sometimes sank under our very feet. I would come home and see wet footprints on the kitchen doorstep, and follow the tracks upstairs to find that Charles had had to swim ashore again. But my mother never even thought we should catch cold when we fell in! A wonderful quality in a mother.

There was also the row-boat *The Griffin*, which was rather heavy to launch. *The Griffin* was the joy and pride of my mother's romantic heart. She was always inventing errands which obliged someone to row her down to Trinity, or to Jolley's old furniture shop by the Town Bridge. Later on, we all saved up our money for a long time and, with the help of a few tips, bought a canoe of our own, *The Escallop*.

We used to fish interesting things out of the river; once we caught seven top-hats in one day. Another time a baker's cart-horse took fright at the Newnham ford and dashed off into the deep place under the mill; the man leapt out in time, but the horse was drowned, and all the bread came floating down and we fed the hens on it for weeks. Once Billy, almost a baby, caught a large eel which had come ashore on the island; he came staggering along, saying it was 'a Mama worm for the chickens', and Secky, our old gardener, said he was 'a reg'lar little Admiral Nelson' to have caught it. Another time when we were playing at Wicked French Governesses on the Big Island, I was so convincing in the title-part, that my terrified pupil, Frances, ran away from me down into the ditch which separates the Island from the Lammas-Land. The mud and water came nearly up to her shoulders, but she managed to scramble out—on the wrong side; and then had to be persuaded to wade back again. It says much for our nurses that they were more frightened than cross, in spite of all the mess.

The queer thing about falling into the river is that you are never surprised when you do it; you feel as if you had known all along that you were going in just at that instant. I remember looking calmly and intelligently at the green bubbles going slowly up past me as I went down head-foremost into the depths, the time when Ralph heroically dived after me, into what proved to be about four feet of water.

For, when I was about seven or eight, two Gods revealed themselves to our worshipping eyes. They were our cousins, Ralph and Felix Wedgwood, and they came up as undergraduates to Trinity, first Ralph and, soon after, Felix. Divine Beings, glorious in their condescension, one or both of them used often to spend whole afternoons playing with us. Then the pirates became more reckless than ever. Sometimes the pirate ship was captained by Ralph, while a land-party, headed by Felix, made great detours, carrying a plank with them, which they threw across the ditches for a bridge, and so turned up in unexpected places and boarded the vessel with incredible valour. Sometimes we made bonfires, and rushed about the islands waving torches made of the straw covers of wine bottles: or we had battles with miniature fire-boats, made out of cardboard boxes and candle-ends and matches. Or there was tree-climbing, roof-climbing, story-telling; everything they did was exciting beyond words. In fact, sometimes it was too exciting and we could not sleep at night afterwards, and Felix had to be asked to moderate the horrors of his stories (but I don't think he did).

There was one story about two South American Indians, Gaucho and Poncho, who were dying of starvation in a jungle; but Gaucho saved them by catching a sackful of big black ants; and Poncho put the mouth of the sack to his mouth, and squeezed the bottom, and the ants all ran down his throat and were very nourishing. In another story someone was lowered down a well, and ghostly, furry bony hands came out of the sides and clutched at him as he went by. This was almost too much for me, told as it was inside the gable part of the roof, where it was pitch dark—the part beyond the boarded attic. You had to seesaw, squeezing yourself through the rafters to get there; and then to be very careful not to walk on the plaster between the beams. Once Ralph himself did go through the plaster, and to our delight he sat astride a beam, with his legs hanging down through the ceiling into the room below, where Nana was giving Billy a bath.

We used to explore the huge cellars under the Grange, where there are places for fabulous numbers of beer barrels; and there Ralph taught us how to write our names on the ceiling in candle smoke; while Felix terrified us by jumping at us out of dark corners. The most superior inscriptions were made in blood, pinched out of a pricked finger; but the ordinary records, such as 'I have been a Prisoner here for forty-five years', or 'I am slowly starving to death', were too expensive in blood, and had to be written in smoke. We came out of the cellars with our hair full of candle-grease, in a delicious state of terror.

Ralph and Felix made fashionable a new and particularly blood-curdling form of hide-and-seek. Our ordinary game was called Scallawag, and was played of a winter's evening all over the house, which was well adapted for the purpose, having two staircases and plenty of passages and complications. All the passage lights were turned out—our parents were wonderfully patient about this—and the Scallawag pounced out of dark corners on the seekers, and chased them as they raced shrieking for Home. I am sorry to say that Charles and I found that we could add zest to this game by making Margaret Scallawag, and then goading and insulting her till she became mad with rage; a thing which was never very difficult to do. We were then really afraid of being caught by her, for the ferocity of her pinches was well known. In battle, Margaret selected a certain very painful part of her victim's upper arm for pinching; I hit with my fists; Charles kicked. This was the accepted practice during hostilities; which, I must say, were not usually very serious.

Ralph's innovation lay in playing hide-and-seek out of doors at night; the party was divided into two sides, and a lantern was placed in the middle of the lawn, to be Home. Tiptoeing about in the rustling blackness of the garden, with a potential enemy behind every bush, was altogether too much for my nerves though, of course, I dared not say so. Yet even through my terror, I enjoyed the strong secrecy of the night, and felt how the power and personality of each tree and plant comes pouring out in the dark. After that first game of hide-and-seek I used, half frightened, to slip out for a moment at night, whenever I could.

The climax of all earthly pleasures came when we received a letter from Ralph, written in invisible ink, inviting us to tea in his rooms in Trinity. After that tea-party poor Charles went through a terrible ordeal, for Felix threw his cap on to the grass in the Great Court, and dared him to go on to it to fetch it. Walking on the sacred college grass is about the worst crime a Cambridge child can commit; however, Charles did it and survived.

Floods were a great source of pleasure to us; when one was imminent we used to watch the height of the water on the boathouse steps, from hour to hour, and grieve if it began to go down. Very soon indeed—long before it had reached the top step of the cellar under the house—the hens had to be rescued from the Big Island, and brought over to lodgings in the Granary. It was such fun catching them, and putting them into sacks and wading through the rising water with them, that we had to be forcibly prevented from moving them far too soon, at the very first sign of a possible flood.

## Sport

We used to climb about all over the roof, too (it was not so dangerous as it sounds), and Charles and I stole a cigarette from the study, and cut it in half, and smoked the halves, sitting astride of a gable in a very dashing way, expecting every moment to be sick.

As a matter of fact I was secretly terrified at all this climbing, and I wished very much that my mother would take fright for once, and would forbid it. But she did not turn a hair, even when she saw us, in the course of a game of hide-and-seek, climb on to the top of the high old wall which separates the Grange garden from the road, and run along it, chasing each other, and finally jump down into the garden at the end. That wall is exactly nine feet high; it makes me feel quite green even now, to think that I was obliged to do such a thing, simply in order not to lose 'face' with the others. For *they* weren't in the least afraid—unless, indeed, they were pretending better than I did. Nora and Frances were great tree-climbers, and used to boast about bringing down birds' eggs in their mouths, quite like people in books. I pretended with all my might that I liked climbing, but it is difficult to be convincing when you feel sick and giddy; and the others knew very well that it was a sham. I was even frightened once when we sat in a row on the top of the high wall to see the Prince of Wales go by. He had been to a review, and came riding along, very stout indeed, with a lot of officers. And one dreadful time, I really *could* not make myself jump down from a trapeze, and Ruth and Nora and Frances jeered at me, and went away and left me in tears, to get down as best I could.

We built a platform of planks, for a house, in the copper beech tree, and went up and down to it by a swinging rope-ladder, which had the special advantage of being too difficult for Margaret and Billy to climb (what horrid creatures children are!). We also bought a cart-load of old bricks from a builder, for ten shillings, and began to build a brick house on the Big Island, using mud for mortar. We mixed earth and water, in a pit, to a most delightful slubious consistency, and then slopped it on the wall and stuck the bricks on; a satisfactory pursuit.

One of the very few times I ever saw Charles really angry was when these brick walls were fairly high. I took a large shovelful of the best mud, and heaved (or should it be *hove?*) it on to the wall, with such enthusiasm that most of it went over on to the other side; where unfortunately I had not noticed that Charles was kneeling. It all went on to his head, and I really thought he would kill me. Another time when I enraged him he was so angry that, being by then too old to hit a girl, he found relief in throwing his shoes into the river. He then had to undress and go in and fetch them out again, which, I suppose, soothed him.

We never finished the brick house because, just when the walls were high enough for us to begin on the roof, Charles was sent away to school, and I had not the heart to go on with it alone. Margaret was not the building sort of person, and was too young anyhow. It did not seem worth while to do anything; for there was no chance of his ever coming back properly again. I was very miserable; I remember crying in bed, just loud enough for Nana to hear from the nursery and to come and comfort me; but not loud enough for anyone else to hear. But soon after that Nana began to be ill; and then she went away, too, and never came back any more. That was the end of my childhood; and I passed on into a much less happy adolescence.

We played the classic games to a certain extent, but we were not very good at them, and I myself was very bad indeed, especially at tennis. On the whole we thought them rather dull, and found it more amusing to invent new games of our own, such as Tenni-croque, in which you had to move croquet balls about by throwing tennis balls at them. However, at school I managed to get into the hockey team; not by skill, but by a kind of terrified ferocity; and because I could run rather fast. I even broke a strange girl's nose in a match; at least, she skidded in the mud during a wild storm of rain, and fell gently forward, nose downwards, on to my stick; and I felt more guilty than if I had hacked her in the face on purpose. But such is guilt. (*See* Religion, page 215.) And I won a race for a hundred yards at the school sports, and at last got my long-coveted book of Milton's *Poems* as a prize. I was not showing off in asking for it; I really wanted it.

The Bicycling craze came in when we were just about at the right age to enjoy it. At first even 'safety' bicycles were too dangerous and improper for ladies to ride, and they had to have tricycles. My mother had (I believe) the first female tricycle in Cambridge; and I had a little one, and we used to go out for family rides, all together; my father in front on a bicycle, and poor Charles standing miserably on the bar behind my mother, holding on for all he was worth. I found it very hard work, pounding away on my hard tyres; a glorious, but not a pleasurable pastime.

Then, one day at lunch, my father said he had just seen a new kind of tyre, filled up with air, and he thought it might be a success. And soon after that everyone had bicycles, ladies and all; and bicycling became the smart thing in Society, and the lords and ladies had their pictures in the papers, riding along in the park, in straw boater hats. We were then promoted to wearing baggy knickerbockers under our frocks, and over our white frilly drawers. We thought this horridly improper, but rather grand; and when a lady (whom I didn't like anyhow) asked me, privately, to lift up my frock so that she might see the strange garments underneath, I thought what a dirty mind she had. I only once saw a woman (not, of course, a *lady*) in real bloomers.

My mother must have fallen off her bicycle pretty often, for I remember seeing, several times, the most appalling cuts and bruises on her legs. But she never complained, and always kept these mis-

The family outing. Charles, my mother, Sancho, me and my father. Charles said afterwards: 'The body is too fat and the arms are too short.' (My mother's body and his own
arms.) Sancho is saying: 'How fast they go; it must be 5 or 6 miles an hour. But of course
they never think of *me*.'

haps to herself. However, the great Mrs. Phillips, our cook, always knew all about them; as indeed she knew practically everything that ever happened. She used to draw us into the servants' hall to tell us privately: 'Her Ladyship had a nasty fall yesterday; she cut both her knees and sprained her wrist, and the front wheel of her bicycle is bent all crooked. But don't let her know I told you.' So we never dared say anything, even if we saw her Ladyship limping. Similar little contretemps used to occur when, at the age of nearly seventy, she insisted on learning to drive a car. She never mastered the art of reversing, and was in every way an unconventional and terrifying driver. Mrs. Phillips used then to tell us, under the seal of secrecy: 'Her Ladyship ran into the back of a milk-cart yesterday; but it wasn't much hurt'; or 'A policeman stopped her Ladyship because she was on the wrong side of the road; but she said she didn't know what the white line on the road meant, so he explained and let her go on.' Mrs. Phillips must have had an excellent Intelligence Service at her command, for the stories were always true enough. But though she was omniscient, she was always very discreet.

How my father did adore those bicycles! Such beautiful machines! They were as carefully tended as if they had been alive; every speck of dust or wet was wiped from them as soon as we came back from a ride; and at night they were all brought into the house, and slung up to the ceiling of the kitchen passage by a series of ingenious pulleys, for fear that the night air in the covered backyard might rust them. His heart would have bled to see the callous way in which we treat our humble necessary beasts of burden nowadays.

Sometimes, with friends, we used to harness four bicycles with ropes to a little four-wheeled wagon, and Margaret was obliged to be passenger in it. The brunt of the duties appertaining to the youngest always fell on Margaret, because Billy was really too small. Anyhow she had as yet no bicycle of her own, so she ought

The four-in-hand, undecided whether to go up the Backs or round by Newnham. In the distance may be seen the lame crossing-sweeper and Sidgwick Avenue. Sancho is saying: 'Of course they'll all be killed, and then they'll say it was my fault. How unjust people always are.'

to have been very thankful to be allowed to be passenger. But she wasn't. The cart was too light; it upset if it were empty, and even with her weight in it, the back wheels banged up and down, in a very alarming way, when we went fast. Sometimes the four postilions quarrelled, and all went different ways, and the cart ran into the curb and upset; and sometimes the ropes all got tangled up and everyone fell off and the cart upset; and sometimes it just upset of its own accord; but Margaret was only terrified and never badly hurt, and after all one expects to pay something for the privilege of playing with older people.

Once the arrogance of the Upper Classes went too far, and the Lower Classes were driven into Red Revolution. We were playing soldiers in a pine-wood with the three Butler boys, and Margaret and the other young ones had been kept far too long on sentry duty, while the Generals (Jim and Charles and I) had been conferring in the tent; so Margaret suddenly mutinied in the most subversive manner, and said that she was going to run away, and would not be a soldier any more. We said, then she would be a Deserter; but when we tried to arrest her, she turned on us in a mad fury, and in the scrimmage *bit* Charles in the middle of his back, so fiercely that her teeth went right through his jacket and shirt and vest, and drew blood. (Biting is always the weapon of the weaker party.) We were absolutely stunned at her wickedness, and said, sanctimoniously, that we would never, NEVER, have anything to do with her again. She then ran away screaming, while the Butlers all watched in consternation. That was what made it so dreadful; that this family scandal should be seen by Jim and Gordon and Nevile. We were really ashamed of our treatment of her, though at the time we maintained that it was her own fault for contravening all the rules of military discipline. I went after her, and found her lying under a tree in a state of hysteria; I brought her firmly home and delivered her to Nana, who calmed her, and bathed Charles's back, and said nothing about the *fracas* to our parents. Neither the Butlers nor we ever referred to this shocking affair again, till many years later.

We weren't great at card games, except for Fighting Demon, when bedlam broke loose. This game has, no doubt, been the ultimate cause to its addicts of many a nervous breakdown in later life; though this is an idea which never seems to have occurred to the psychologists. There was also the more soothing Muggins, suitable alike for extreme youth and incipient senility (though Uncle Richard could not *even* play Muggins!). And there was National Gallery (or Nat. Gal.). This was played like Happy Families, with a set of cards of very blurry photographs of the English pictures at the National Gallery. Thus we grew familiar with such works as 'Ulysses (de)riding Polyphemus', where you could neither make out Ulysses, nor see what he was riding on; or 'The Fighting *Temeraire*'—which we took to be the little black tug in front; or 'Uncle Toby and Widow Wadman (Uncle Tob. and Wid. Wad.); or Landseer's 'Dignity and Impudence' (Dig. and Imp.); or mysterious pictures such as 'Sigismonda grieving over the heart of Guiscardo', where Sig. (as she was called) was holding a kind of soup tureen, and there was no heart anywhere.

But our chief intellectual exercise was the Letter Game: word-making and word-taking. At this we became practically professional; and sometimes, in the holidays, the game would have gone on all night, if the teams had not been sent to bed in a state of exhaustion, while the letters were left on the table, for the game to be finished in the morning. Many an expert must have blessed the sound education given him by the Letter Game when, later in life, his self-respect obliged him to do *The Times* Crossword every day.

We gradually developed a regular word-game technique, and the rules were perfected to cover all exigencies. Any dictionary word was allowed, but no proper names, and a word could be stolen by adding a letter *and* changing the meaning. Many words known only to dictionaries were of great value: such as ZAX (a slate-cutter's tool); and other words such as PYX or WAX which were held to be practically unstealable. It was a recognized fact, for instance, that the only steal for FOX was CRUCIFIXION—which needs eight extra letters, most unlikely to occur simultaneously. Then there were regular expected sequences of steals, such as MIX, MINX, MIXEN, EXAMINE; and as any part of a verb was allowed, provided the meaning was changed, by the end of a hard-fought game, the board would be strewn with such splendid words as (thou) REASSESSEDST; or (he or she) DECONTAMINATETH. The finest play of the game lay in the ETHS and EDSTS of the verbal endings.

This game can be very embarrassing at times. Suppose, for instance, that one side had the innocent word TRUMPET, and an S was turned up, you could see all the older people getting red in the face in their efforts not to say STRUMPET. Heavens! how Aunt Bessy's fingers did fumble and flutter, when Margaret (it *would* be Margaret) shouted in triumph: 'STRUMPET; what does that mean?' But Aunt Bessy replied, with her usual dignity: 'It's a word we don't generally use.' (I should guess that she did not quite know herself what it meant.) The word was probably forbidden for Aunt Bessy's sake; but it is such a good example of the way a word might run, if it were to follow its own natural and licentious course, that I give it here. It would probably start as RUM; and go on RUMP, TRUMP, TRUMPET, STRUMPET, (thou) TRUMPEDST, (he or she) STRUMPETED, (thou) TRUMPETEDST, (thou) STRUMPETEDST; and I cannot get it any farther, though a real virtuoso, such as Charles, might be able to do so.

This had been a Down game originally, and legends had grown up around it, such as that of the nameless person who had set his heart on getting HIPPOPOTAMUS, and who, in consequence never got a word at all. (I have always believed, without evidence, that this must have been Uncle Richard.) Then there was the story of my grandfather (C.D.) who, on seeing the word MOTHER on the board, looked at it for a long time, and then said 'MOE-THER; there's no word MOETHER.' I feel that the Psychologists might get a great deal of fun out of this anecdote—I beg their pardons, I don't mean fun, but Important Information; clues to the conception of the *Origin of Species* on the one hand, or to his ill health on the other; both of which developments could doubtless be proved by this story to be the direct consequences of the early death of his own MOETHER.

I had a solitary game of my own, played at bedtime; it was called 'Being Kind to Poor Pamela'. Pamela was a child with whom I sometimes played, but whom I rather despised. The game was played by getting out of bed and lying on the floor, until you were as cold as you could bear to be. During that time you were Poor Pamela, lying out in the snow in her nightgown, owing to the cruelty of her parents. She was starving and the wolves were howling in the woods all round. Then you became yourself again, and went out into the cold and rescued poor Pamela—the wolves were getting very near—and you put her into your own bed and warmed her, and fed her, and comforted her most tenderly. This made you feel frightfully good and kind; and you could do it over and over again, until you could keep awake no longer. On showing this passage to Margaret, she revealed that she had independently practised a variety of this sport, when put to bed with a hot-water bottle, because she had a cold; only it was not Pamela whom she impersonated by lying naked on the oil-cloth, but a mother with a baby (a doll). A good cure for a cold.

But when I met Pamela again in real life, I was just as nasty to her as ever. This fortunately was not very often, as she did not live in Cambridge. She was the sort of person one was always nasty to;

because, however hard one tried to be nice to her, she always managed to give you a remorseful feeling that you had not really understood her. It was just a quality she had. Once when I went to tea with her alone, we were given a special little feast; and among the good things were some raspberries. They turned out to be full of maggots, but Pamela ate them all up, both hers and mine. Without saying anything, she implied that she so seldom had anything nice

Poor Pamela; the wolves are getting very near.

for tea, that she was glad even of maggotty raspberries; while no doubt I, lucky I, had delicious fruit every day of my life (which was very far indeed from being true). I think now, that there was not the faintest reason to believe that her parents were at all unkind to her; but in a patient, tolerant, uncomplaining way, she certainly made me think so then; and all without a word being said on the subject.

In this quality of hers, Pamela always reminded me of our dog

246

# Sport

Sancho (pronounced—correctly—San-tcho. Sometimes pedantic visitors tried to call him Sanko, and were despised by us for their ignorance of Spanish). He was a brown water-spaniel, rather like Dog Tray in *Struwwel Peter*, and with the same reproachful

Sancho and me in the garden. I am saying: 'Oh, Sancho, I do think you might let me have *one* of my own biscuits. You know you've had five already.' Sancho is saying: 'But I hardly ever have anything to eat, and I *did* think you were a kind person.' He ate enormously and was much too fat anyhow.

expression. He was obviously born to be a martyr, and it was hard on him that he had to manage to be one without the necessary ill-treatment: like making bricks without straw. But he did very well, for he had a wonderful power of putting other people in the wrong. He would sit there staring at you; brown and fat and

smelly; slobbering, and sometimes giving a heavy sigh; and however long a walk you had taken him, he made you feel that it ought
to have been longer; and however many biscuits he had had, he
made you feel that he ought to have had more. Frances tells me
that there was a legend in her family that Sancho was nearly always
kept chained up; this was entirely untrue, but it just shows the force
of his character that he was able to impose this idea on them from a
distance. In other respects, he was a worthy, but boring dog, and
appallingly faithful. We had at different times several more interesting dogs; but, just because I have a weak conscience, Sancho remains in my memory as the principal dog of my childhood.

Of course the Pamela game was a form of one of the acting games
we were always playing. I never played with dolls at all, except
when they were useful for acting—to be sailors in a shipwreck, or
human sacrifices. We had a whole mythology of Gods, of whom
the chief was Great Pompadella Bim, and they all required frequent
human sacrifices; though they often had to be content with spent
shot-gun cartridges, which we collected to represent soldiers. They
weren't very nice Gods—Norse Gods, with a dash of the more unpleasant Greek Gods in them; and more than a *soupçon* of Jehovah.

From the far beginnings of dumb crambo and charades, we
gradually climbed to the heights of the Christmas play. This was
written in Committee, by us all together, and was the principal
event of the year. As soon as one play was acted we instantly began
planning the next one, even upon Boxing Day! They were performed in our house, on the evening of Christmas Day, and were
followed by the Christmas dinner, which was attended by all the
family then in Cambridge, and by no one else at all.

These plays were built up on a good solid foundation of Gilbert
and Sullivan, and were full of topical allusions. They always had a
Chorus, in which we all took part, whenever we were not on the

stage in some other capacity, because we were short of actors. Bernard wrote and recited the Prologue, but he was too grown-up to act with us; Erasmus disliked acting and refused to take part. Charles probably disliked it quite as much, but public opinion always compelled him to be the Prince and to wear the beautiful Russian boots—a present from Felix—which were the Prince's insignia, and the glory of our dressing-up box. Nora was considered the prettiest of us (to her disgust), so she generally had to be the Princess, which was very dull for her. Ruth and Margaret were celebrated actresses and had character parts; and the rest of us were Witches, Professors, Ghosts or whatever was required. I did a good deal of the costume designing, and used to cut out dresses by the simple process of laying the patient down on a piece of butter muslin, and cutting out round his edges. But we had a pretty good stock of curious cast-off odds and ends to fall back on. There was no scenery, and only a screen for a curtain. The plots were incredibly complicated; no one really understood them; but that was no matter; for the success of the play depended entirely on the wit, and the verses. The dialogue was in prose, and full of jokes; the verses were mostly written by Ruth and Frances. Here is the opening chorus of *The Magic Snowboot*, which was written when Nora, Frances and I were round about thirteen and fourteen. It was spoken by a *Chorus of the Cooks* of the Princess Lavinia Plantagenet:

| THOMAS: | *You must know our situation* |
| | *Is the highest in the nation;* |
| | *On a close examination* |
| ALL: | *Of a heraldery book,* |
| THOMAS: | *You'll find there's not a badge in it* |
| | *So noble as Plantagenet;* |
| | *And though you won't imagine it,* |
| ALL: | *I am that household's cook.* |

## Sport

THOMAS:
*So we cook and wash the crockery,*
*Go out and weed the rockery;*
*This service is no mockery,*

ALL:
*You probably infer;*

THOMAS:
*Yet we condescend to dish-up*
*For a baron or a bishop,*
*And we'll sometimes send the fish up*

ALL:
*For an ordinary Sir.*

I fancy that the character of Princess Lavinia must have been founded on that of my mother, who certainly would have thought weeding the rockery quite a suitable occupation for the cook; and who, like the Princess, was able to put her ideas across, as no one else could have done.

Here is the end of a lecture by the *Witch of Curses*, delivered at the Sorcery Institute to a *Chorus of Ghosts*. It contains allusions to the boredom of the Sunday afternoon calls of shy undergraduates, who were perfectly miserable, but quite unable to go away.

THE WITCH:
*My Experiment One makes e'en undergraduates laugh,*
*Though their collars and general depression be quite un-*
*impeachable;*
*'Twill reach to their stony young hearts in a minute, or*
*even a half;*
*Provided their stony young, stolid young, stupid young*
*hearts are made reachable.*

GHOSTS:
*Nervous freshmen in a row,*
*Kind of, sort of, don't you know,*

250

## Sport

*As the Sunday onward wears,*
*Sitting swallowing in chairs,*
*O take a moral from this song*
*And never, never stay too long.*

Once the play had to be put off, because we all had influenza and the aunts were in a terrible Darwin fuss about it, which annoyed and shamed us very much. When the play was finally acted, Bernard's Prologue contained these lines:

*Fell Influenza, stalking through the land,*
*From this devoted house has held its hand.*
*See how each Mother, with a touching pride,*
*Lays the well-worn thermometer aside.*
*No less than seven Darwins, be it said,*
*Are simultaneously out of bed!*

Bernard used to write whole plays for us, too. There was *The Apterix* and *The Bishop of South-West Equatorial Mesopotamia*. This last was a summer play, to be acted in the garden; but Alas! it was an exclusive Wychfield production, in which Ruth and Nora (who lived near by) took part, but of which I was only a dazzled and jealous spectator. We had the advantage of having the river in our garden; but we had the great disadvantage of living over a mile from the others.

Ruth was the Bishop—or rather an Imp impersonating the Bishop—and she came riding through the garden on to the stage on a tricycle. She was dressed in episcopal clothes, and her long hair was tucked down the back of her neck; but a blue woollen tail hanging out behind betrayed her infernal origin. There had been some trouble about this, and Aunt Ida had only allowed Ruth to act under protest; but whether it was the male dress, or the clerical dress, or the tail, to which she objected, we never knew. There were only near relations in the audience to see the shocking sight, anyhow. The text had also been bowdlerized; for in the original draft, the Bishop had brought with him, as specimens of the handiwork of his only convert, a waste-paper basket, and *a pair of bathing-drawers*; but during rehearsal an orange had been substituted for the bathing-drawers, by order of the Censor.

As we grew older the plays grew more informal, but we still always acted some half-impromptu skit on Christmas Day. The year that Frances got engaged to Francis Cornford, I wrote the play myself: *The Importance of being Frank*. In this all the characters were called Francis or Frances, which caused great confusion, until the hero allowed himself to be called Frank; a solution which the Cornfords did not adopt in real life.

I believe this was the last of the regular plays; after that we got married or turned our attentions to other diversions.

# CHAPTER XIII

# *Clothes*

Clothes were a major cause of rows, naughtiness, misery and all unpleasantness, right through my whole youth. The difficulties were caused, not only by best clothes, but by practically everything we wore.

In her own way my mother took a good deal of trouble about dress, not only about her own, but about ours, too. She used to spend hours and hours superintending a humble daily dressmaker in cutting old dresses to pieces, and putting them together again in new permutations and combinations; for that marble-hearted fiend Economy, who was her evil angel, was always putting in his spoke and preventing her from having things made at a good shop. Sometimes the results of this home manufacture were rather clumsy; but as far as my mother was concerned it really did not matter much, as she always managed to look attractive, even if it were in spite of, rather than because of, her dress. For one thing she had a very fair idea of what became her; she never wore those dreadful hard boater hats, when they were so fashionable; and she knew that soft floppy things suited her better than tailor-made suits. She was in her glory in a 'tea-gown'; or in a summer dress, with a feather boa, ostrich-plume hat and parasol.

My share of the dressmaking industry was the unpicking of the old dresses, which I did most unwillingly. Sometimes, when it went on for too long, Good God, there was such a scene! But even that was not so bad as when I had to try on a new frock myself. It seemed to me then that I was kept standing on the table for whole days at a time (I suppose it may have been about twenty minutes), while she and the dressmaker fumbled about, with their mouths full of pins; cutting with ice-cold scissors against my bare neck, and

The Torturers. The daily dressmaker is on the left; my mother
in her most implacable mood kneels on the right.

constantly saying: 'Now *please* stand up straight for a minute'; or 'For Goodness' sake do keep still'; until at last there was a real explosion.

Once, when I could not endure it a single instant longer, I went completely mad and, seizing between my teeth the pink cotton

frock they were fitting on, I bit it all to pieces. I suppose I was pun-
ished for this, but I cannot remember anything except my triumphant satisfaction in my crime. Another time I fairly liquidated a
hat. My mother had brought back some hats for us from Paris.
They had yellow straw crowns and frilly white paper brims, and
were supposed to look like daisies. After an argument, one Sunday
morning, Margaret and I were made to go to King's Chapel wearing them, and a sulkier pair of daisies you never saw. But once
inside, and safe in the stalls—for Walter the Verger always put us
in the High Places, though we really had no connection with King's
—once safe inside, I say, where grown-up reactions had all to be
put into cold storage and their human accounts were frozen . . . I
took off my hat and STOOD on it, and squashed it as flat as ever St.
George squashed the Dragon; and no one could ever wear it again.
Glory, glory hallelujah.

For, in spite of my mother's efforts, I thought all my clothes
horrible. I can't remember liking a single coat or hat or frock in all
my youth, except for one pinafore with pink edges. There is a
theory that we always admire the present-day fashions, and think
those which are recently past vulgar, till lapse of time gives them
a period romance again. This cannot always be true; for I certainly
thought that the dresses my mother had worn in the 'eighties were
rather charming, while all the fashions from 1890 till 1914 seemed
to me then, and seem to me still, preposterous, hideous and uncomfortable.

I remember, when I was at school in 1902, walking at the back
of our Sunday crocodile, and seeing all the girls in front of me,
very smart and Sundayfied, going down the hill to church. And I
thought (I am afraid, with a touch of superiority): 'How frightful
they all look, and what a lot of trouble they have taken to make
themselves still more frightful. I am sure I look every bit as hideous,
but at any rate I haven't taken any trouble about it at all.' I thought

them much 'the worse for dress', as Uncle Lenny once said of an over-dressed lady of his acquaintance. The thought comes back to me perfectly clear, every time I get a whiff of something which reminds me of the empty, damp, suburban, Sunday-morning smell of Wimbledon Common; and then I see again their beribboned top-heavy hats, stuck on to the top of the hair they had spent so long in frizzling and puffing out; and their tightly corseted, bell-shaped figures wobbling down the hill, as they chattered their way to church.

I suppose that, in spite of the fashions, there must have been *some* elegant women in the 'nineties; but even if any of them lived in Cambridge (which is doubtful) we should certainly have failed to appreciate them. Cambridge was not well-dressed; Darwins were far from smart; and we cousins despised, or affected to despise, dress. Four of us really did, largely because our clothes were imposed on us from above, without even the power of veto. Frances alone had a secret wish to be prettily dressed; but she had to pretend to be above such things; for interest in clothes showed a low moral nature. Whenever we were telling stories, if the story-teller said: 'She was a very fashionable lady,' we all knew at once that *she* was the villainess of the piece.

In a less explicit way this was the attitude to dress of all born Darwins, and of most of the married-in Darwins, too. Dressing well was a Duty, and not a pleasure: your duty to that state of life to which it had pleased God to call you. Dresses designed solely with an eye to the wearer's age and position are apt to be rather serious affairs; but at any rate every aunt managed to look extremely dignified in one of her 'best gowns'. Aunt Ida always looked like a duchess, anyhow—one of the best kind of duchesses of the real old aristocracy; and Aunt Etty was magnificent on occasion. Her dresses were beautiful, too, even in that unpromising age, and her little lace caps were charming. As always, she made her position perfectly clear; she would say: 'I shall wear my pearl necklace and then they'll know that I've done my best.' White gloves were also a sign that one was doing one's best.

My mother, on the other hand, frankly enjoyed dress. She tells in a letter how she set out to pay some visits, '*George in his high hat, which he only wears in London and Paris, and I in my red cloth. We both went off feeling very comfortable in our best clothes. Clothes do give you assurance, there is no doubt about it.*' There, in a nutshell, lies the difference between her and me. For she could never have believed that this feeling was entirely unknown to me. Nor, with the best intentions in the world, did she understand that I needed very special treatment to be made tolerable; that what suited her, did not suit me.

Once, when I was about eighteen, I was made into a fat, blue-satin bridesmaid for a cousin's wedding. It is really astonishing that I did not cast a curse over that bridal pair, such were the blackness and venom of my feelings in the church. However, the marriage has been a success, in spite of this inauspicious opening. But I can here and now lay my hand on my heart and say that I always—when I thought about it—felt a great ill-dressed lump; and when I went to boarding-school, and they all despised me, I thought they were perfectly right. In a sort of way that is; for I simultaneously thought them quite wrong, about appearances in general.

My clothes were particularly unsuccessful just then. I had a new green tweed coat and skirt, badly made by the poor little daily dressmaker; and the skirt had been lined with bright buttercup-yellow cotton, which showed round the edges whenever I moved. This was because, at the Christmas party that year, there had appeared an enormous yellow pumpkin, which suddenly split open to reveal Billy and all the Christmas presents inside it; and so my mother had economically used up the pumpkin material to line my skirt.

I endured the criticisms of the girls at school for some time—and girls are very outspoken about such matters—but at last I turned at bay. I simply made up my mind that as I could not be good-looking or well-dressed, I would never again think about my appearance at all. I would have enough clothes to be decent, but I would try to be as nearly invisible as possible, and would live for the rest of my life like a sort of disembodied spirit. Of course I knew that this was not the best possible solution, but it was the only one that seemed to me practicable. And at any rate this decision did really set me free; I hardly ever thought about my clothes or my looks any more at all; and, except sometimes at the beginning of a party, nearly always forgot to be self-conscious.

One of the difficulties in illustrating this book is that if I draw the people as they really were, they simply look impossible. Not quaint, or old-fashioned or uncomfortable or even ugly; but just simply impossible. If I draw young men in bowler hats and high collars and black coats in a canoe on the river, no one will believe that (a) they were gentlemen; or (b) that if they were, they could look like that. I have some snapshots of May Week picnics, where the girls are dressed in tight-bodiced, high-collared, long-skirted silk dresses, which you would think only suitable for an afternoon party at Buckingham Palace; while their hats are terrific compilations of fruit, flowers and feathers. And we wore the most incredible clothes for bicycling or playing tennis.

The thought of the discomfort, restraint and pain, which we had to endure from our clothes, makes me even angrier now than it did then; for in those days nearly everyone accepted their inconveniences as inevitable. Except for the most small-waisted, naturally dumb-bell-shaped females, the ladies never seemed at ease, or even quite as if they were wearing their own clothes. For their dresses were always made too tight, and the bodices wrinkled laterally from the strain; and their stays showed in a sharp ledge across the middles of their backs. And in spite of whalebone, they were apt to bulge below the waist in front; for, poor dears, they were but human after all, and they had to expand somewhere. How my heart went out to a fat French lady we met once in a train, who said she was going into the country for a holiday 'pour prendre mes aises sans corset'. Whenever I went to stay with Aunt Etty, soon after my arrival, I would feel her fingers fumbling in my waist-belt, to make sure that I was not tight-lacing; for she suspected every young person of a wish to be fashionable. She used to tell us a dreadful moral tale about a lady who laced herself so hard that she cut her liver *right in half*, and died in consequence. (I don't really think that there was much danger of my dying in that way.)

We knew it was almost hopeless—we were outnumbered and outflanked on every side—but we *did* rebel against stays. Margaret says that the first time she was put into them—when she was about thirteen—she ran round and round the nursery screaming with rage. I did not do that. I simply went away and took them off; endured sullenly the row which ensued, when my soft-shelled condition was discovered; was forcibly re-corsetted; and, as soon as possible went away and took them off again. One of my governesses used to weep over my wickedness in this respect. I had a bad figure, and to me they were real instruments of torture; they prevented me from breathing, and dug deep holes into my softer parts on every side. I am sure no hair-shirt could have been worse to me.

After the torture of stays came the torture of hats, the enormous over-trimmed hats, which were fixed to the armature of one's puffed-out hair by long and murderous pins. On the top of an open bus, in a wind, their mighty sails flapped agonizingly at their anchorage, and pulled out one's hair by the handful.

Males and females alike, we had always to wear something on our heads out of doors. Even for children playing in the garden, this was absolutely necessary. According to the weather, we were told, that we should catch cold, or get sunstroke, if we went bare-headed. But the real reason was that it was proper—that the hat was an essential part of the dress.

Skirts were more tiresome than painful, but they could be very tiresome indeed. By the time I was eighteen, my skirts came right down to the ground, and Sunday dresses had to have little trains behind. It was difficult to walk freely in the heavy tweed 'walking skirts', which kept on catching between the knees. Round the bottom of these skirts I had, with my own hands, sewn two and a half yards of 'brush braid', to collect the worst of the mud; for they inevitably swept the roads, however carefully I might hold them up behind; and the roads were then much muddier than the tarred roads are now. Afterwards the crusted mud had to be brushed off, which might take an hour or more to do. There can be no more futile job, imposed by an idiotic convention, than that of perpetual skirt-brushing. This was the only work that ever made me wish that I had a maid; otherwise I despised people who could not look after themselves.

Once I asked Aunt Etty what it had been like to wear a crinoline. 'Oh, it was delightful,' she said. 'I've never been so comfortable since they went out. It kept your petticoats away from your legs, and made walking so light and easy.'

One of our governesses, thinking to be very modern and dashing, once ordered a new skirt, which cleared the ground by quite two inches. But when it came she was too bashful to wear it, and finally only solved the difficulty by always wearing spats with it. For, of course, ankles ought never to be seen at all and, if they were, the lady they belonged to was not quite a nice lady. Legs had no value, except that of impropriety.

This was the reason why quite well-dressed, but respectable, women did not seem to mind wearing shabby shoes and stockings—though even the most proper lady could not help letting her shoes peep out sometimes. Well-brought-up young men were taught by careful mothers to get over a stile *before* a lady, and then stand with their backs to it, looking at the view, while they stuck out an anonymous hand sideways to help her out of her embarrassing position.

Of course, this was because the switch-over from the hair-mindedness of the mid-Victorian period to the leg-mindedness of the twentieth century had not yet taken place. Hair was still an asset in the 'nineties, though it was not what it once had been. No longer did ladies flaunt enormous masses of well-brushed hair over their shoulders, as they used to do when they were going to be painted by Rossetti, or photographed by Mrs. Cameron. There is even a photograph of the 'sixties of Aunt Etty—surely the least vain person in the world—dressed for a party, with her hair all over her shoulders.

Good manners.

My mother's lovely golden-brown hair came down nearly to the ground, it was the longest I have ever seen—though even so, I don't believe that Browning could have wrapped it 'three times her little neck around', as he says he did when he strangled Porphyria. But my mother was not so proud of it, as she would have been twenty years earlier; she even had bits cut out, as she said her plaits were too heavy. Hair in the 'nineties was worn all in coils and plaits, and was often very prettily arranged. In the nineteen hundreds it had to be puffed out in hideous lumps and bumps, over cushions or frames. It was important still, but no longer the crown of a woman's glory as it had once been.

As for the men, those maned and bearded lions, who had roared and tossed their tangled doormats in the 'sixties, had now somewhat tempered their magnificence; though even in the 'seventies Aunt Etty wrote with pride of Uncle Richard's 'unusually long thick brown beard'; and in the 'eighties my mother still thought that Mr. T.'s plentiful hair and 'nice *soft* brown beard' were attractions. But beards were yearly growing smaller and the younger men were likely only to cultivate moustaches. Whiskers were definitely relics of the past, and every year the area devoted to them grew less, as the razor went further inland among the bristles. In the 'nineties the hair on their manly heads was cut to a reasonable length, half-way between the exuberance of the 'sixties and the horrid two-day's growth of prickles on the back of the head, which is, unfortunately, to-day's style.

But though hair was going out, respectable female legs had not yet come in. That revolution needed a World War to set going. Nowadays we spend far too much on the thinnest possible stockings, in which we are very cold in the winter; and we say casually: 'She's got rather pretty hair'; but with enthusiasm: 'She's got *lovely* legs'; for good ankles matter more than anything else.

It fairly makes my heart bleed to see photograph after photograph of ourselves as children, playing in the garden in high summer, always in thick, black, woolly stockings and high boots. We wore, too, very long, full overalls with long sleeves, and of course hats or caps of some sort. All the same we were luckier than our cousins, because in warm weather we were sometimes allowed to play out-of-doors with bare feet, and they hardly ever were. There is a pathetic story of Erasmus, Ruth and Nora. They once, in the holidays, found a little brook and, quite innocently, began to paddle in it. Then their poor consciences began to work, and one of them was sent back to the house to ask permission. They were told Certainly not; and they had to put on their black woollen stockings and hot tight boots again.

As I grew older, my mother began to say that it was not proper for me to walk about with bare legs any more, even in the country.

# Clothes

'There, Gwen, that man's seen you. I don't know what he'll think of a big girl like you, going about like that.' But though this made me shy and uncomfortable, I defied propriety, and went on walking barefoot whenever I dared. It is still quite dreadful to me to reflect that during at least fifty years of my life, Propriety has hardly ever allowed me to enjoy one of the simplest and most innocent of sensual pleasures: the air blowing on my bare ankles. What a waste of the only life I have!

I wish, too, that I had been allowed then to have proper boys' boots, with little brass hooks for the laces; for I wanted them then so passionately, and now it is too late; I don't want them any more. I always had button boots, which I thought effeminate. They were made to measure by Mr. Flack the shoemaker, who ran a tickly pencil round our toes, in his shop looking over the Round Church graveyard. We never had ready-made boots. There was a grand row once, when Charles was made to wear a pair of my old button-boots, and we both thought it an insult to his sex. I was much the angrier of the two, and made a terrible scene on his behalf; while he bore with the indignity of the buttons with his usual aloofness. They must have been the very same boots which he was forbidden to take off, once when we were acting a barefoot play in the garden at Down, and he had a cold. He was, as usual, to be the Fairy Prince —a role which he detested, but which his sex made it inevitable that he should play—so it was felt that the entire production was in danger. Whoever heard of a Fairy Prince in black button boots? Then someone thought of sticking flowers—scabiouses—into all the buttonholes of the boots; and the play was saved.

There must have been something aristocratic about buttons in those days, for everything that could possibly button and unbutton was made to do so: buttons all down the front of one's night-gown, buttons on the sleeves, buttons on one's bodices and drawers, buttons everywhere. That anonymous genius, who discovered that clothes could be slipped over one's head, had not yet been born; nor had his twin brother, who discovered elastic.

Women were incredibly modest then, even with each other. You could see a friend in her petticoat, but nothing below that was considered decent. At school, the sight of a person in her white frilly drawers caused shrieks of outraged virtue; and I should have thought it impossible to be seen downstairs in my dressing-gown. As a consequence decent women did not take very much trouble about their underclothes, which were apt to be rather Jaeger and patched; but they were often extremely complicated. This is what a young lady wore, with whom I shared a room one night—beginning at the bottom, or scratch:

1. Thick, long-legged, long-sleeved woollen combinations.
2. Over them, white cotton combinations, with plenty of buttons and frills.
3. Very serious, bony, grey stays, with suspenders.
4. Black woollen stockings.
5. White cotton drawers, with buttons and frills.
6. White cotton 'petticoat-bodice', with embroidery, buttons and frills.
7. Rather short, white flannel, petticoat.
8. Long alpaca petticoat, with a flounce round the bottom.
9. Pink flannel blouse.
10. High, starched, white collar, fastened on with studs.
11. Navy-blue tie.
12. Blue skirt, touching the ground, and fastened tightly to the blouse with a safety-pin behind.
13. Leather belt, very tight.
14. High button boots.

I watched her under my eyelashes as I lay in bed. She would have been horrified if she had known that I was awake.

Warm underclothes were very important. This is what my

# Clothes

American grandmother wrote to my mother, soon after she came
to live in England: '*Do you wear thick warm flannels? I do think Queen
Victoria has a great deal to answer for, in making the ladies wear low—*

'She uses Face Powder! Can she be really Respectable?'

*neck dresses at her receptions, thus setting the fashion of so dressing, which
I believe has sent many a young and delicate woman to her grave.*'
Children were generally far too warmly dressed, but our cousins

265

suffered more than we did from parental solicitude. They were always too hot.

Dress-hangers were unknown in my youth—at any rate to me. And I well remember the first time I ever saw face-powder. It was on the dressing-table of a most venerable lady, in whose house we were playing hide-and-seek at a small children's party. I cannot imagine how I knew what it was; but I did know, and was very much shocked at the sight of it. *Could Mrs. H. really be respectable?* If you could only have seen her! The kind, elderly, intellectual wife of a kind, elderly, intellectual don. Even now it surprises me that she knew about powder!

My astonishment was probably due to the fact that my mother never used it; her clear pink-and-white complexion needed no such help. I believe that people used to discuss whether she were made up or not. I can vouch for it that she was not. However, obviously, less favoured ladies did use powder, with discretion; but never young girls. And never, never rouge or lipstick. That was definitely only for actresses, or 'certain kinds of women', or the wickedest sort of 'fashionable lady'.

Rupert Brooke once told us a story, which had been told him by a friend at King's, as having happened to himself. This young man said that he had been brought up with a cousin, a girl of whom he was very fond. When she was about seventeen this girl suddenly died. The boy had been exceedingly sorry, but at the time of her death he had been much occupied with his tripos and other matters, so that he had not been so much shattered as he might otherwise have been. But some months later he had a dream which showed what a blow her death had really been to him. He saw in his dream this young girl standing before a mirror; and he thought, with an indescribable shock of horror and incredulity, that she appeared to be making up her face. This seemed to him so impossible that he crept up behind her, and then saw clearly in the glass that she was

# Clothes

indeed painting her face, but that she was *dead*. She was trying to cover up the ravages of death on a decaying face. He woke to the dreadful knowledge of the meaning of mortality. It was in 1912 that Rupert told us that story; but you could not tell it now. The point of it—the impossibility of a young girl making up before a mirror—would be entirely missed.

When I was eighteen I was given a dress-allowance of £60 a year. This was to cover everything, all my clothes and my own private expenses—books, presents, travel, drawing materials. This was a very good allowance, and I should have felt extremely rich if I had been able to spend as little as I wished on clothes. But the authorities required me to lay out on dress sums that I considered enormous. I had always to have at least three really good (and horribly ugly) evening dresses ready to wear; and lots of long white kid gloves, which were very expensive; and never nice again after they had once got dirty. And always at least one pair of silk stockings. They cost ten shillings, I remember! What a bother and a waste of good money it all was.

After writing so bitterly about the clothes of my youth, I must now be just, and admit that they had one great advantage over the clothes we wear nowadays. We had *Pockets*. What lovely hoards I kept in them: always pencils and india-rubbers and a small sketch-book and a very large pocket-knife; beside string, nails, horse-chestnuts, lumps of sugar, bits of bread-and-butter, a pair of scissors, and many other useful objects. Sometimes even a handkerchief. For a year or two I also carried about a small book of Rembrandt's etchings, for purposes of worship.

Why mayn't we have Pockets? Who forbids it? We have got Woman's Suffrage, but why must we still always be inferior to Men?

# CHAPTER XIV

## *Society*

D ancing class was the worst of the social events which I dreaded as a child. It was worse than Parties and worse than Church. It was the indignity of it that I minded so much, not only the terrible waste of time, or the dressing-up, bad though that was. In the abstract, so to speak, I thought my white frock and pink sash extremely beautiful; but *not on me*. When I wore them I felt a fool, and I went on feeling a fool all the time I had them on. I knew I was fat and clumsy and plain, and the white frock made it worse. And, on top of that, the fiendish Dancing Woman wanted me to hop, and wave my arms about, and stick out my legs, and do idiotic things with skipping ropes and castanets, in public. Degrading antics. I always felt exactly like a lion at a circus, when he is made to ride a bicycle with a pink ribbon round his neck; and I resented it exceedingly.

Strangely enough many of the other children seemed to like the class; and even my cousins, whom I admired more than anyone else in the world, didn't mind it much. Frances was quite distinguished at the Double Through, in skipping. But I felt a shame for them which they didn't feel for themselves. Sometimes one of the best dancers, generally Dolly, would be called out to do a star turn in front of the class; and when she had finished, Miss Ratcliffe's voice would rise in a long crescendo scream, with a drop at the end, as she called:

NOW CHILDREN ALL TOGETHAR

It was then that I hated her worst of all; and I stood there wishing death, torture, and the undying worm on the poor lady.

So, in revenge, I did it all as badly as possible; kicked the heels of the child in front of me when we were marching; and toppled over sideways when we were kneeling on one knee and supposed to be making graceful semicircles with our arms. But when we came to the polka or the barn dance, I used to relieve my feelings by choosing a congenial partner and getting round the room as fast as we possibly could. Then we would be sent out of the room for 'racing'; but that I liked. Or I would divert myself by squabbling with one of the boys who disgraced his manly sex by wearing yellow plush knickerbockers and girl's shoes. The lynx-eyed mothers and nurses sat around the room, with shawls on their laps and rivalry in their hearts, while the jangly piano unceasingly churned out jiggetty tunes. Last indignity of all, fuzzy, tickly, Shetland shawls were put over our mouths, so that we should not catch cold when we went home through the Cambridge fog; and the wool got full of little drops of water from our breath. The only thing tolerable about the whole business was the ceiling of the room. It was made in a pattern of pink and blue plaster mouldings, and looked as if it might have been good to eat. As if a kind, but rather mawkish, angel had made a roof out of Turkish Delight.

I am sure that Charles hated the dancing just as much as I did; but he did not get so angry about it, for he always seemed able to remain above such futilities, and to go on appearing to dance, while he was really thinking calmly about prime numbers and electricity, and all that sort of thing; the sort of stuff I carefully did not listen to when he and my father were talking together. I shut my mind up tight as soon as they began.

However, since those days, this dancing problem has been solved by one of Charles's sons in a very satisfactory way. After a series of colds and stomach-aches which came on regularly on Monday afternoons, he was told that he would have to go to the next dancing class, whatever the state of his health. There were neither tears nor prayers, and he went off quite quietly on the appointed day; but when he got there he just lay down on the floor; and stayed

The Dancing Class. Oh no, my dear contemporaries, I know very well that neither you, This is a Psychological picture; it is what it felt like to me at the time. You are none of

lying down. You can't make a person jig and amble when they go on lying on the ground. I wish I had thought of this myself; but it needs a man, and perhaps a genius, to invent anything so simple; and, anyhow, I should never have had the strength of mind to carry it through properly. This was, no doubt, an hereditary reaction on the part of Charles's son, for Nora says that she can remember Charles himself, during some altercation with a nursemaid, lying immovable on the ground in the Backs, surrounded by shocked and admiring female relations.

As I grew older the horrors of Dancing Class grew rather less, though the resentment remained; until at last I stopped going altogether; but the horrors of Parties, which had been intermittent

nor your mothers, nor your nurses, nor even Miss Ratcliffe herself, ever looked like this. you in the picture; nor am I, because I have just been sent out of the room in disgrace.

while we were young, became constantly more frequent and distressing. What I really need on these public occasions is Protective Colouring and plenty of cover. In these respects parties are not quite so bad as Dancing Class. The unpleasant clothes are the same for both, and they are in no sense protective; but at a Party you can often manage to spend part of the time under the stairs, or behind the window curtains, or in the lavatory; and you are hardly ever obliged to prance about in public; whereas, at Dancing Class, there is never any cover at all. Then, too, there is frequently good food at a party; only unfortunately I was always so rattled by the company that I hardly knew what I was eating. If only I could have taken it away to eat under the stairs! Also, sometimes my cousins were at the party, too, and then we made a bee line for a quiet corner and all jabbered away together, just as if we were at home; only we were always scolded for it and told that it was bad manners to do so. I have no doubt that we must have seemed very arrogant and exclusive, but really we were only very shy. I can never remember enjoying a party in those days, and I am always surprised when I see modern children go off quite cheerfully to some gruesome festivity; and I offer them a great deal of sympathy, which they don't seem to need in the least.

Going out to tea with children we knew was not so bad. In fact, it was sometimes rather fun; for we generally had tea in the decent seclusion of the nursery, and then Nana was there, too. This was a great protection, and we were not too much frightened to enjoy the food.

Tea at Trinity Lodge was great fun. We used to hope to go there directly after the quarterly visit of the Judge for the Assizes. For the Judge, as representative of the King, turns the Master out of part of his lodge, and takes possession of certain rooms for himself and his servants; and even has his own kitchen and cook. The Master and Fellows used to greet him ceremonially and feed him on mulled port and a special sort of sweet biscuit, which we believed to be the only kind a Judge could eat. And the nursery had the remains of the biscuits after he had left. Then the Master, Dr. Montagu Butler, used sometimes to come to the nursery while we were having tea; and on Jim's birthday, when we had tea in the great dining-room, he would make a short but elegant speech, which we thought very grand. After tea, Jim would read us the last few hundred lines which he had added to his epic poem on the Siege of

Troy; and then we would settle down to hide-and-seek, all over the rambling, dimly lighted house: through the great drawing-room full of seventeenth-century portraits; and under the Judge's bed; or tiptoe down a romantic underground passage, which joins one part of the complicated old house to another; and we even sometimes got a glimpse down into the College Hall, through the· little window in the panelling behind the Master's bed. I believe I could even now find my way in the dark, and on all fours, right across the great dust-sheeted drawing-room. But, of course, that wasn't a party, that was fun.

We must have seen a good many Great Men in our youth, but most of them seemed to me very uninteresting. There was Lord Kelvin; he looked very fine, but he seemed to be always absorbed in his own thoughts, and never opened his mouth, except once. That was when poor Charles, at a very young age, was made to recite to him '*The Charge of the Light Brigade*'. 'Into the Jaws of Deff rode the Six Hundred,' said Charles, and then: 'What's Jaws of Deff?' to which Lord Kelvin, living up to his part as a Great Man, replied: 'Doing your Duty, my Boy.'

An amusing recollection of this very young age is of overhearing scraps of conversation about 'that foolish young man, Ralph Vaughan Williams', who *would* go on working at music when 'he was so hopelessly bad at it'. This memory is confirmed by a letter of Aunt Etty's: '*He has been playing all his life, and for six months hard, and yet he can't play the simplest thing decently. They say it will simply break his heart if he is told that he is too bad to hope to make anything of it.*' She held much the same opinion of the early writings of E. M. Forster, a family friend: '*His novel is really not good; and it's too unpleasant for the girls to read. I very much hope he will turn to something else, though I am sure I don't know what.*' But, of course, these two were not great men then; this is what you have to go through to become great.

*L'Entente Cordiale.* Margaret is carefully noting every intonation of the Ambassador's voice, with a view to 'doing' him later on. I am most miserably conscious of my spectacles and the hairpins sticking straight into my head, and of all my horrible brand-new grown-up clothes. Monsieur Cambon is wondering if he can make his list of immoral animals last out till lunch-time.

But Francis Galton was both pleasant and impressive, with his bushy, twitching eyebrows. We went to his house once to have our fingerprints taken for some experiment on the classification of fingerprints, on which he was working. He did not provide us with any means of washing off the printers' ink, and we had to go about all day in London with sticky black hands. Lord Rayleigh was pleasant, too. Once, when we were older, he came to call when the elders happened to be out; and he sat on the sofa like a great ginger cat and told us very funny stories: how his barber had said to him: 'Wonderful things brains, my lord, so good for the roots of the 'air.' My father said afterwards: 'That came out of Rayleigh's own factory of stories. He makes up all the best ones himself.'

And then there was Monsieur Paul Cambon, the French Ambassador. He came to Cambridge for some ceremony and lunched with us. He had just lost his wife and was in deep mourning: he wore a top-hat and the most beautiful frock-coat; and black kid gloves, which he never took off. Margaret and I were sent to show him the garden before lunch, and he entertained us with a monologue suitable for *jeunes filles*. It was all about *la morale*. 'C'est la morale qui soutient l'homme. Le chat, le chameau'[I particularly remember the immorality of the camels] 'le lion, le tigre—etc., etc. —n'ont pas de morale. Enfin c'est la morale qui soutient l'homme.' Margaret and I walked respectfully on either side of him, making polite interjections, and wondering whether French girls often had to swallow this sort of stuff. I dare say he was wondering whether Englishmen often had to endure such dumb, ill-dressed, lumps of girls.

I have had many doubts as to whether Monsieur Cambon actually said *le moral* or *la morale*; the question is terribly involved, because the words have different meanings, and while *le moral* in French is best translated by *morale* in English, *la morale* in French corresponds more nearly to the English meaning of *morals*. On the whole, I think he must have said *la morale*, because *morals* rather than *morale* are what young ladies and animals are so sadly in need of, (particularly camels). In fact, the Ambassador was trying, in his curious Gallic way, to express the idea which Bishop Wykeham, so long ago, made into an epigram: 'Manners makyth Man.'

## Society

As I grew older, parties grew steadily worse. My mother saw that we were shy and bad mixers, and thought that seeing more people would be good for us; and so, in our adolescence, she grew more and more autocratic about forcing us to go out. Of course, she was perfectly right in principle, only it did not work out well in practice.

It was a difficult situation both for her and for me. The kind of girl she understood was gay and pretty and charming, and had lots of love-affairs and told her all about them; and she never understood that I could not—really *could* not—fill this role. It was part of her indomitable courage never to admit defeat, so she grew more and more inexorable in trying to force a square peg into a round hole, and in driving me into society for my own good; and I grew more and more miserable. It was really pathetic to see her pleasure when, later on, a niece of her own came on a long visit, and exactly filled the place that Margaret or I ought to have taken.

I am certain that she never understood the agonies I went through. Shyness was so alien to her that she could not take it seriously, and could only laugh at me, or scold me mildly, which made me feel guilty as well as shy. 'It is so *silly!*' [Of course it was, I knew that perfectly well, but it didn't make any difference.] 'People can't eat you!' [No, but *look* at you, which was much worse.]

My cowardice sometimes rose to such a pitch that once, when I had been invited to spend a weekend with a charming and friendly family, I simply could not bring myself to go over the edge, at zero hour on the Saturday morning; and I telegraphed that I was ill and could not come. My mother was away from home, or this would have been impossible. I was ashamed afterwards, and knew I had been idiotic: 'for,' thought I, 'I might have met there a young man, who would have fallen head over ears in love with me at first sight, and how lovely that would be; or I might have made real friends

276

with one of the girls; all kinds of nice things might have happened. What a donkey I am!'

I dreaded the servants at strange houses quite as much as the hosts themselves. One could not hide from the servants; they came and looked at you in bed, and, very rightly, despised your tooth-brush and your underclothes; every privacy lay open before them. Anyhow, I always hated being waited on personally; why should I, a healthy girl of eighteen, have tea brought to me in bed by a tired woman of double my own age?

Even when I had made up my mind to face the music and not be a coward, it only meant that I put my head down and charged blindly on to the assegais of the assembled impis, with such deter-mination that I nearly frightened them into fits. It was the only way I could do it. I am sure I don't know what ought to be done with idiots like me; but I am very glad that I was not my own mother. I have mercifully not had to deal with the problem myself, as my own daughters being half French were born knowing by instinct all the things I shall never learn. It was *they* who had to deal with *me*, though they soon gave me up as a bad job. But though I de-feated my French daughters, I think possibly a French mother might have made something of me. I have seen the most grotesque lumps of French girls turned into charming young women; not beautiful perhaps, but intriguing, characteristic—personalities in fact. But to do that you have to work with the grain of the wood. My mother did not understand that wood has a grain in it at all.

She could never have believed it possible that it was out of un-controllable panic that I upset a whole dish of spinach into my lap, at one of the first dinner-parties I ever went to. I was about eigh-teen, and I had on my best green satin evening dress, very smart and tight and shiny. I mopped away at the mess with my long white kid gloves, and made it much worse. The kind parlour-maid tried to help me; but my neighbours, instead of making a joke of it, pretended that they did not see; no doubt from the best of motives, but it was not the right treatment. Oh dear, Oh dear, how I did wish to fall down dead that very instant! But it was a horrible dress anyhow; I had been allowed no choice in colour or make; and I was glad when it was found to be spoilt for ever.

I was never good at tennis, and at a tennis party I became quite unable to serve a ball over the net at all. At a river picnic I simply rowed and rowed; so that I always thought of picnics as Hard Labour; but rowing was much less painful than having to talk to people. I felt sick for several days before my first dances, for fear that I should be shamed in public by not having enough partners. However, in time, I did, with economy and skill, generally manage to get enough dances engaged to look decent; and by degrees I got to dance fairly well and acquired a clientèle of young men who liked dancing, and to whom I did not have to talk very much. But I did not enjoy dances.

Once, after we were grown-up, my mother insisted on having rather a large picnic: 'Because you really ought to get to know the young people of your own age.' We sulkily pointed out that we didn't get to know them at picnics; but it was no good, it had to be; and as it was to be a specially grand affair, we were to drive to the Ouse in a private motor-bus, instead of going on the Cam as usual. The open-topped motor-bus was the best part of the business to our minds, for we had seldom been in a motor-bus then, and going bowling along the Huntingdon Road on the roof was rather splendid.

It was at this picnic that I first beheld true heroism. Probably everyone concerned will remember the story in a different way; that is human nature; but I can only tell the story as I remember it myself.

Well, it all went off with the usual kind of grisly brightness, and the picnic part and all its dreary sports were over: the sham cricket with a bun for a ball, the fighting with paddles, the airy badinage about catching crabs: it had all at last drawn to its longed-for close, and everyone was packing up the baskets to go home. I must observe that we liked a Free Picnic, with spontaneous sports and lots of cousins, well enough; it was only the forced labour of a Compulsory picnic which made everything seem so dismal. I hope the guests did not feel it too much; we did try to be agreeable, but I am afraid we were not very good at concealing our feelings.

Now among our guests were two sisters, whom I shall call Cordelia and Jane. The boats were moored in very deep water, beneath a steep bank, perhaps four or five feet high, and Cordelia and I had scrambled into one of them to receive the baskets, when Jane appeared at the top of the bank. A man, standing in my boat, held out his hand and said brightly: 'Jump in.' So Jane simply jumped! From that height! She hit the edge of the boat, which would certainly have upset if I had not instinctively thrown all my weight over on the other side. After wobbling wildly for a moment both she and the man, who tried to hold her, fell with a terrific splash into the deep water. Then, by my side, Cordelia rose grandly to her feet, and with a ringing cry of, 'Oh, Jane!' simply *stepped* into the river, no doubt preferring a watery grave to living on alone; and thus illustrating the verse:

> *Decisive action in the hour of need*
> *Denotes the hero, but does not succeed.*

Then might have been seen the glorious spectacle of English Manhood at its best; one gentleman was already swimming about in the flood; another dived splendidly into the stream, and then found that he had chosen a place which was not really deep enough for diving; and Charles, who had been at some distance away, arriving on the bank when the rescue was already well in hand, obviously felt that, as a host, he must not be behindhand in getting wet. So he waded in, at a shallow place, till the water came just below his watch-chain—(I saw his hand on his watch)—and thus honour was satisfied. There were hardly enough drowning young ladies to go round, and 'one poor Tiger didn't get a Christian'; especially as Cordelia managed to climb back into the boat by herself; but for a minute the Ouse was rather like Alice's Pool of Tears, when all the animals were swimming about. But at last everyone was saved. Even the people who had not jumped—or walked—into the water, were nearly as wet as the heroes and heroines, from helping them to climb into the boats; and when at last a friendly house was found—and it was not very near—there were only enough dry clothes for Jane, and they belonged to a very old lady; the rest of us had to drive home as we were. All this made us very late, but finally the two girls, Jane muffled in her borrowed dress, were smuggled in at the kitchen door of their house; and though their mother was told all about it, the adventure, with her connivance, was for ever concealed from their father, who was very ill at the time.

But we felt that anyhow *that* picnic had been worth while.

Not long after this we ourselves organized a picnic, which no one could call a success. It was just before Frances' wedding; Uncle Frank was very gloomy at the idea of losing her, and Frances thought that something ought to be done to cheer him up, and to entertain the uncles and aunts assembled in Cambridge for the occasion. So a river picnic was arranged, entirely for their sakes; a family party, given by the young for the old.

It was a grey, cold, gusty day in June. The aunts sat huddled in furs in the boats, their heavy hats flapping in the wind. The uncles, in coats and cloaks and mufflers, were wretchedly uncomfortable on the hard, cramped seats, and they hardly even tried to pretend that they were not catching their deaths of cold. But it was still worse when they had to sit down to have tea on the damp, thistly grass near Grantchester Mill. There were so many miseries which we young ones had never noticed at all: nettles, ants, cow-pats . . . besides that all-penetrating wind. The tea had been put into bottles wrapped in flannels (there were no Thermos flasks then); and the climax came

Heroic survivors of the picnic. Left to right: Uncle Frank, Uncle Horace, Aunt Etty, Aunt Ida, my mother. My father has shamefully given in already, unable to face any more hardships, and has started off alone to walk home. Aunt Ida alone has still a gallant smile glued to her lips; the others are just enduring. The trees of Byron's Pool can be seen in the distance.

when it was found that it had all been sugared beforehand. This was an inexpressible calamity. They all hated sugar in their tea. Besides it was Immoral. Uncle Frank said, with extreme bitterness: 'It's not the sugar I mind, but the Folly of it.' This was half a joke; but at his words the hopelessness and the hollowness of a world where everything goes wrong, came flooding over us; and we cut our losses and made all possible haste to get them home to a good fire.

## Society

Frances was the first of us girls to be married, and her marriage was the end of an epoch. After that we were really grown up. I had already been allowed to stop trying to be a young lady; and I was now very happy, living in London, alone with Uncle William, and working at the Slade School.

When I look back on those years when I was neither fish nor flesh, between the ages of sixteen and twenty-two, I remember them as an uncomfortable time, and sometimes a very unhappy one. Now that I have certainly attained the status of Good Red Herring, I may at last be allowed to say: Oh dear, Oh dear, how horrid it was being young, and how nice it is being old and not having to mind what people think.

## Ann Arbor Paperbacks

"Gwen Raverat, a granddaughter of Charles Darwin, has been looking back over the first twenty years of her li... ...d the consequence for us is a book en... *Piece*, every page of which is a delight. ...ry page. . . . As if the text of *Period Piece* were not bounty enough, Mrs. Raverat has illuminated her recollections with line drawings, and these too are joyous, offhand, and intensely her own, with captions that add up to a sort of private book within a book."

—*The New Yorker*

"The affectionate, high-spirited account of life as it was lived in the Darwin Circle. . . . Her drawings, her delicious wit and judgment, give every incentive for turning these pages."

—*The Atlantic*

At the close of 1952, Bertrand Russell wrote to Gwen Raverat that he had been reading *Period Piece* "with the very greatest delight." Raverat's memoirs of childhood and coming of age during the final years of Victoria's reign capture a young woman's impressions of dons, eccentrics, and tradespeople in Cambridge during the 1890s. With astonishing power *Period Piece* brings us into the real presence of the late Victorian past.

## THE UNIVERSITY OF MICHIGAN PRESS

ISBN 0-472-06475-4

9 780472 064755

90000>

ANN ARBOR PAPERBACKS